Sergio Aragonés
GROO™
Fray of the Gods

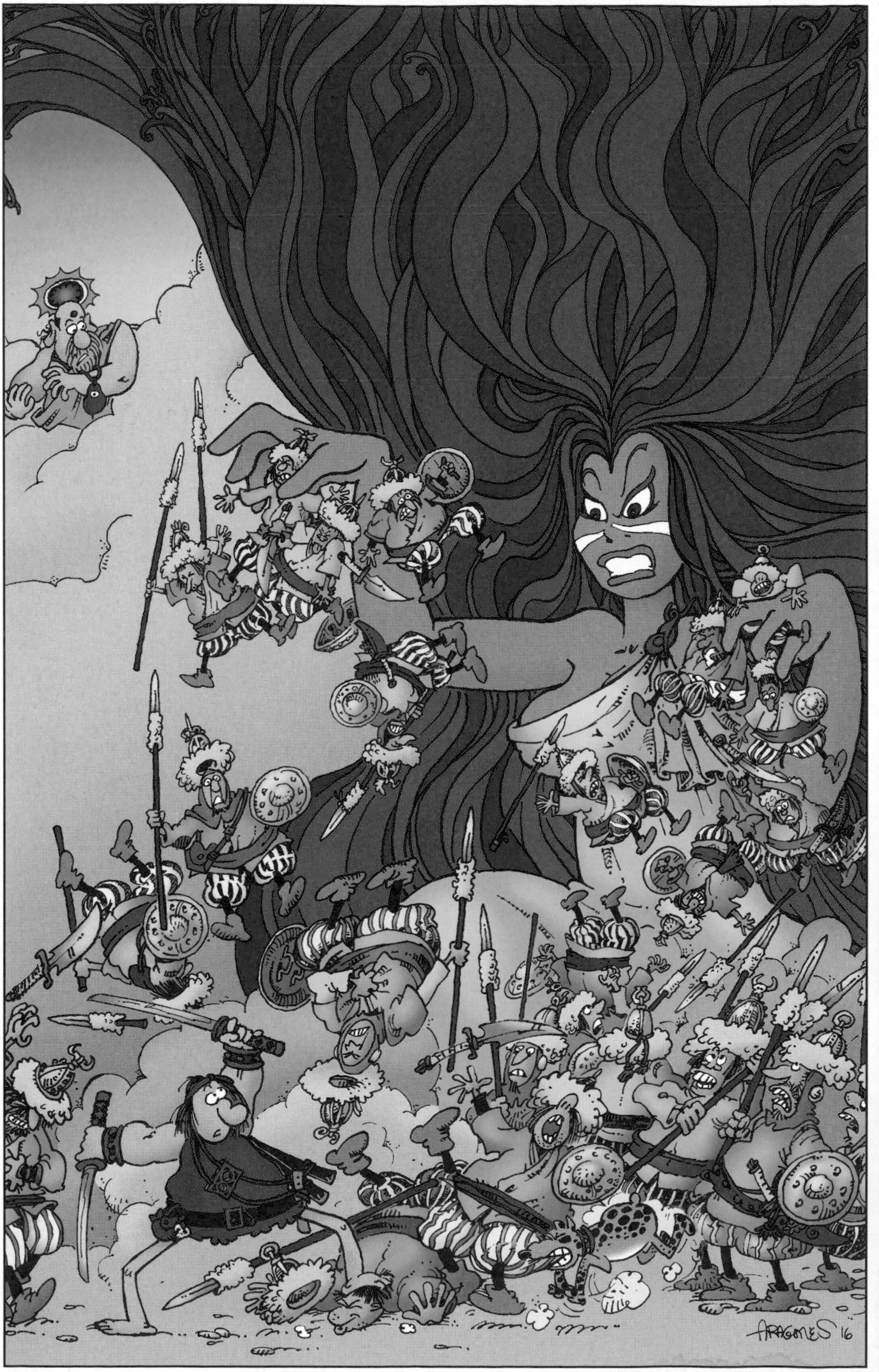
ARAGONES '16

Sergio Aragonés
GROO™
Fray of the Gods

by **Sergio Aragonés**

wordsmith
Mark Evanier

letterer
Stan Sakai

colorist
Tom Luth

Dark Horse Books

president & publisher **Mike Richardson**

editor **Patrick Thorpe**

assistant editor **Cardner Clark**

designer **Brennan Thome**

digital art technician **Adam Pruett**

Special thanks to Annie Gullion.

Published by Dark Horse Books
A division of Dark Horse Comics, Inc.
10956 SE Main Street
Milwaukie, OR 97222

DarkHorse.com

To find a comic shop in your area, call the Comic Shop
Locator Service toll-free at (888) 266-4226.
International Licensing: (503) 905-2377

First edition: April 2017
ISBN 978-1-50670-241-4

1 3 5 7 9 10 8 6 4 2
Printed in China

SERGIO ARAGONÉS GROO™: FRAY OF THE GODS

This volume collects issues #1–#4 of the Dark Horse Comics miniseries *Groo: Fray of the Gods*.

Names: Aragonés, Sergio, 1937- author, illustrator. | Evanier, Mark, author.
| Sakai, Stan, letterer. | Luth, Tom, colourist.
Title: Groo : fray of the gods / by Sergio Aragonés ; wordsmith, Mark Evanier
; letterer, Stan Sakai ; colorist, Tom Luth.
Description: First edition. | Milwaukie, OR : Dark Horse Books, 2017. | "This
volume collects issues #1-#4 of the Dark Horse Comics miniseries Groo:
Fray of the Gods."
Identifiers: LCCN 2016039397 | ISBN 9781506702414 (paperback)
Subjects: LCSH: Comic books, strips, etc. | BISAC: HUMOR / Form / Comic
Strips & Cartoons. | COMICS & GRAPHIC NOVELS / Fantasy.
Classification: LCC PN6728.G786 A63 2017 | DDC 741.5/973--dc23
LC record available at https://lccn.loc.gov/2016039397

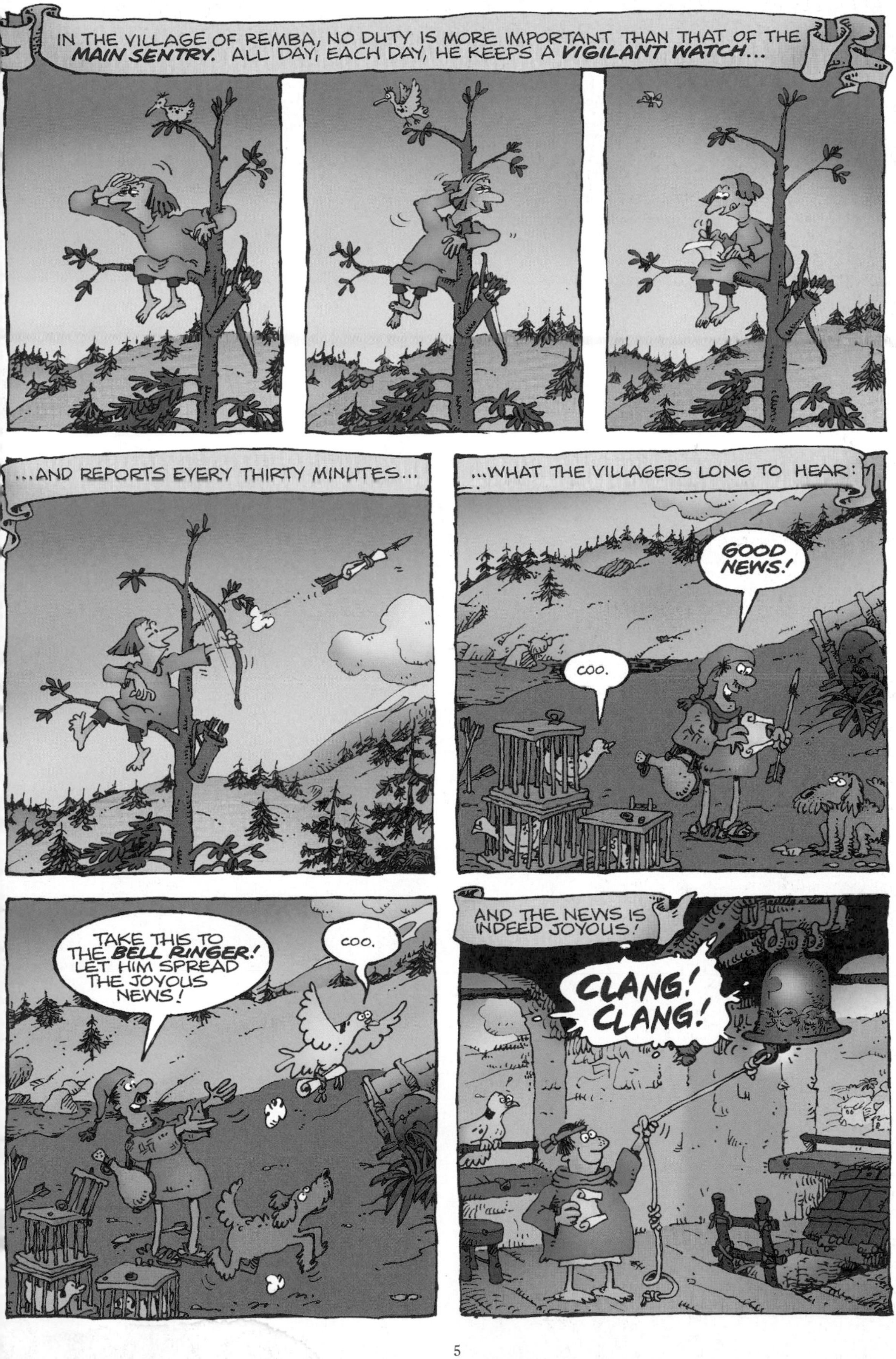
IN THE VILLAGE OF REMBA, NO DUTY IS MORE IMPORTANT THAN THAT OF THE MAIN SENTRY. ALL DAY, EACH DAY, HE KEEPS A VIGILANT WATCH...
...AND REPORTS EVERY THIRTY MINUTES...
...WHAT THE VILLAGERS LONG TO HEAR:
GOOD NEWS!
COO.
TAKE THIS TO THE BELL RINGER! LET HIM SPREAD THE JOYOUS NEWS!
COO.
AND THE NEWS IS INDEED JOYOUS!
CLANG! CLANG!

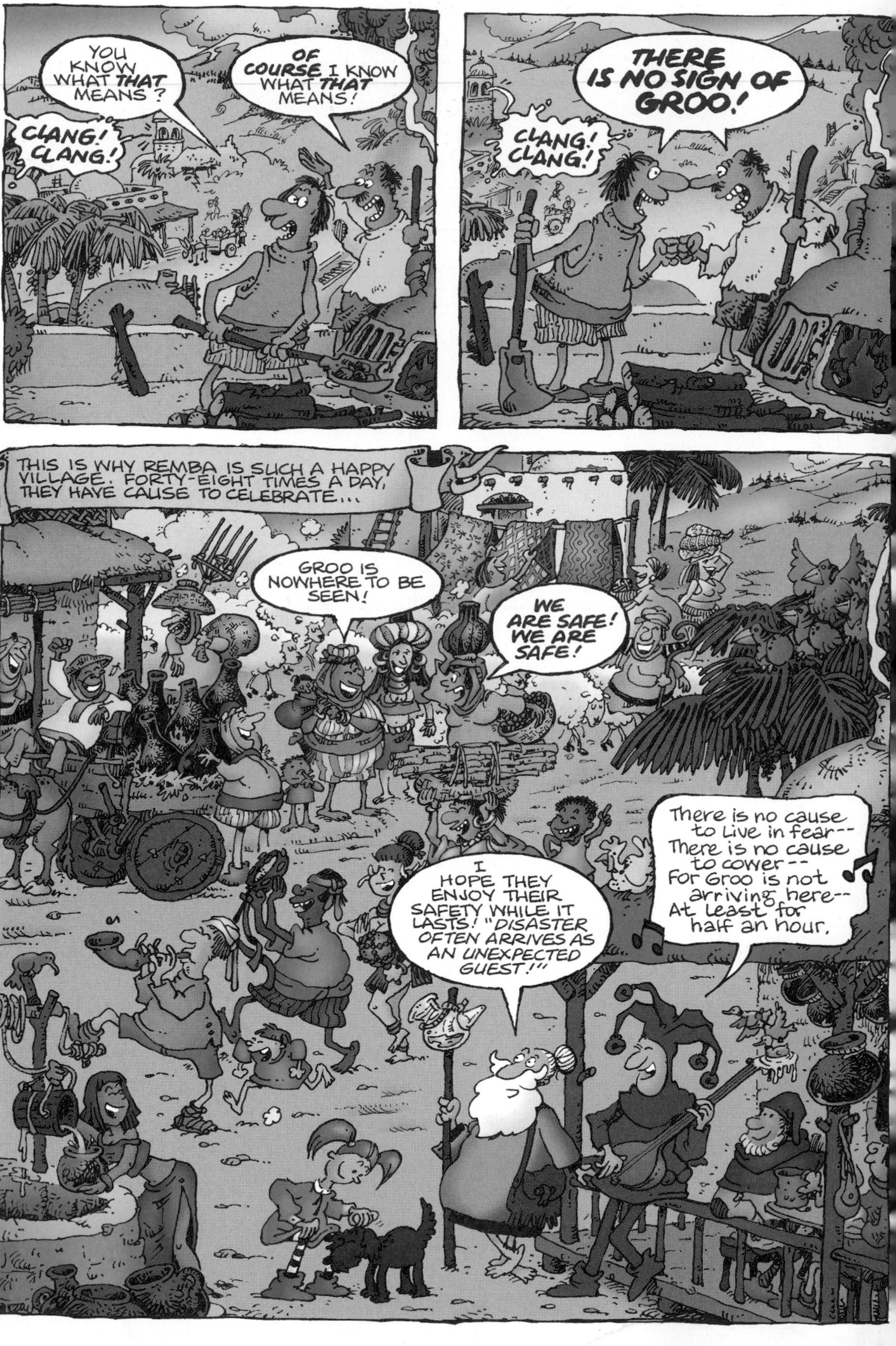
CLANG! CLANG!
YOU KNOW WHAT THAT MEANS?
OF COURSE I KNOW WHAT THAT MEANS!
CLANG! CLANG!
THERE IS NO SIGN OF GROO!
THIS IS WHY REMBA IS SUCH A HAPPY VILLAGE. FORTY-EIGHT TIMES A DAY, THEY HAVE CAUSE TO CELEBRATE...
GROO IS NOWHERE TO BE SEEN!
WE ARE SAFE! WE ARE SAFE!
There is no cause to Live in fear-- There is no cause to cower-- For Groo is not arriving here-- At Least for half an hour.
I HOPE THEY ENJOY THEIR SAFETY WHILE IT LASTS! "DISASTER OFTEN ARRIVES AS AN UNEXPECTED GUEST!"

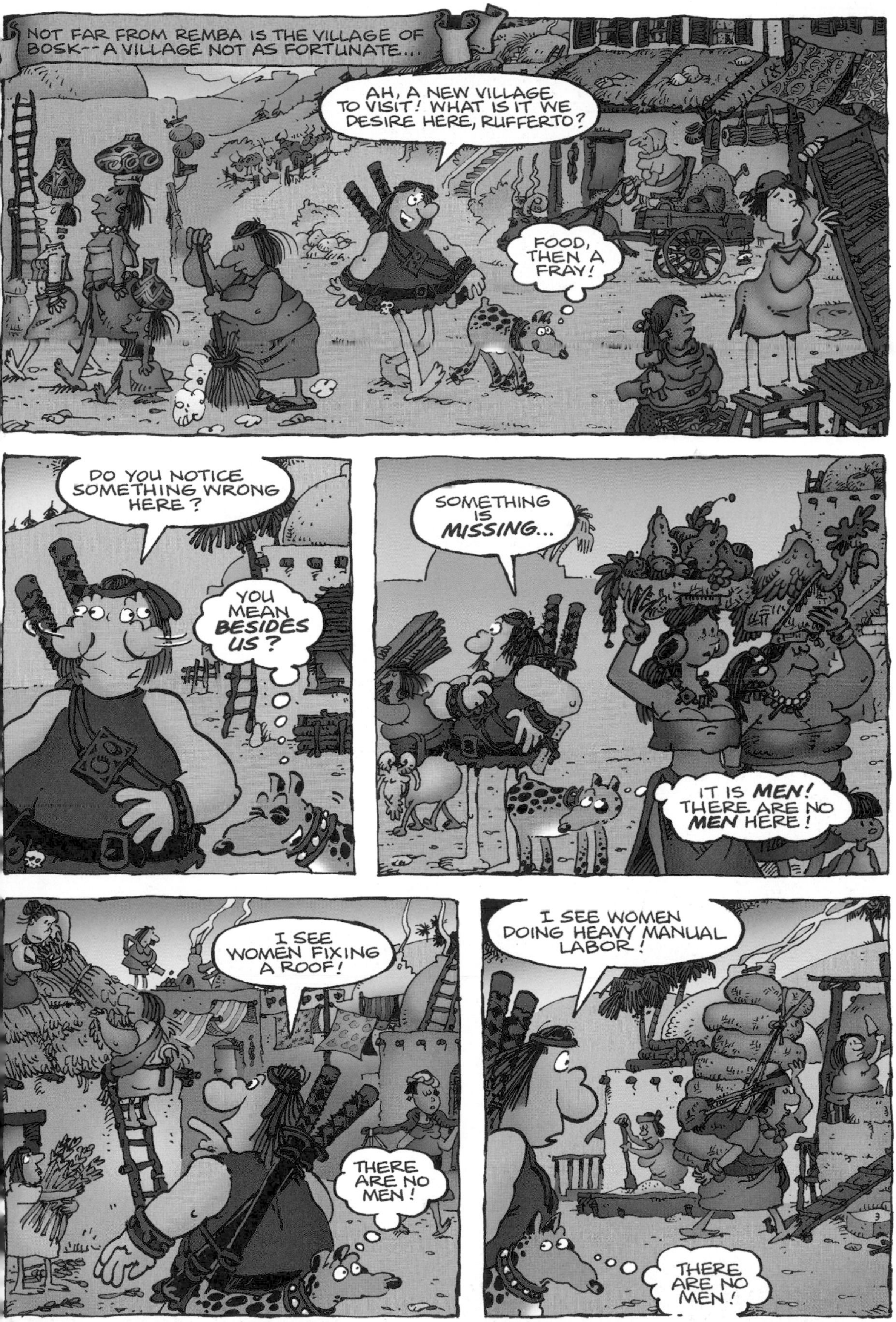
NOT FAR FROM REMBA IS THE VILLAGE OF BOSK--A VILLAGE NOT AS FORTUNATE...
AH, A NEW VILLAGE TO VISIT! WHAT IS IT WE DESIRE HERE, RUFFERTO?
FOOD, THEN A FRAY!
DO YOU NOTICE SOMETHING WRONG HERE?
YOU MEAN *BESIDES US*?
SOMETHING IS *MISSING*...
IT IS *MEN*! THERE ARE NO *MEN* HERE!
I SEE WOMEN FIXING A ROOF!
THERE ARE NO MEN!
I SEE WOMEN DOING HEAVY MANUAL LABOR!
THERE ARE NO MEN!

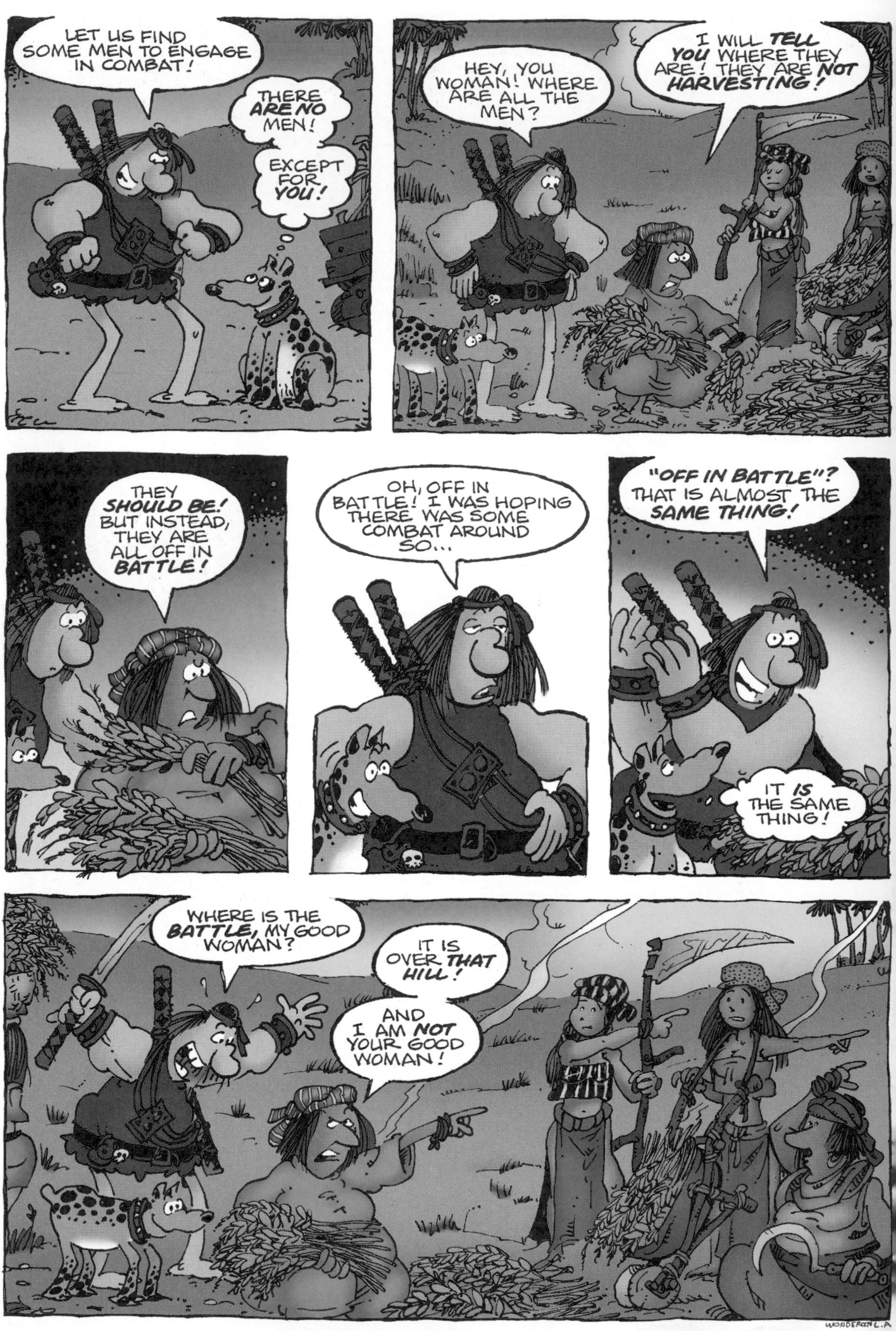

LET US FIND SOME MEN TO ENGAGE IN COMBAT!
THERE ARE NO MEN!
EXCEPT FOR YOU!
HEY, YOU WOMAN! WHERE ARE ALL THE MEN?
I WILL TELL YOU WHERE THEY ARE! THEY ARE NOT HARVESTING!
THEY SHOULD BE! BUT INSTEAD, THEY ARE ALL OFF IN BATTLE!
OH, OFF IN BATTLE! I WAS HOPING THERE WAS SOME COMBAT AROUND SO...
"OFF IN BATTLE"? THAT IS ALMOST THE SAME THING!
IT IS THE SAME THING!
WHERE IS THE BATTLE, MY GOOD WOMAN?
IT IS OVER THAT HILL!
AND I AM NOT YOUR GOOD WOMAN!
WONDERCOMIL.A

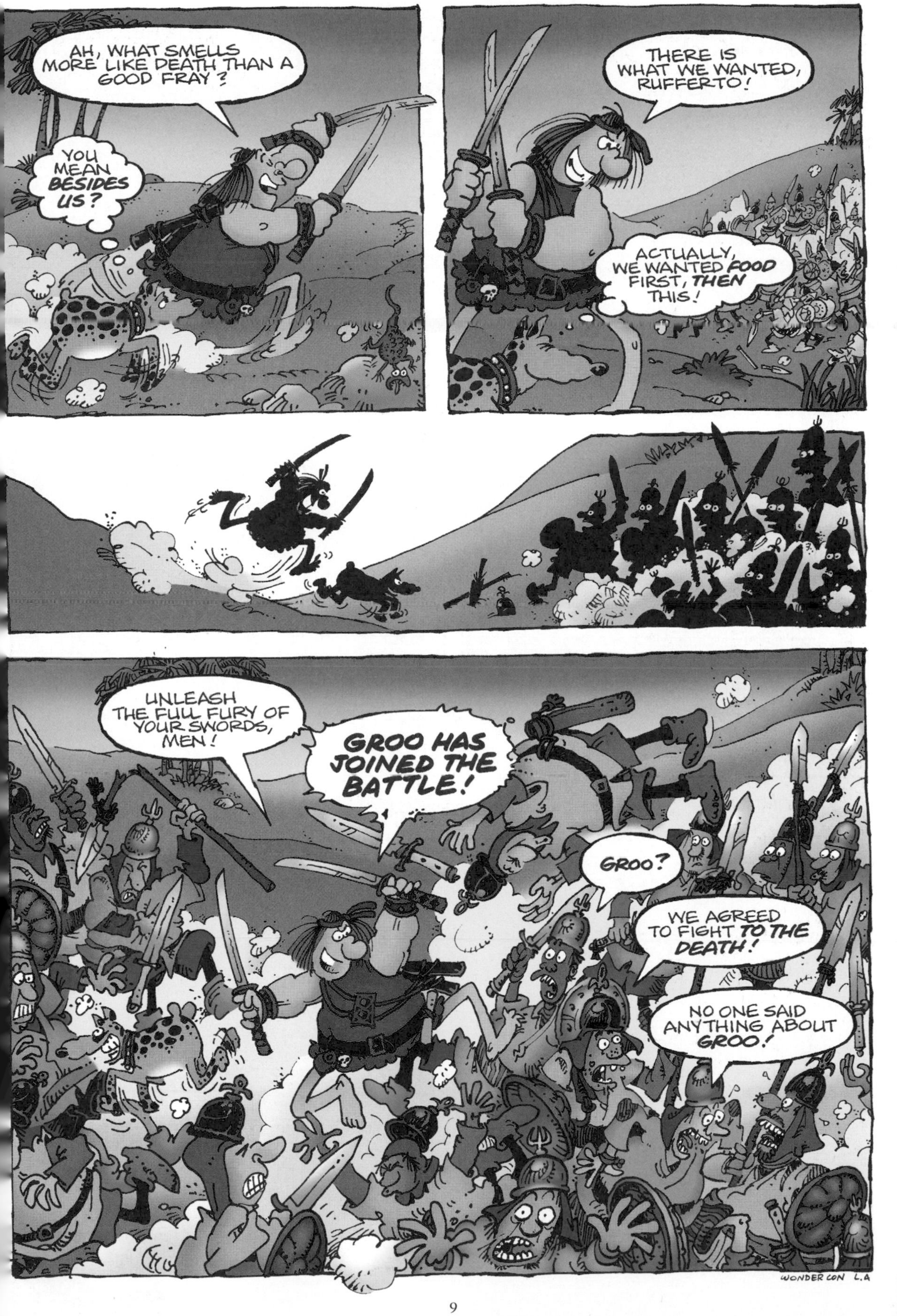
AH, WHAT SMELLS MORE LIKE DEATH THAN A GOOD FRAY?
YOU MEAN BESIDES US?
THERE IS WHAT WE WANTED, RUFFERTO!
ACTUALLY, WE WANTED FOOD FIRST, THEN THIS!
UNLEASH THE FULL FURY OF YOUR SWORDS, MEN!
GROO HAS JOINED THE BATTLE!
GROO?
WE AGREED TO FIGHT TO THE DEATH!
NO ONE SAID ANYTHING ABOUT GROO!
WONDER CON L.A

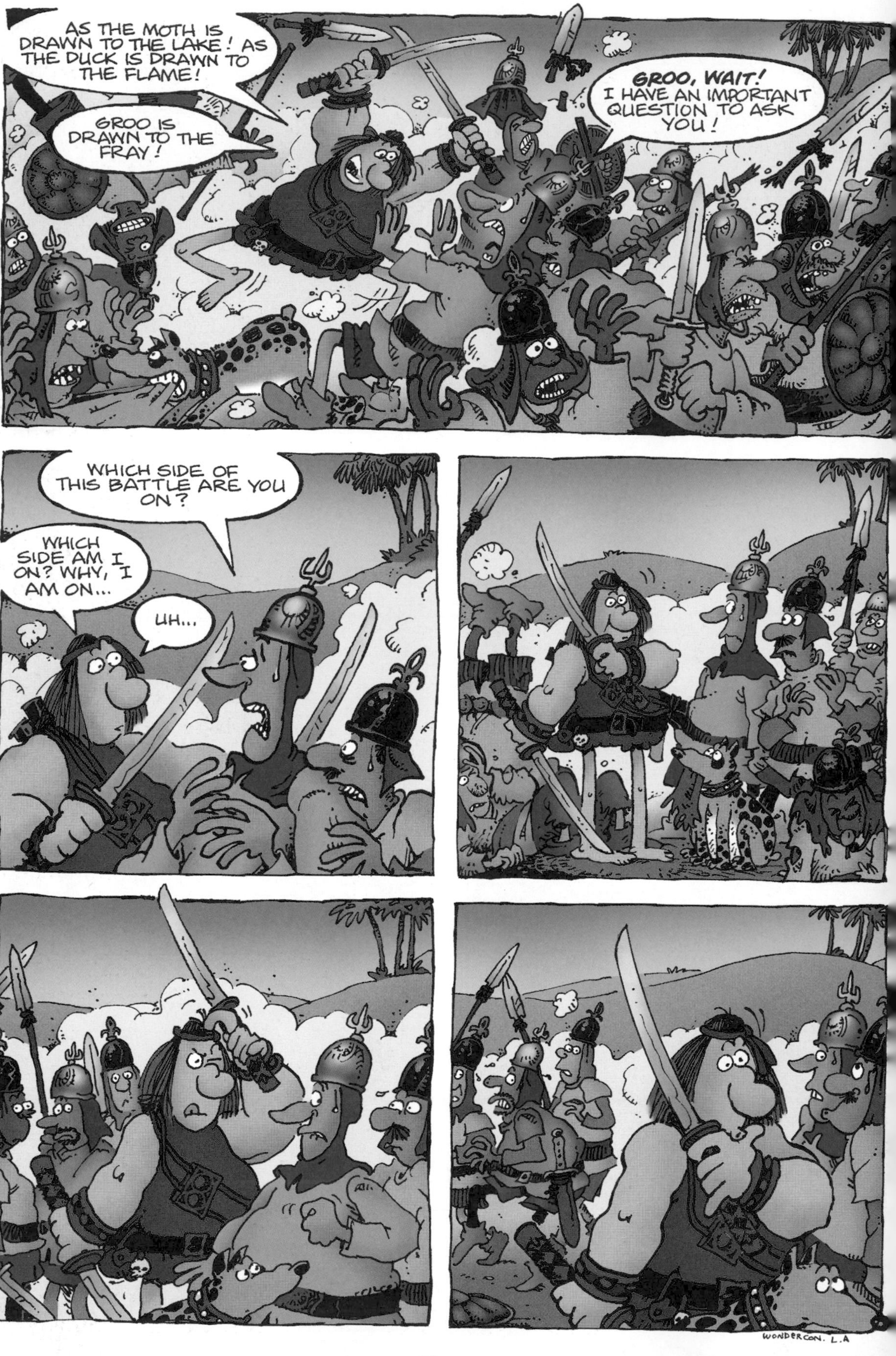
AS THE MOTH IS DRAWN TO THE LAKE! AS THE DUCK IS DRAWN TO THE FLAME!
GROO IS DRAWN TO THE FRAY!
GROO, WAIT! I HAVE AN IMPORTANT QUESTION TO ASK YOU!
WHICH SIDE OF THIS BATTLE ARE YOU ON?
WHICH SIDE AM I ON? WHY, I AM ON...
UH...
WONDERCON. L.A

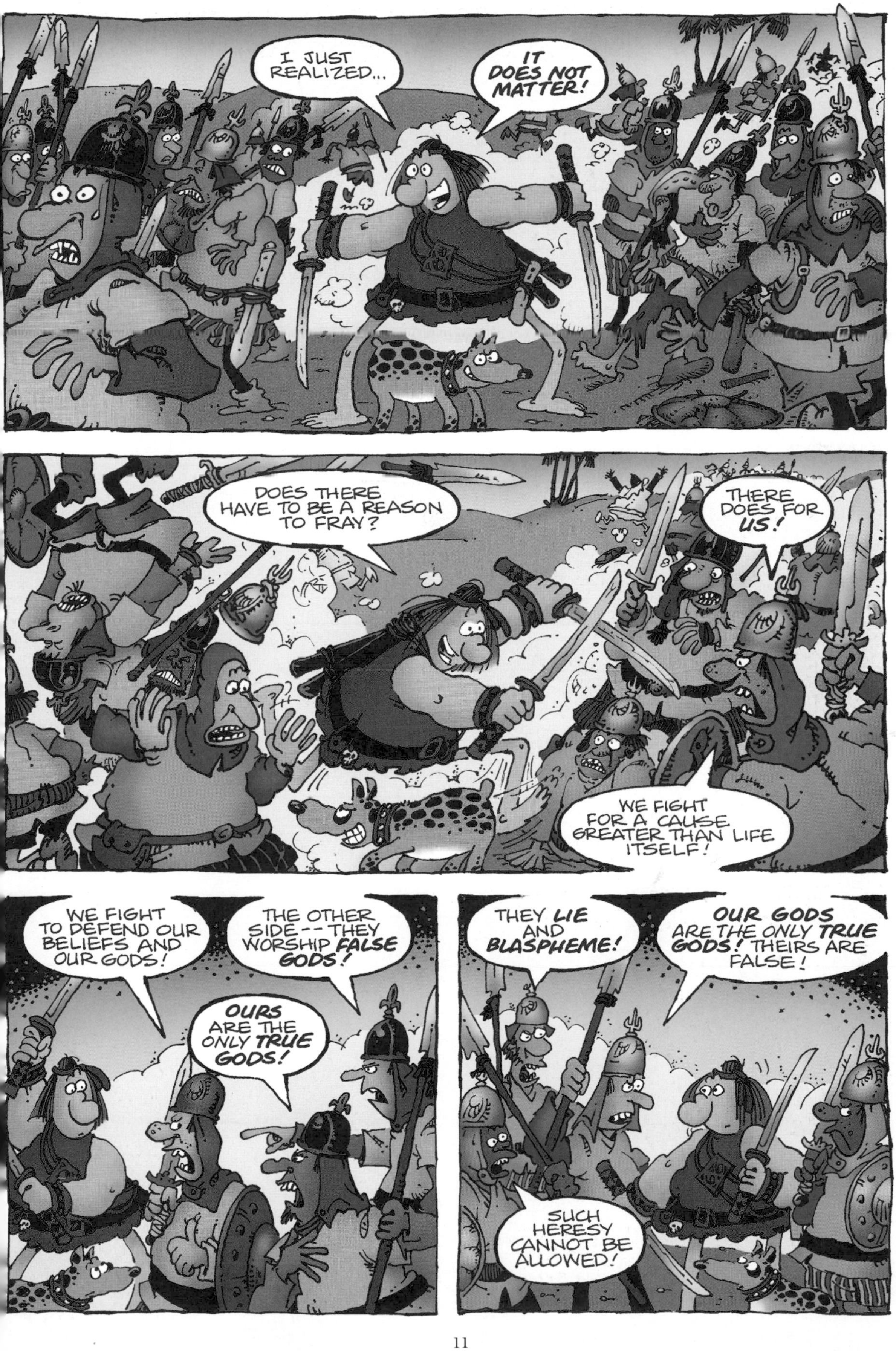
I JUST REALIZED...
IT DOES NOT MATTER!
DOES THERE HAVE TO BE A REASON TO FRAY?
THERE DOES FOR US!
WE FIGHT FOR A CAUSE GREATER THAN LIFE ITSELF!
WE FIGHT TO DEFEND OUR BELIEFS AND OUR GODS!
THE OTHER SIDE-- THEY WORSHIP FALSE GODS!
OURS ARE THE ONLY TRUE GODS!
THEY LIE AND BLASPHEME!
OUR GODS ARE THE ONLY TRUE GODS! THEIRS ARE FALSE!
SUCH HERESY CANNOT BE ALLOWED!

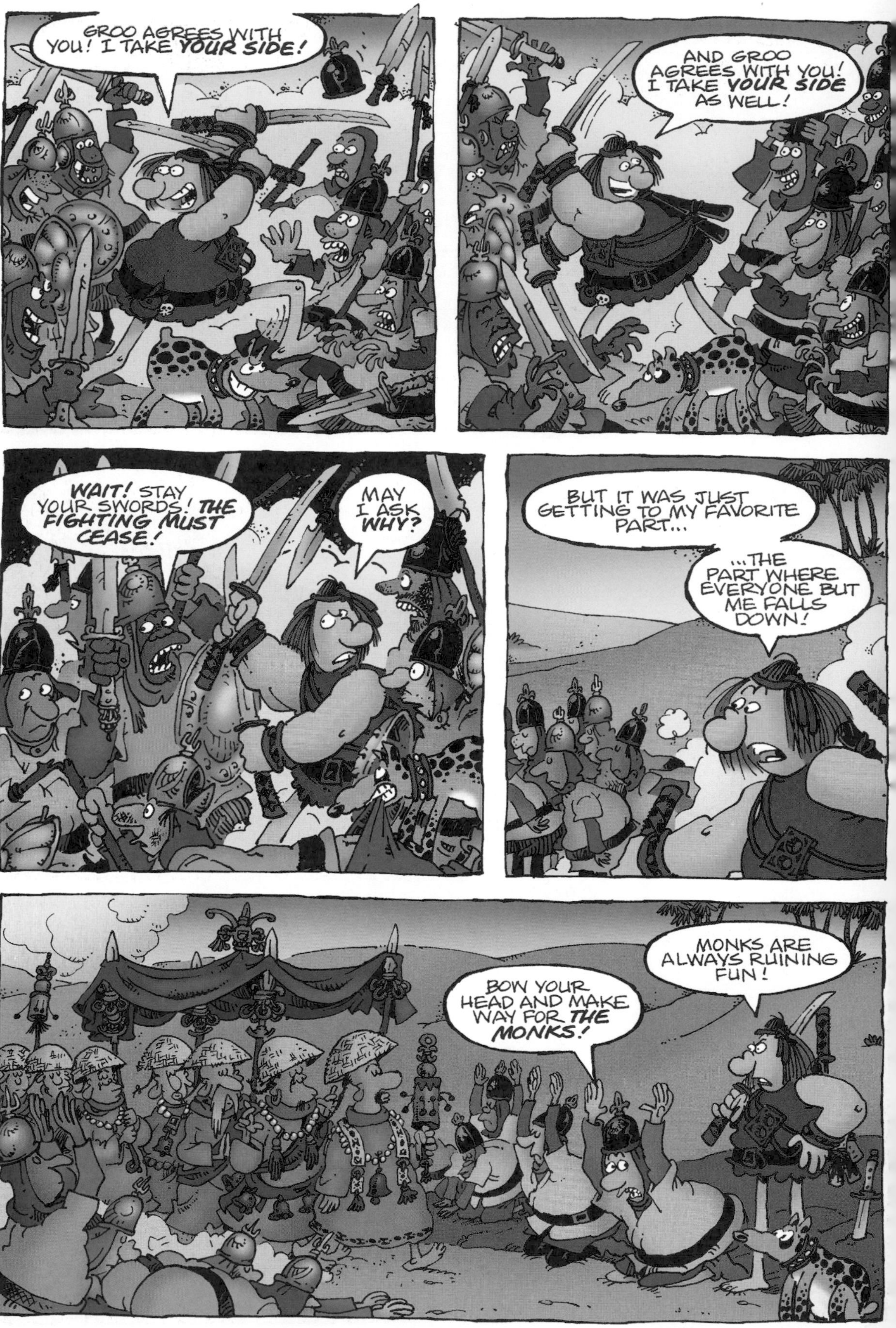
GROO AGREES WITH YOU! I TAKE YOUR SIDE!
AND GROO AGREES WITH YOU! I TAKE YOUR SIDE AS WELL!
WAIT! STAY YOUR SWORDS! THE FIGHTING MUST CEASE!
MAY I ASK WHY?
BUT IT WAS JUST GETTING TO MY FAVORITE PART...
...THE PART WHERE EVERYONE BUT ME FALLS DOWN!
BOW YOUR HEAD AND MAKE WAY FOR THE MONKS!
MONKS ARE ALWAYS RUINING FUN!

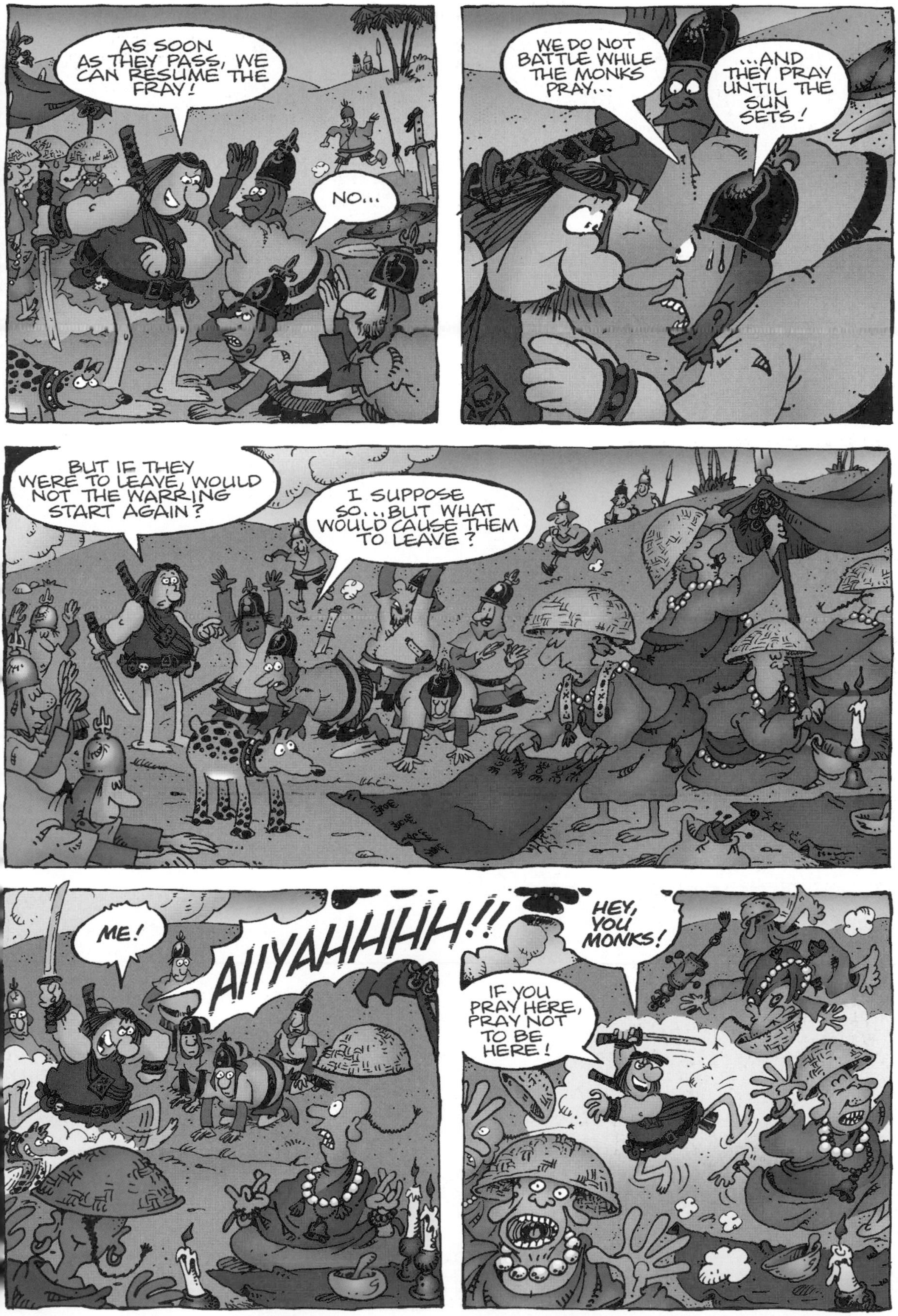
AS SOON AS THEY PASS, WE CAN RESUME THE FRAY!
NO...
WE DO NOT BATTLE WHILE THE MONKS PRAY...
...AND THEY PRAY UNTIL THE SUN SETS!
BUT IF THEY WERE TO LEAVE, WOULD NOT THE WARRING START AGAIN?
I SUPPOSE SO...BUT WHAT WOULD CAUSE THEM TO LEAVE?
ME!
AIIYAHHHH!!
HEY, YOU MONKS!
IF YOU PRAY HERE, PRAY NOT TO BE HERE!

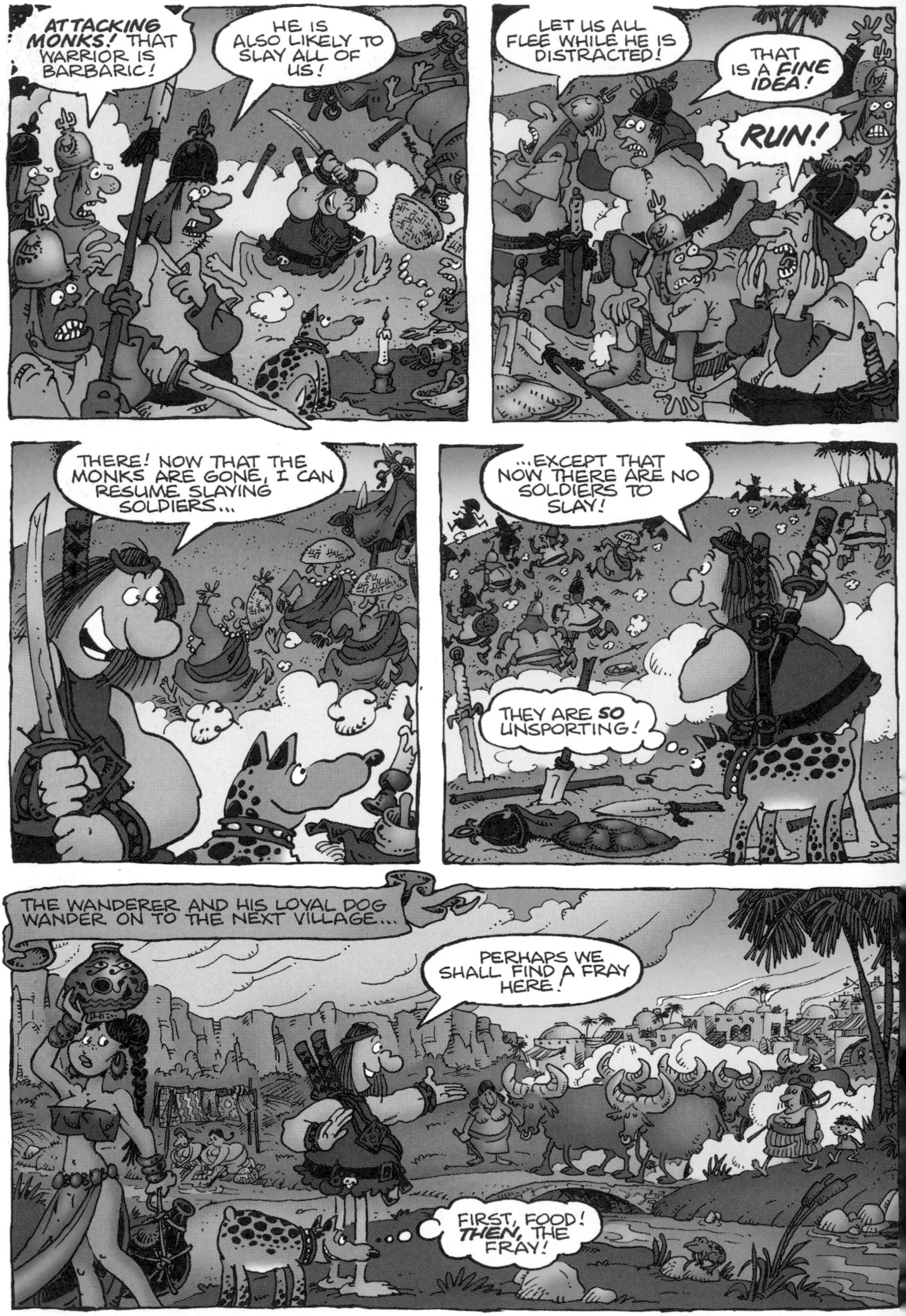
ATTACKING MONKS! THAT WARRIOR IS BARBARIC!
HE IS ALSO LIKELY TO SLAY ALL OF US!
LET US ALL FLEE WHILE HE IS DISTRACTED!
THAT IS A FINE IDEA!
RUN!
THERE! NOW THAT THE MONKS ARE GONE, I CAN RESUME SLAYING SOLDIERS...
...EXCEPT THAT NOW THERE ARE NO SOLDIERS TO SLAY!
THEY ARE SO UNSPORTING!
THE WANDERER AND HIS LOYAL DOG WANDER ON TO THE NEXT VILLAGE...
PERHAPS WE SHALL FIND A FRAY HERE!
FIRST, FOOD! THEN, THE FRAY!

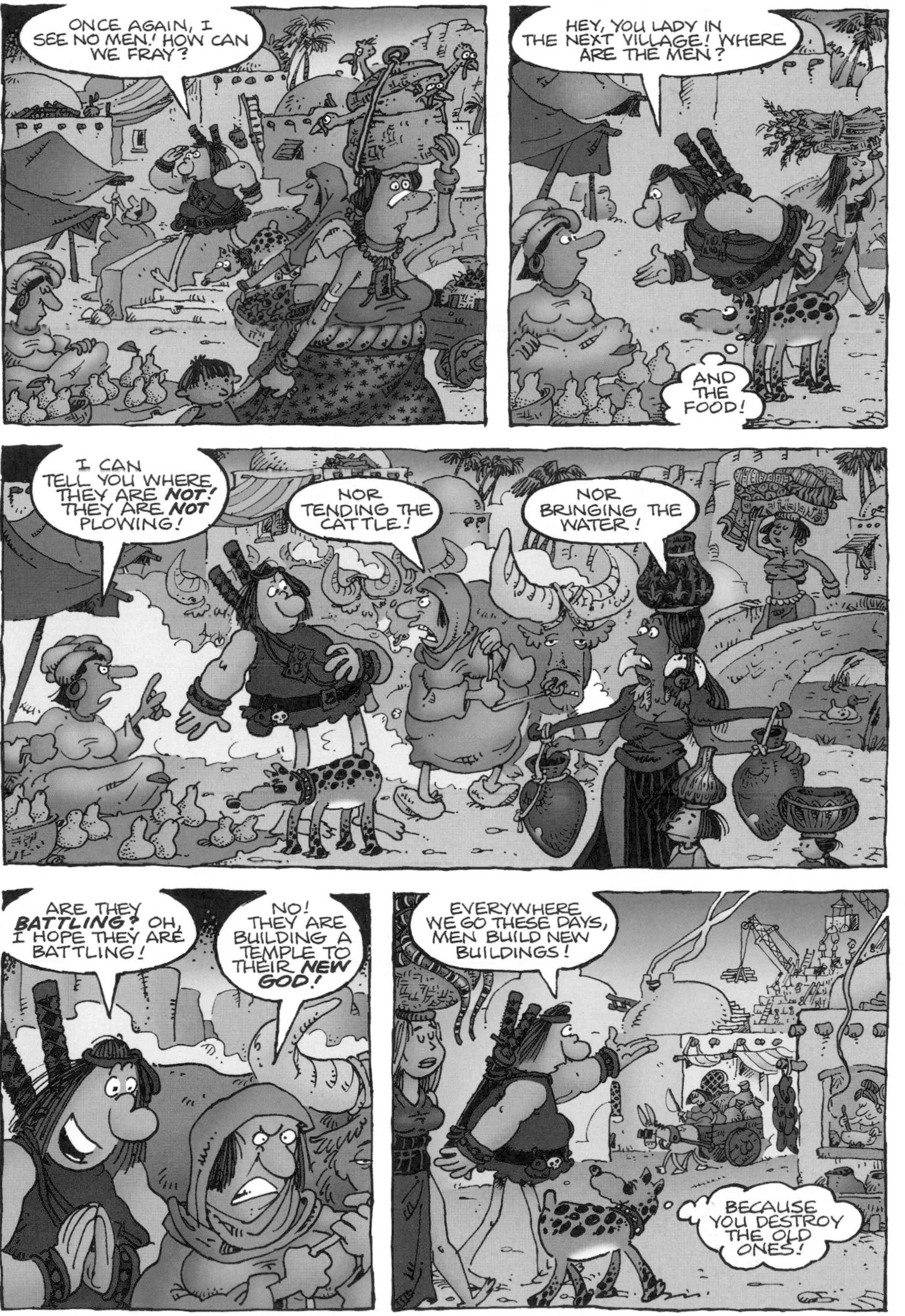
ONCE AGAIN, I SEE NO MEN! HOW CAN WE FRAY?
HEY, YOU LADY IN THE NEXT VILLAGE! WHERE ARE THE MEN?
AND THE FOOD!
I CAN TELL YOU WHERE THEY ARE **NOT**! THEY ARE **NOT** PLOWING!
NOR TENDING THE CATTLE!
NOR BRINGING THE WATER!
ARE THEY **BATTLING?** OH, I HOPE THEY ARE BATTLING!
NO! THEY ARE BUILDING A TEMPLE TO THEIR **NEW GOD**!
EVERYWHERE WE GO THESE DAYS, MEN BUILD NEW BUILDINGS!
BECAUSE YOU DESTROY THE OLD ONES!

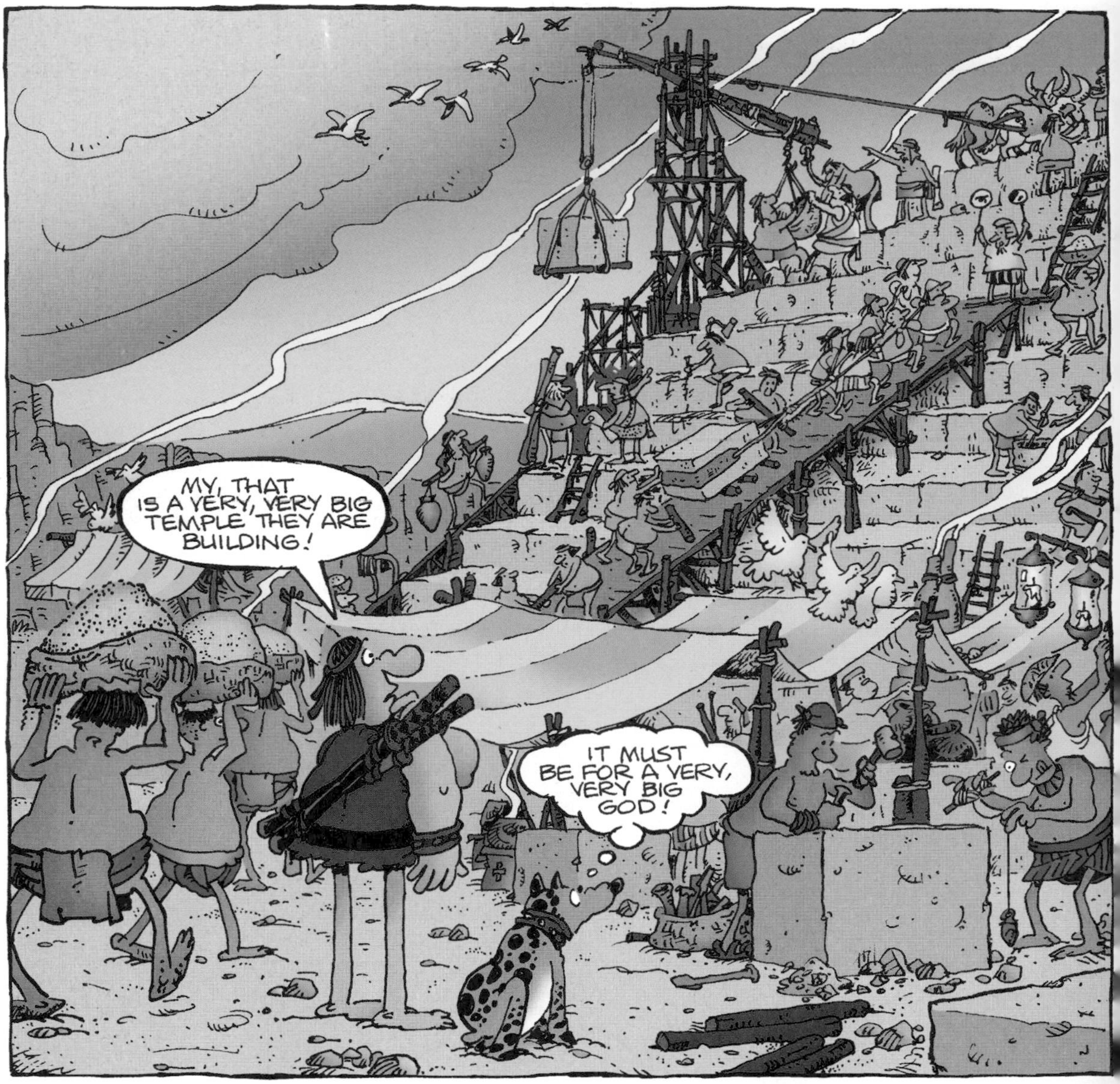
MY, THAT IS A VERY, VERY BIG TEMPLE THEY ARE BUILDING!
IT MUST BE FOR A VERY, VERY BIG GOD!

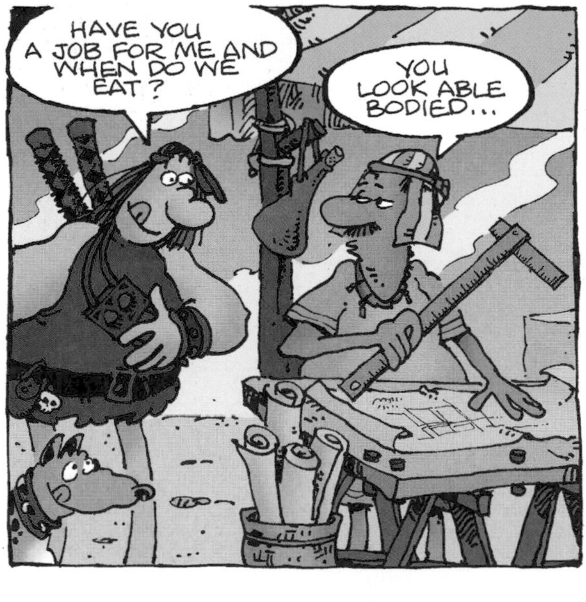
HAVE YOU A JOB FOR ME AND WHEN DO WE EAT?
YOU LOOK ABLE BODIED...

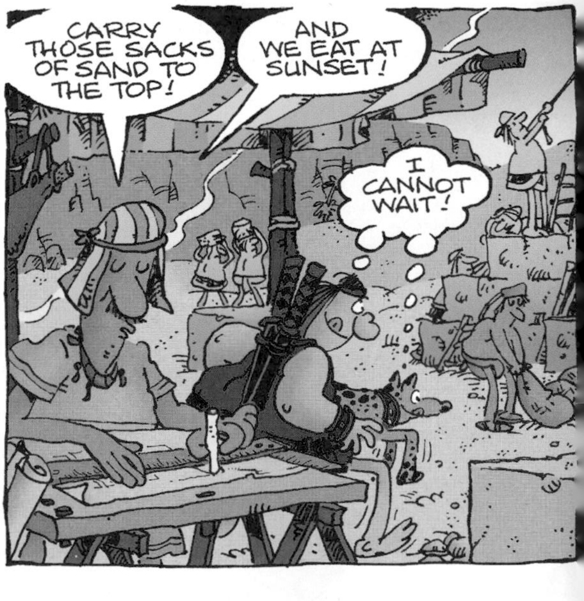
CARRY THOSE SACKS OF SAND TO THE TOP!
AND WE EAT AT SUNSET!
I CANNOT WAIT!

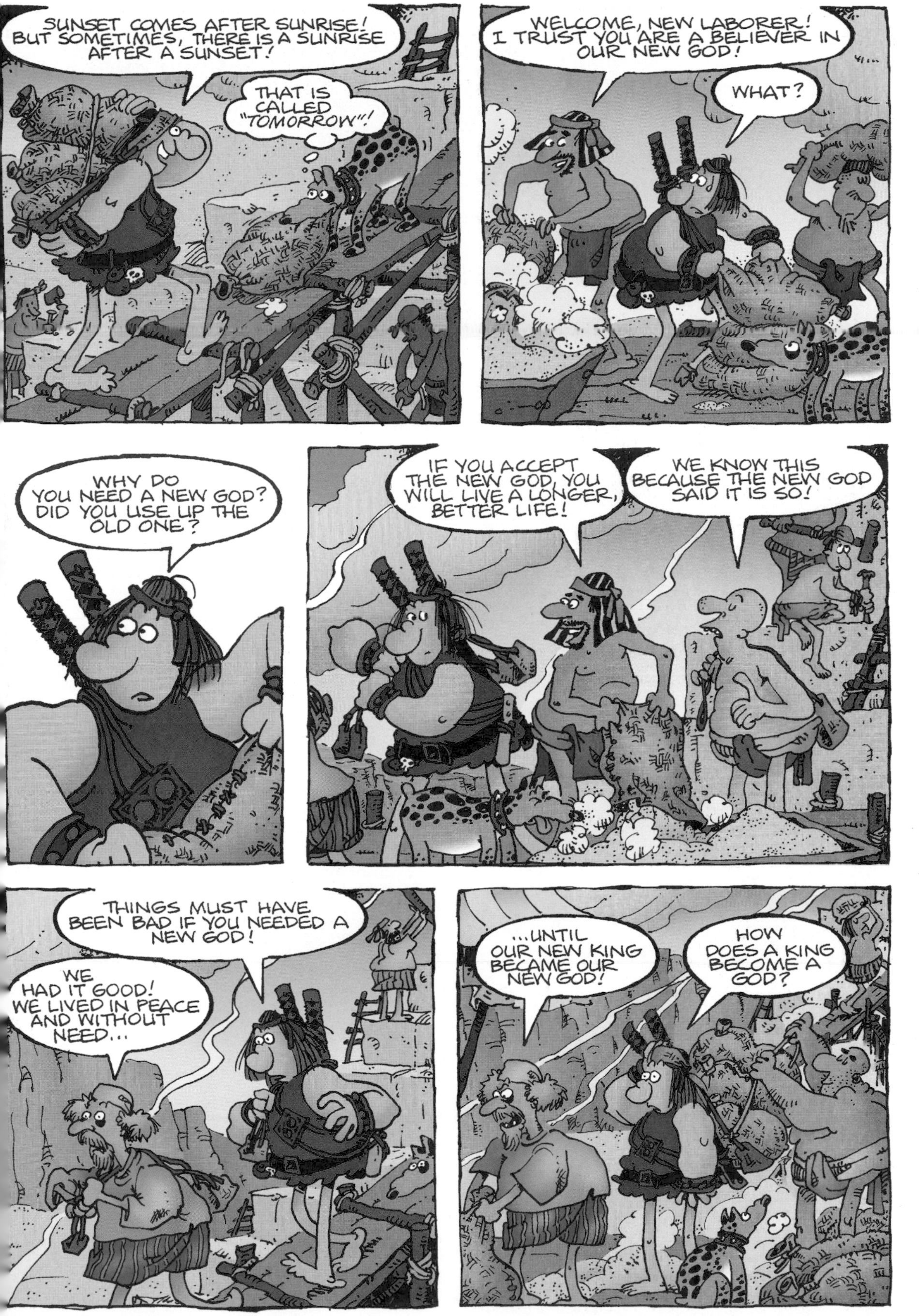
SUNSET COMES AFTER SUNRISE! BUT SOMETIMES, THERE IS A SUNRISE AFTER A SUNSET!
THAT IS CALLED "TOMORROW"!
WELCOME, NEW LABORER! I TRUST YOU ARE A BELIEVER IN OUR NEW GOD!
WHAT?
WHY DO YOU NEED A NEW GOD? DID YOU USE UP THE OLD ONE?
IF YOU ACCEPT THE NEW GOD, YOU WILL LIVE A LONGER, BETTER LIFE!
WE KNOW THIS BECAUSE THE NEW GOD SAID IT IS SO!
THINGS MUST HAVE BEEN BAD IF YOU NEEDED A NEW GOD!
WE HAD IT GOOD! WE LIVED IN PEACE AND WITHOUT NEED...
...UNTIL OUR NEW KING BECAME OUR NEW GOD!
HOW DOES A KING BECOME A GOD?

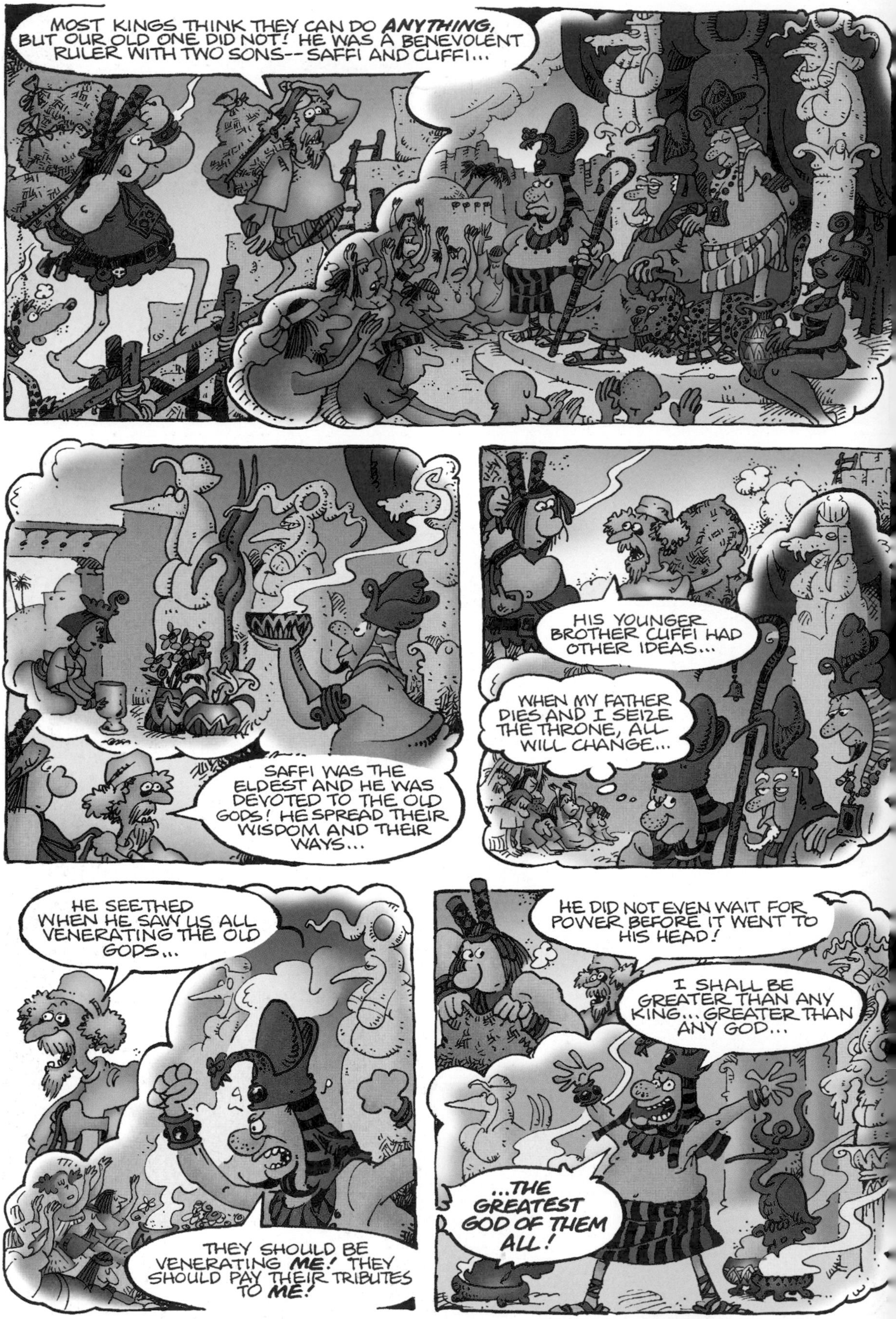
MOST KINGS THINK THEY CAN DO ANYTHING, BUT OUR OLD ONE DID NOT! HE WAS A BENEVOLENT RULER WITH TWO SONS-- SAFFI AND CUFFI...
SAFFI WAS THE ELDEST AND HE WAS DEVOTED TO THE OLD GODS! HE SPREAD THEIR WISDOM AND THEIR WAYS...
HIS YOUNGER BROTHER CUFFI HAD OTHER IDEAS...
WHEN MY FATHER DIES AND I SEIZE THE THRONE, ALL WILL CHANGE...
HE SEETHED WHEN HE SAW US ALL VENERATING THE OLD GODS...
THEY SHOULD BE VENERATING ME! THEY SHOULD PAY THEIR TRIBUTES TO ME!
HE DID NOT EVEN WAIT FOR POWER BEFORE IT WENT TO HIS HEAD!
I SHALL BE GREATER THAN ANY KING... GREATER THAN ANY GOD...
...THE GREATEST GOD OF THEM ALL!

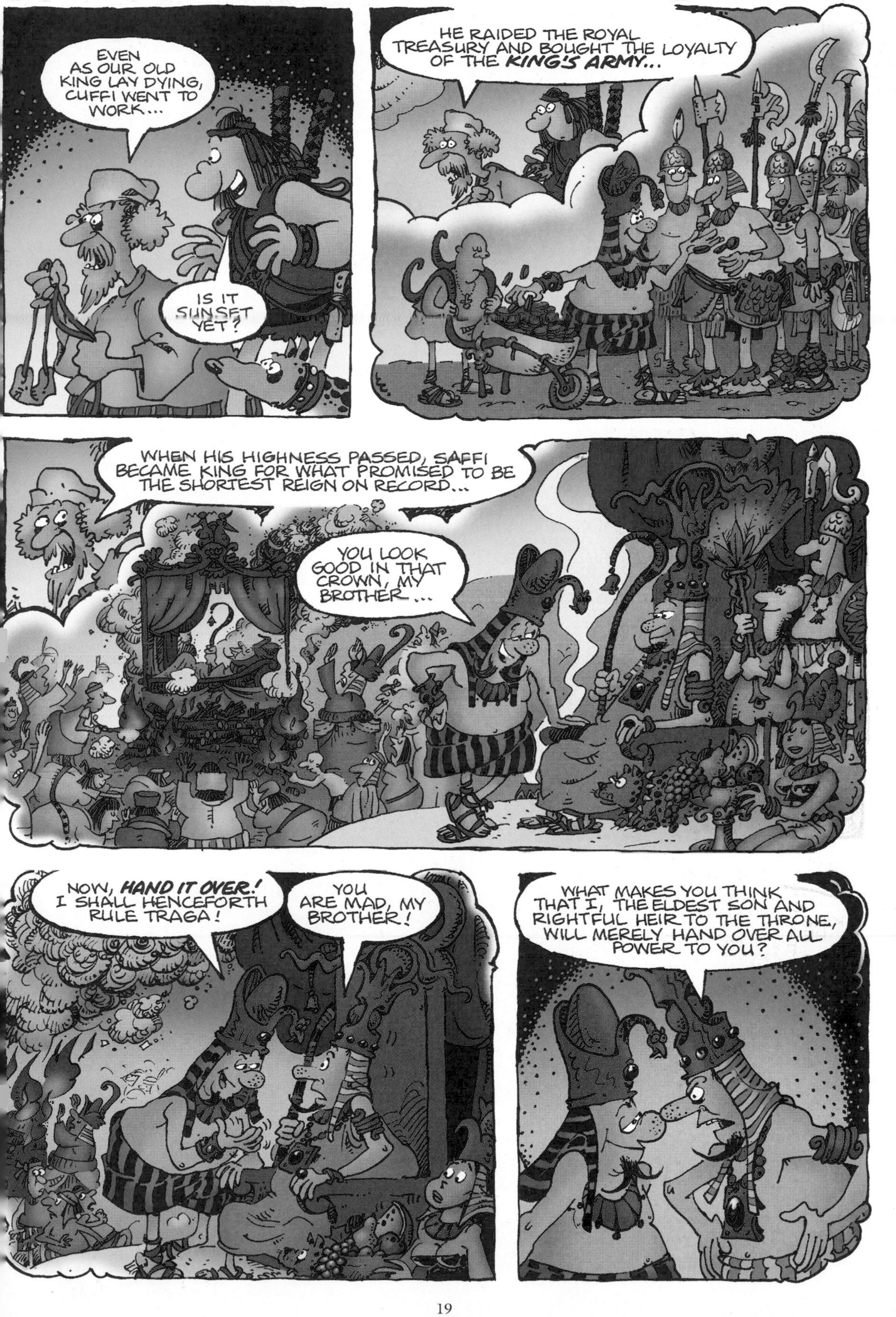
EVEN AS OUR OLD KING LAY DYING, CUFFI WENT TO WORK...
IS IT SUNSET YET?
HE RAIDED THE ROYAL TREASURY AND BOUGHT THE LOYALTY OF THE KING'S ARMY...
WHEN HIS HIGHNESS PASSED, SAFFI BECAME KING FOR WHAT PROMISED TO BE THE SHORTEST REIGN ON RECORD...
YOU LOOK GOOD IN THAT CROWN, MY BROTHER...
NOW, HAND IT OVER! I SHALL HENCEFORTH RULE TRAGA!
YOU ARE MAD, MY BROTHER!
WHAT MAKES YOU THINK THAT I, THE ELDEST SON AND RIGHTFUL HEIR TO THE THRONE, WILL MERELY HAND OVER ALL POWER TO YOU?

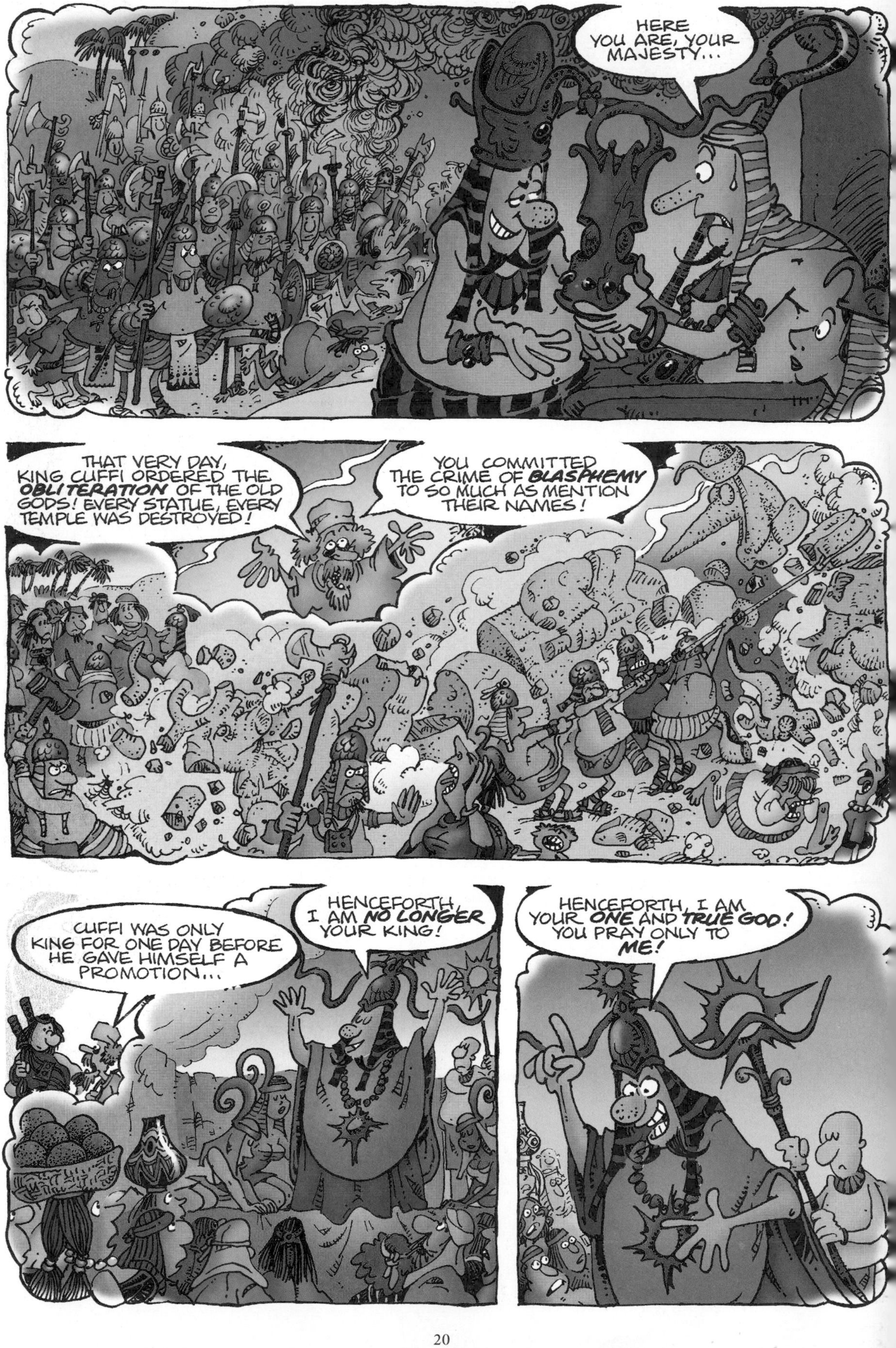
HERE YOU ARE, YOUR MAJESTY...
THAT VERY DAY, KING CUFFI ORDERED THE OBLITERATION OF THE OLD GODS! EVERY STATUE, EVERY TEMPLE WAS DESTROYED!
YOU COMMITTED THE CRIME OF BLASPHEMY TO SO MUCH AS MENTION THEIR NAMES!
CUFFI WAS ONLY KING FOR ONE DAY BEFORE HE GAVE HIMSELF A PROMOTION...
HENCEFORTH, I AM NO LONGER YOUR KING!
HENCEFORTH, I AM YOUR ONE AND TRUE GOD! YOU PRAY ONLY TO ME!

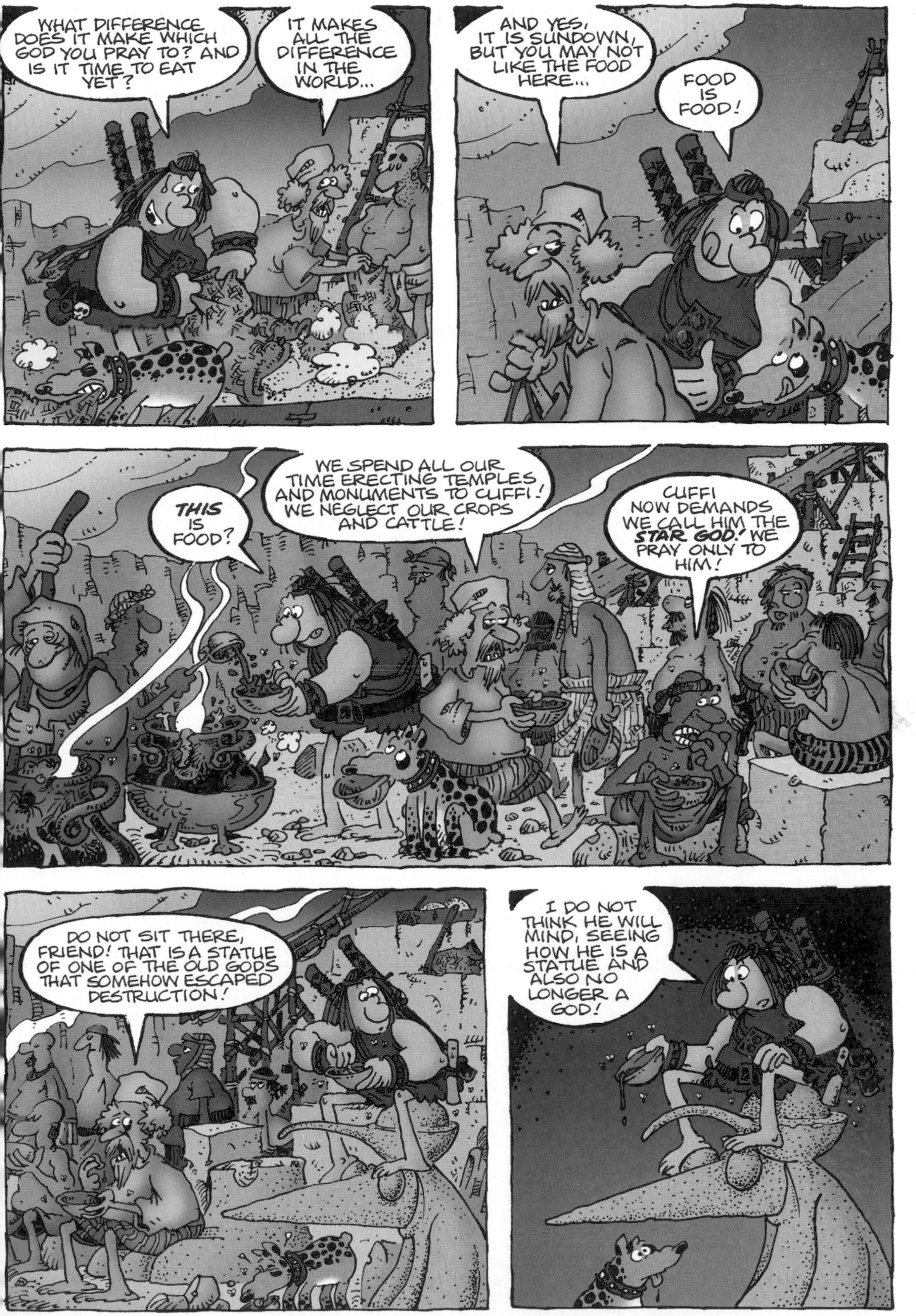

WHAT DIFFERENCE DOES IT MAKE WHICH GOD YOU PRAY TO? AND IS IT TIME TO EAT YET?
IT MAKES ALL THE DIFFERENCE IN THE WORLD...
AND YES, IT IS SUNDOWN, BUT YOU MAY NOT LIKE THE FOOD HERE...
FOOD IS FOOD!
THIS IS FOOD?
WE SPEND ALL OUR TIME ERECTING TEMPLES AND MONUMENTS TO CUFFI! WE NEGLECT OUR CROPS AND CATTLE!
CUFFI NOW DEMANDS WE CALL HIM THE **STAR GOD!** WE PRAY ONLY TO HIM!
DO NOT SIT THERE, FRIEND! THAT IS A STATUE OF ONE OF THE OLD GODS THAT SOMEHOW ESCAPED DESTRUCTION!
I DO NOT THINK HE WILL MIND, SEEING HOW HE IS A STATUE AND ALSO NO LONGER A GOD!

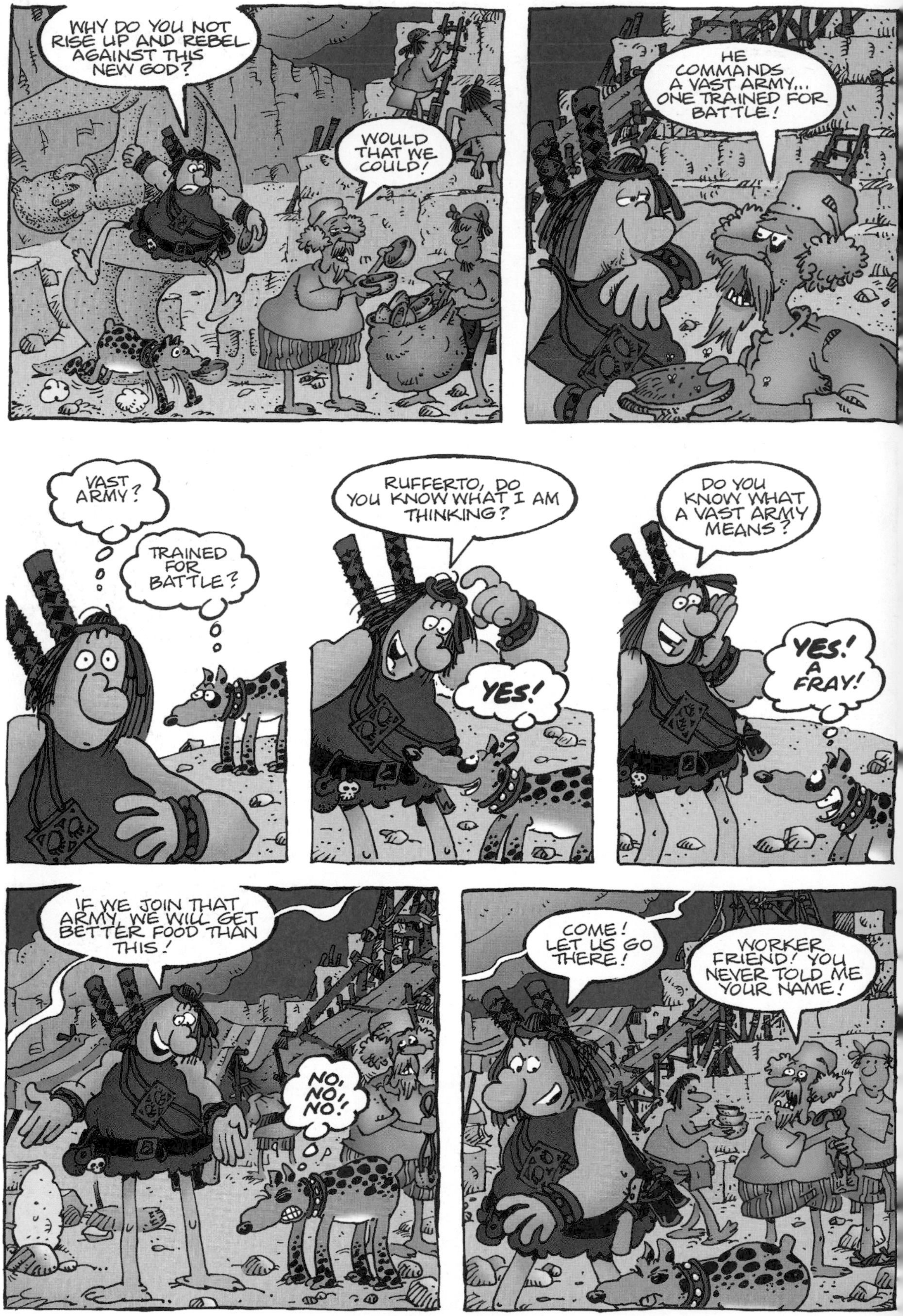
WHY DO YOU NOT RISE UP AND REBEL AGAINST THIS NEW GOD?
WOULD THAT WE COULD!
HE COMMANDS A VAST ARMY... ONE TRAINED FOR BATTLE!
VAST ARMY?
TRAINED FOR BATTLE?
RUFFERTO, DO YOU KNOW WHAT I AM THINKING?
YES!
DO YOU KNOW WHAT A VAST ARMY MEANS?
YES! A FRAY!
IF WE JOIN THAT ARMY, WE WILL GET BETTER FOOD THAN THIS!
NO, NO, NO!
COME! LET US GO THERE!
WORKER FRIEND! YOU NEVER TOLD ME YOUR NAME!

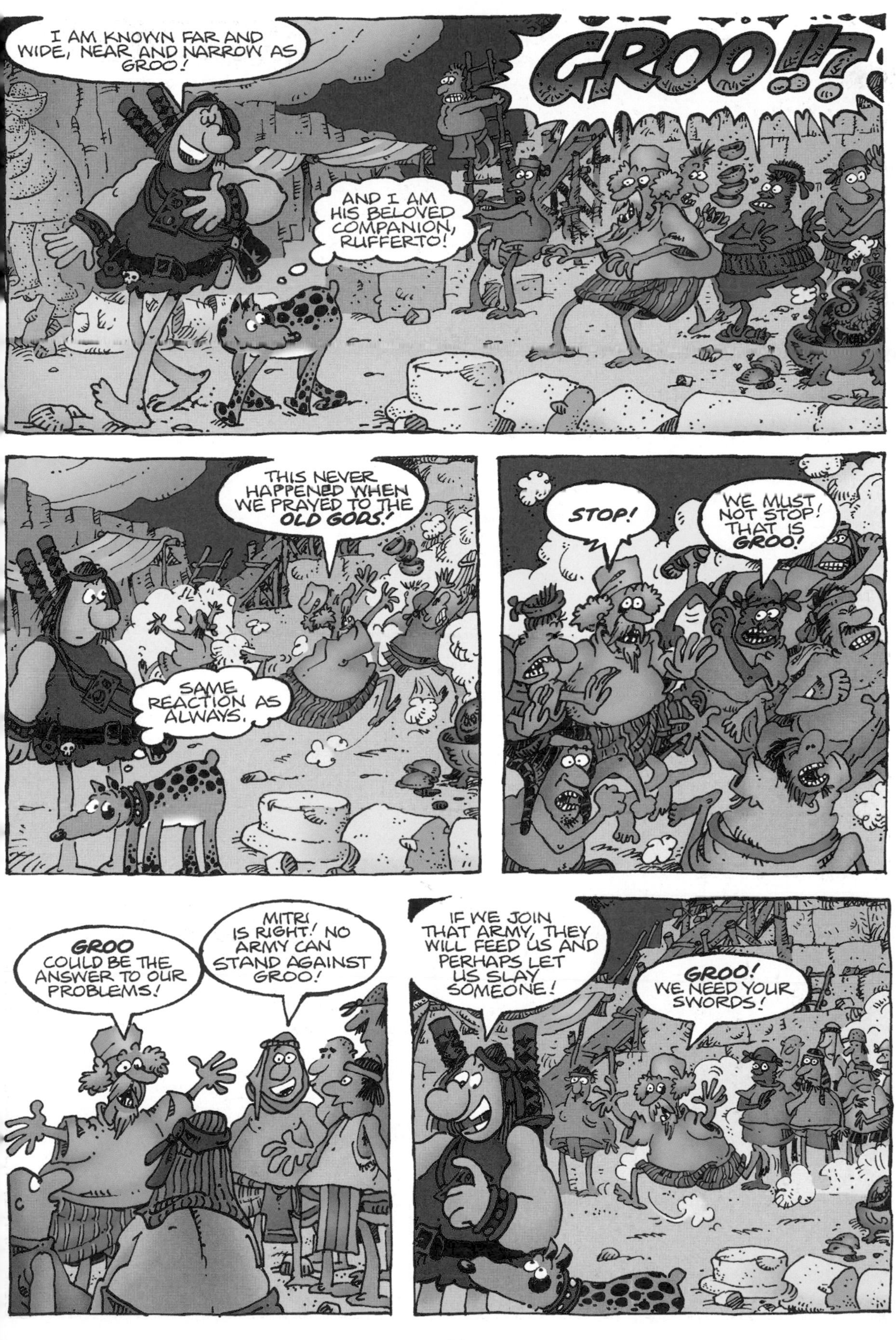
I AM KNOWN FAR AND WIDE, NEAR AND NARROW AS GROO!
GROO!!?
AND I AM HIS BELOVED COMPANION, RUFFERTO!
THIS NEVER HAPPENED WHEN WE PRAYED TO THE OLD GODS!
SAME REACTION AS ALWAYS.
STOP!
WE MUST NOT STOP! THAT IS GROO!
GROO COULD BE THE ANSWER TO OUR PROBLEMS!
MITRI IS RIGHT! NO ARMY CAN STAND AGAINST GROO!
IF WE JOIN THAT ARMY, THEY WILL FEED US AND PERHAPS LET US SLAY SOMEONE!
GROO! WE NEED YOUR SWORDS!

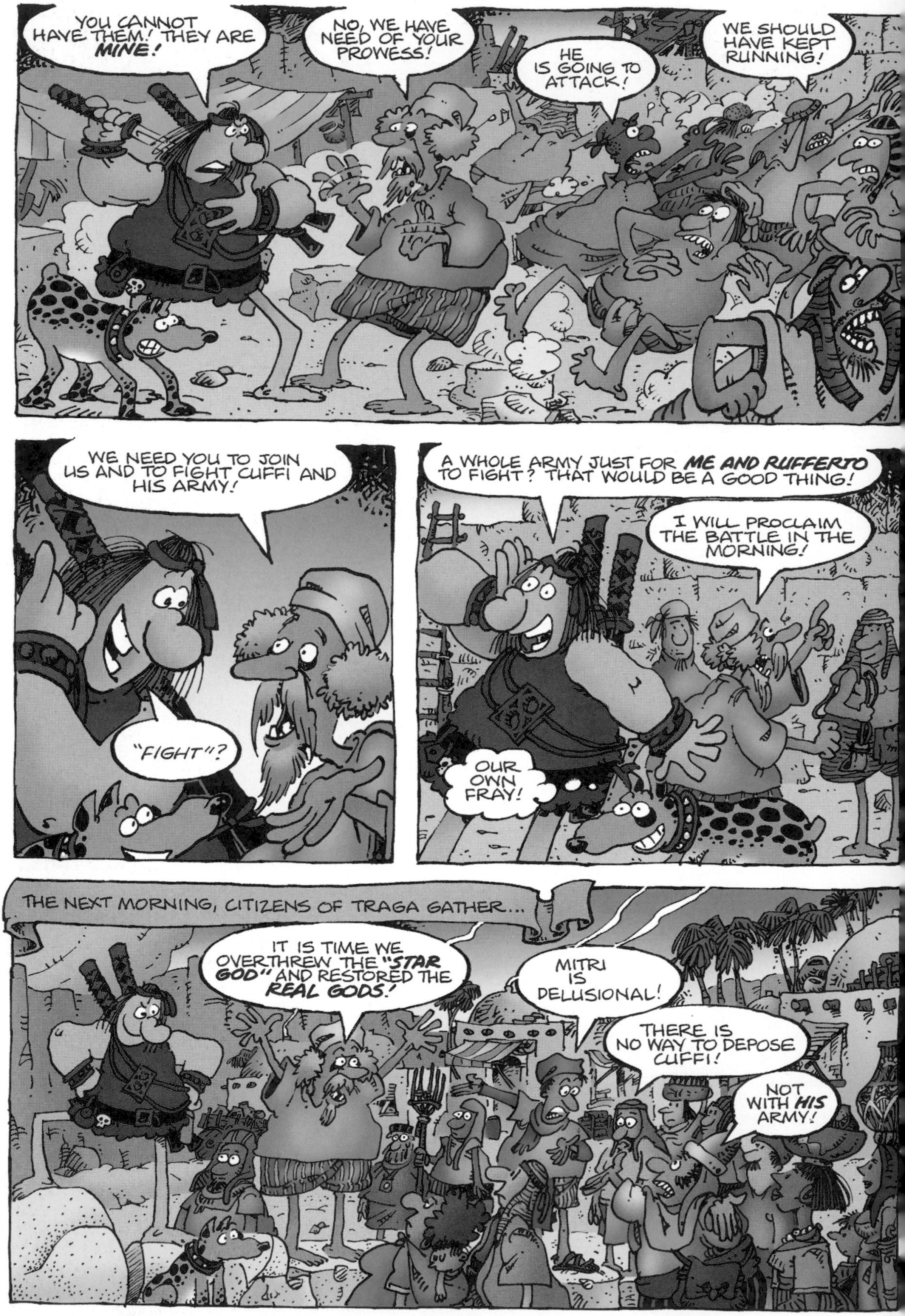
YOU CANNOT HAVE THEM! THEY ARE MINE!
NO, WE HAVE NEED OF YOUR PROWESS!
HE IS GOING TO ATTACK!
WE SHOULD HAVE KEPT RUNNING!
WE NEED YOU TO JOIN US AND TO FIGHT CUFFI AND HIS ARMY!
"FIGHT"?
A WHOLE ARMY JUST FOR ME AND RUFFERTO TO FIGHT? THAT WOULD BE A GOOD THING!
I WILL PROCLAIM THE BATTLE IN THE MORNING!
OUR OWN FRAY!
THE NEXT MORNING, CITIZENS OF TRAGA GATHER...
IT IS TIME WE OVERTHREW THE "STAR GOD" AND RESTORED THE REAL GODS!
MITRI IS DELUSIONAL!
THERE IS NO WAY TO DEPOSE CUFFI!
NOT WITH HIS ARMY!

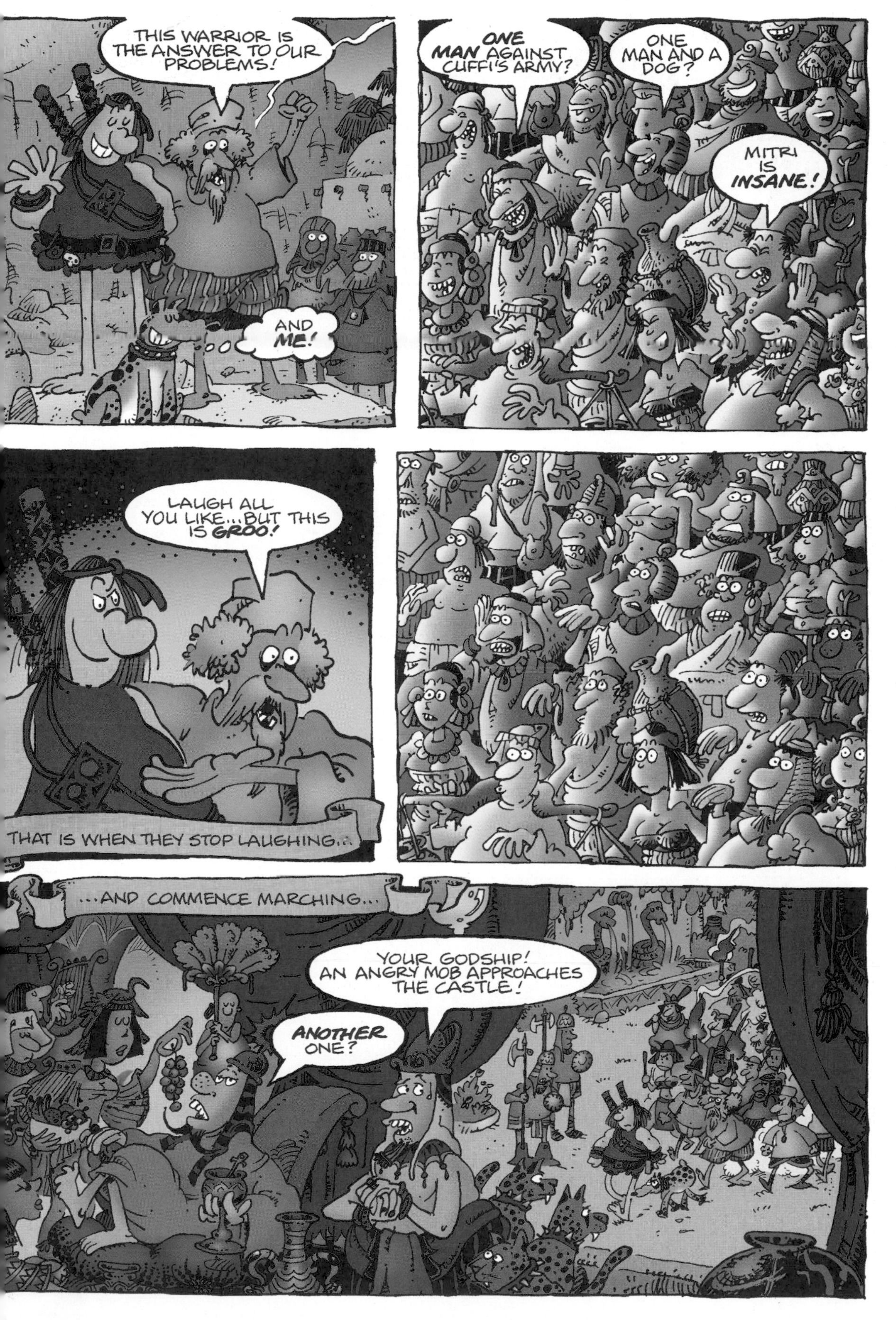
THIS WARRIOR IS THE ANSWER TO OUR PROBLEMS!
AND ME!
ONE MAN AGAINST CUFFI'S ARMY?
ONE MAN AND A DOG?
MITRI IS INSANE!
LAUGH ALL YOU LIKE...BUT THIS IS GROO!
THAT IS WHEN THEY STOP LAUGHING...
...AND COMMENCE MARCHING...
YOUR GODSHIP! AN ANGRY MOB APPROACHES THE CASTLE!
ANOTHER ONE?

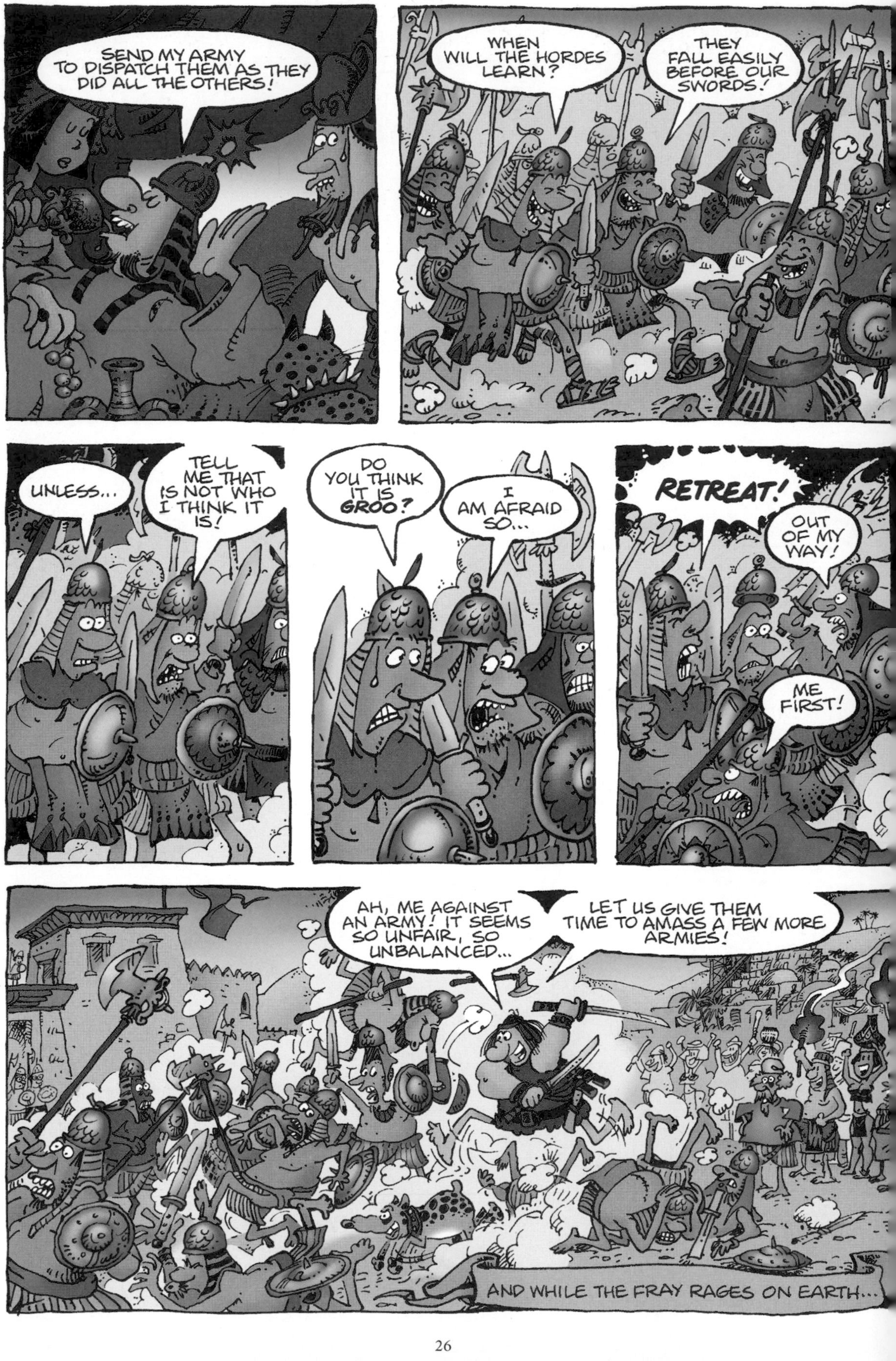
SEND MY ARMY TO DISPATCH THEM AS THEY DID ALL THE OTHERS!
WHEN WILL THE HORDES LEARN?
THEY FALL EASILY BEFORE OUR SWORDS!
UNLESS...
TELL ME THAT IS NOT WHO I THINK IT IS!
DO YOU THINK IT IS GROO?
I AM AFRAID SO...
RETREAT!
OUT OF MY WAY!
ME FIRST!
AH, ME AGAINST AN ARMY! IT SEEMS SO UNFAIR, SO UNBALANCED...
LET US GIVE THEM TIME TO AMASS A FEW MORE ARMIES!
AND WHILE THE FRAY RAGES ON EARTH...

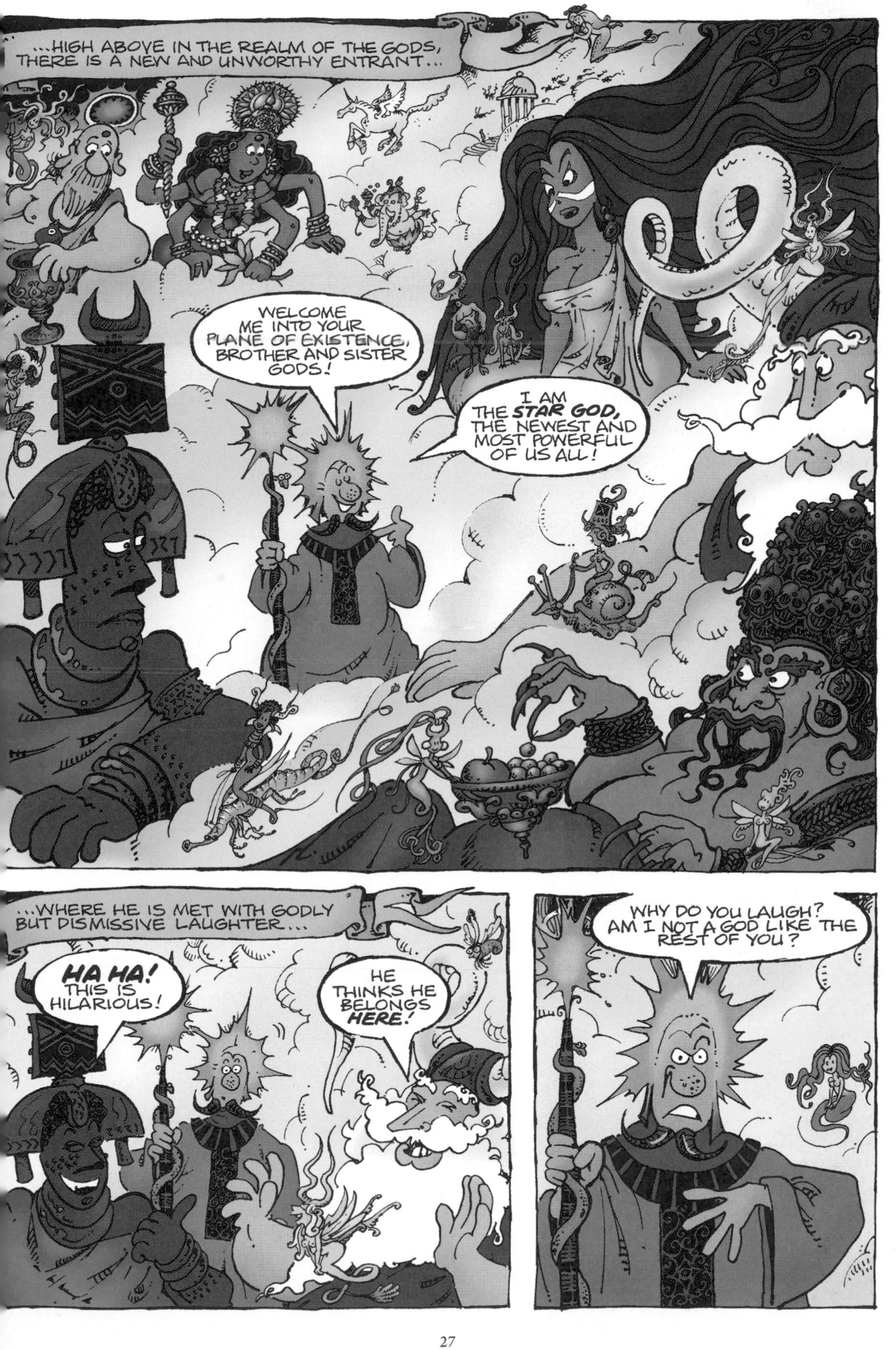
...HIGH ABOVE IN THE REALM OF THE GODS, THERE IS A NEW AND UNWORTHY ENTRANT...
WELCOME ME INTO YOUR PLANE OF EXISTENCE, BROTHER AND SISTER GODS!
I AM THE STAR GOD, THE NEWEST AND MOST POWERFUL OF US ALL!
...WHERE HE IS MET WITH GODLY BUT DISMISSIVE LAUGHTER...
HA HA! THIS IS HILARIOUS!
HE THINKS HE BELONGS HERE!
WHY DO YOU LAUGH? AM I NOT A GOD LIKE THE REST OF YOU?

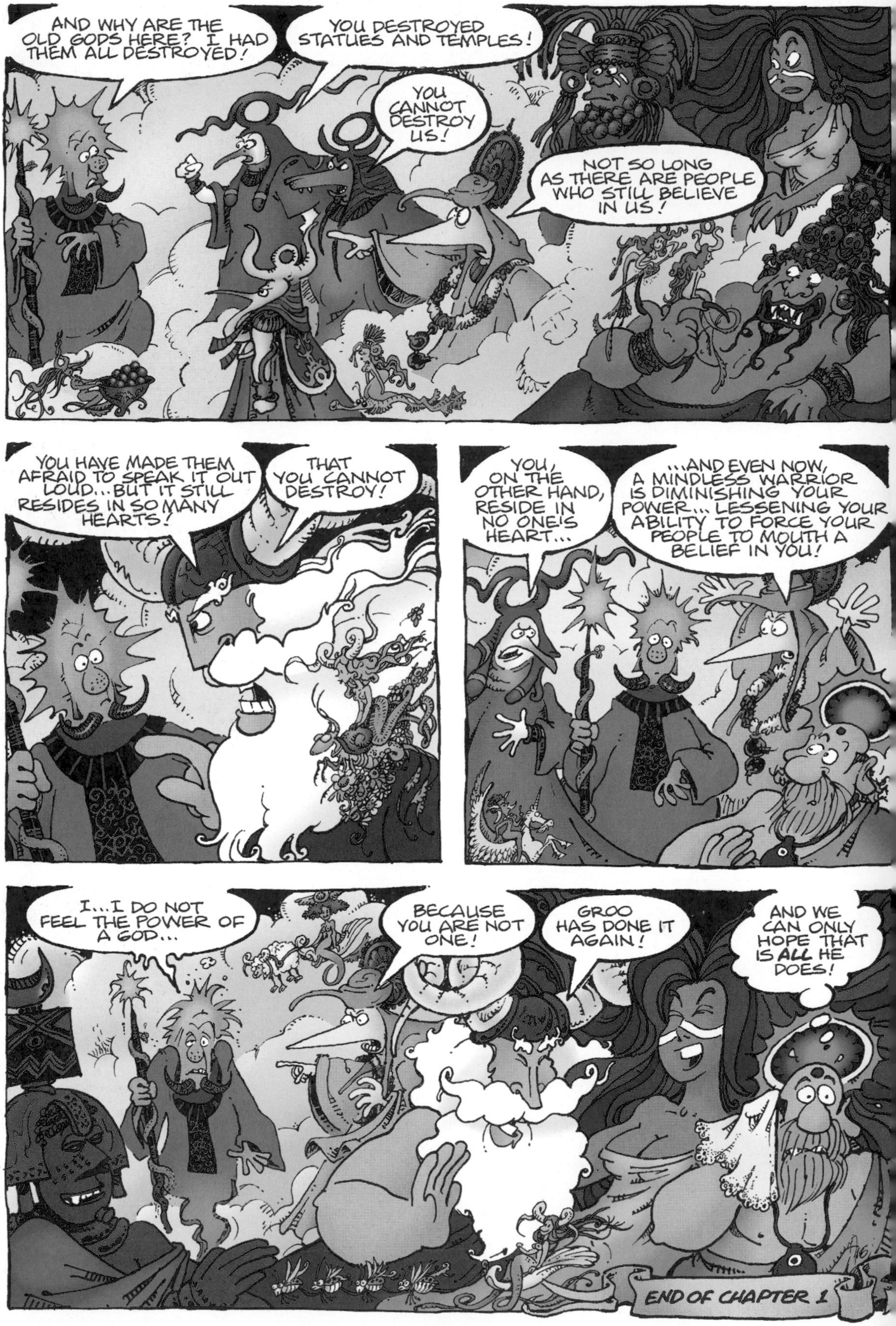
AND WHY ARE THE OLD GODS HERE? I HAD THEM ALL DESTROYED!
YOU DESTROYED STATUES AND TEMPLES!
YOU CANNOT DESTROY US!
NOT SO LONG AS THERE ARE PEOPLE WHO STILL BELIEVE IN US!
YOU HAVE MADE THEM AFRAID TO SPEAK IT OUT LOUD... BUT IT STILL RESIDES IN SO MANY HEARTS!
THAT YOU CANNOT DESTROY!
YOU, ON THE OTHER HAND, RESIDE IN NO ONE'S HEART...
...AND EVEN NOW, A MINDLESS WARRIOR IS DIMINISHING YOUR POWER... LESSENING YOUR ABILITY TO FORCE YOUR PEOPLE TO MOUTH A BELIEF IN YOU!
I...I DO NOT FEEL THE POWER OF A GOD...
BECAUSE YOU ARE NOT ONE!
GROO HAS DONE IT AGAIN!
AND WE CAN ONLY HOPE THAT IS ALL HE DOES!
END OF CHAPTER 1

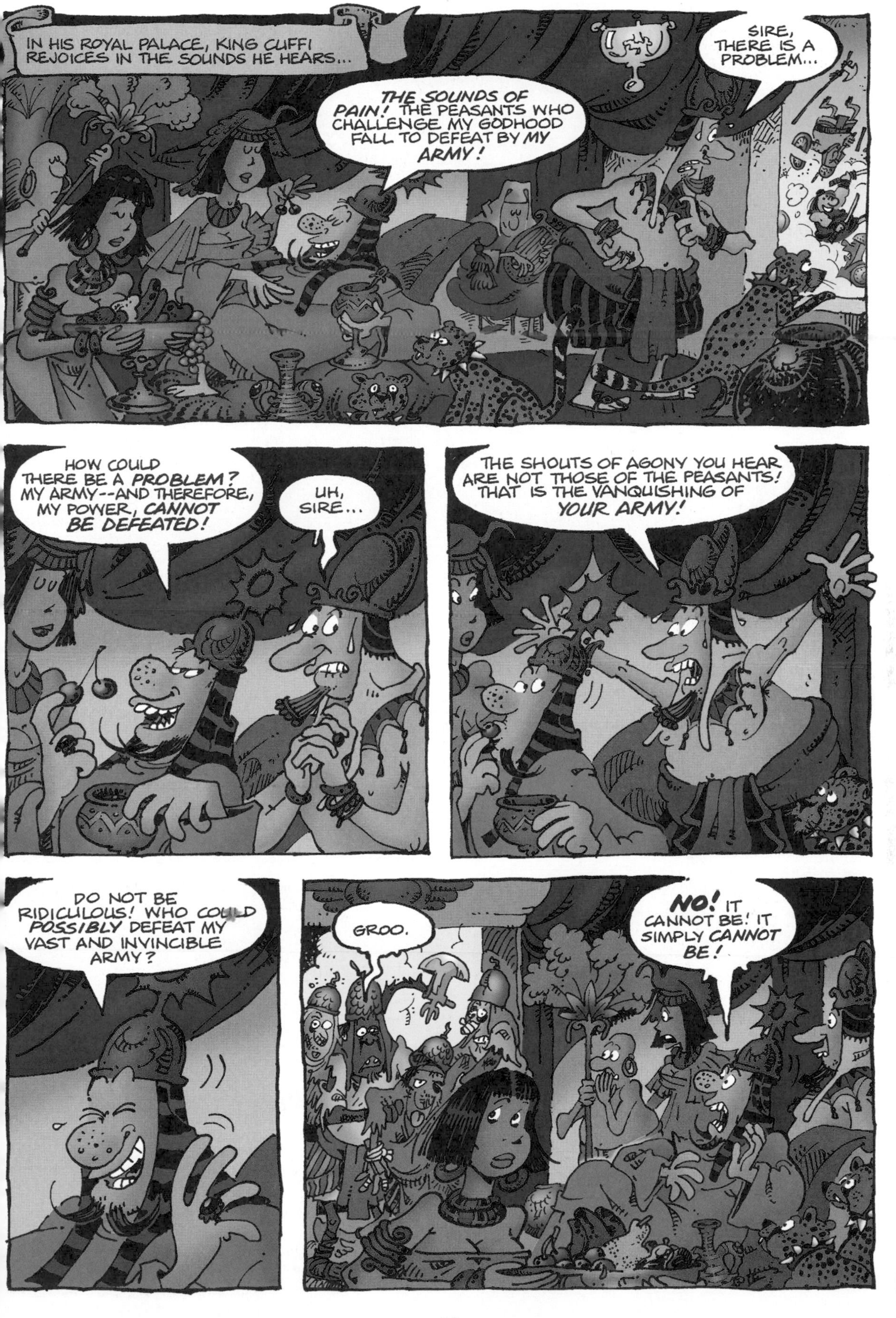
IN HIS ROYAL PALACE, KING CUFFI REJOICES IN THE SOUNDS HE HEARS...
THE SOUNDS OF PAIN! THE PEASANTS WHO CHALLENGE MY GODHOOD FALL TO DEFEAT BY *MY ARMY!*
SIRE, THERE IS A PROBLEM...
HOW COULD THERE BE A *PROBLEM?* MY ARMY--AND THEREFORE, MY POWER, *CANNOT BE DEFEATED!*
UH, SIRE...
THE SHOUTS OF AGONY YOU HEAR ARE NOT THOSE OF THE PEASANTS! THAT IS THE VANQUISHING OF *YOUR ARMY!*
DO NOT BE RIDICULOUS! WHO COULD *POSSIBLY* DEFEAT MY VAST AND INVINCIBLE ARMY?
GROO.
NO! IT CANNOT BE! IT SIMPLY *CANNOT BE!*

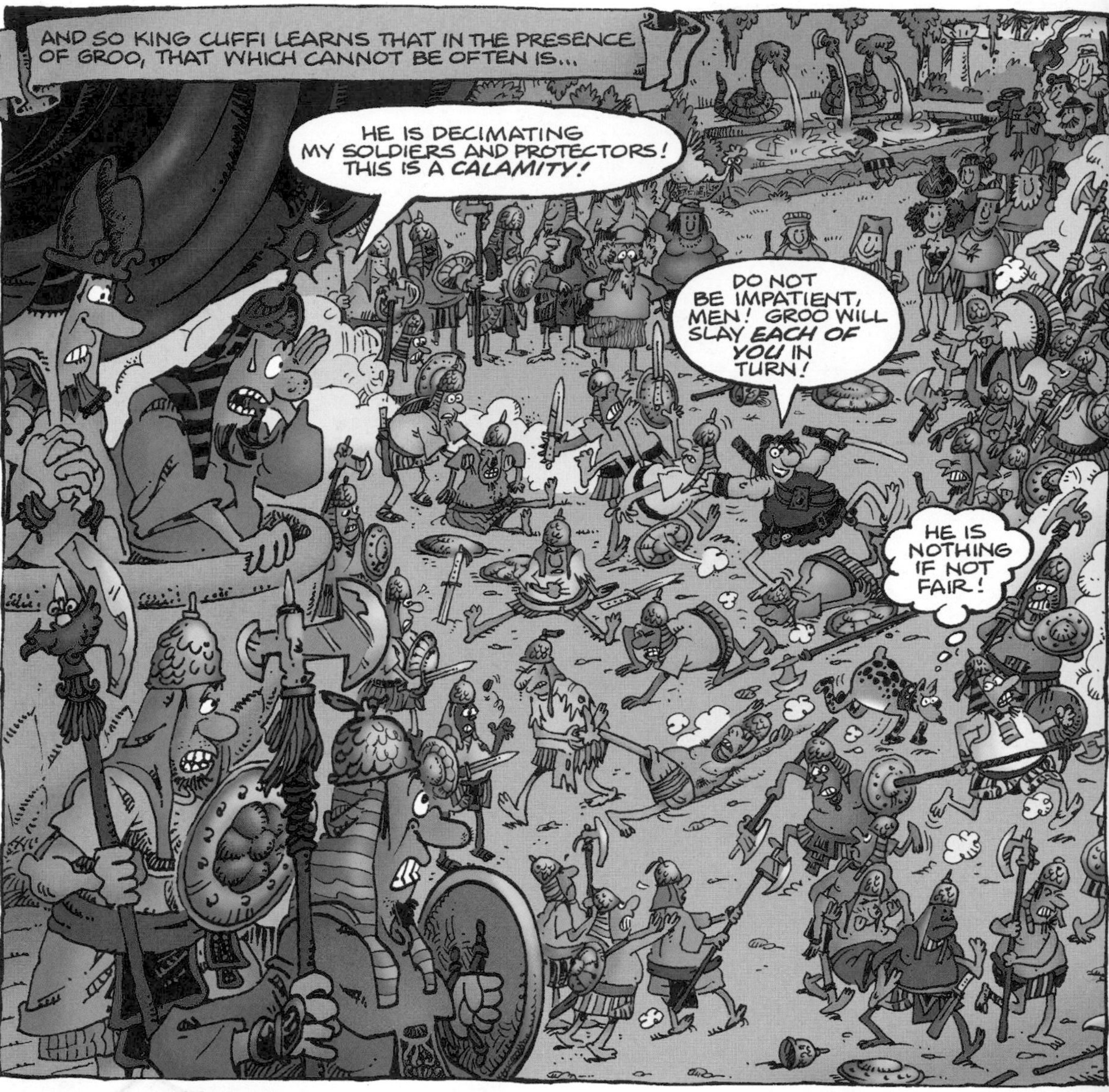
AND SO KING CUFFI LEARNS THAT IN THE PRESENCE OF GROO, THAT WHICH CANNOT BE OFTEN IS...
HE IS DECIMATING MY SOLDIERS AND PROTECTORS! THIS IS A CALAMITY!
DO NOT BE IMPATIENT, MEN! GROO WILL SLAY EACH OF YOU IN TURN!
HE IS NOTHING IF NOT FAIR!

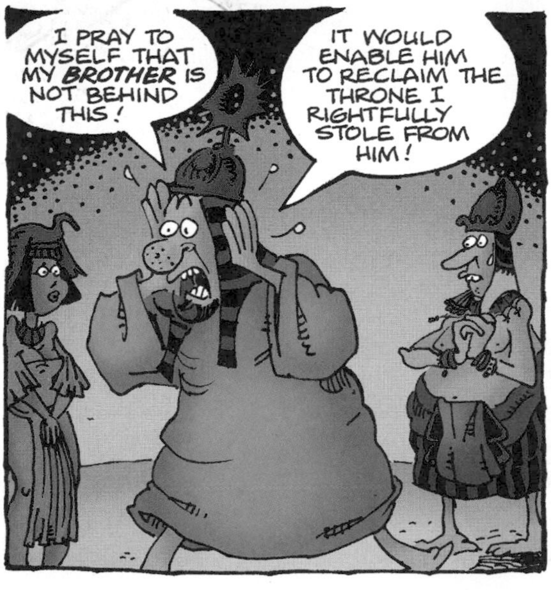
I PRAY TO MYSELF THAT MY BROTHER IS NOT BEHIND THIS!
IT WOULD ENABLE HIM TO RECLAIM THE THRONE I RIGHTFULLY STOLE FROM HIM!

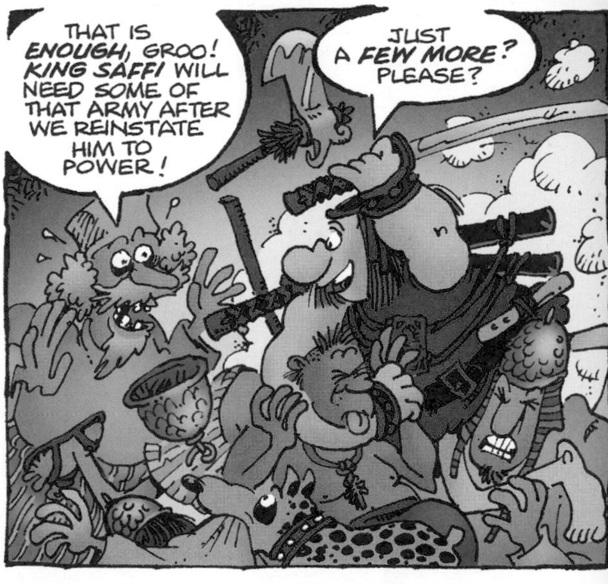
THAT IS ENOUGH, GROO! KING SAFFI WILL NEED SOME OF THAT ARMY AFTER WE REINSTATE HIM TO POWER!
JUST A FEW MORE? PLEASE?

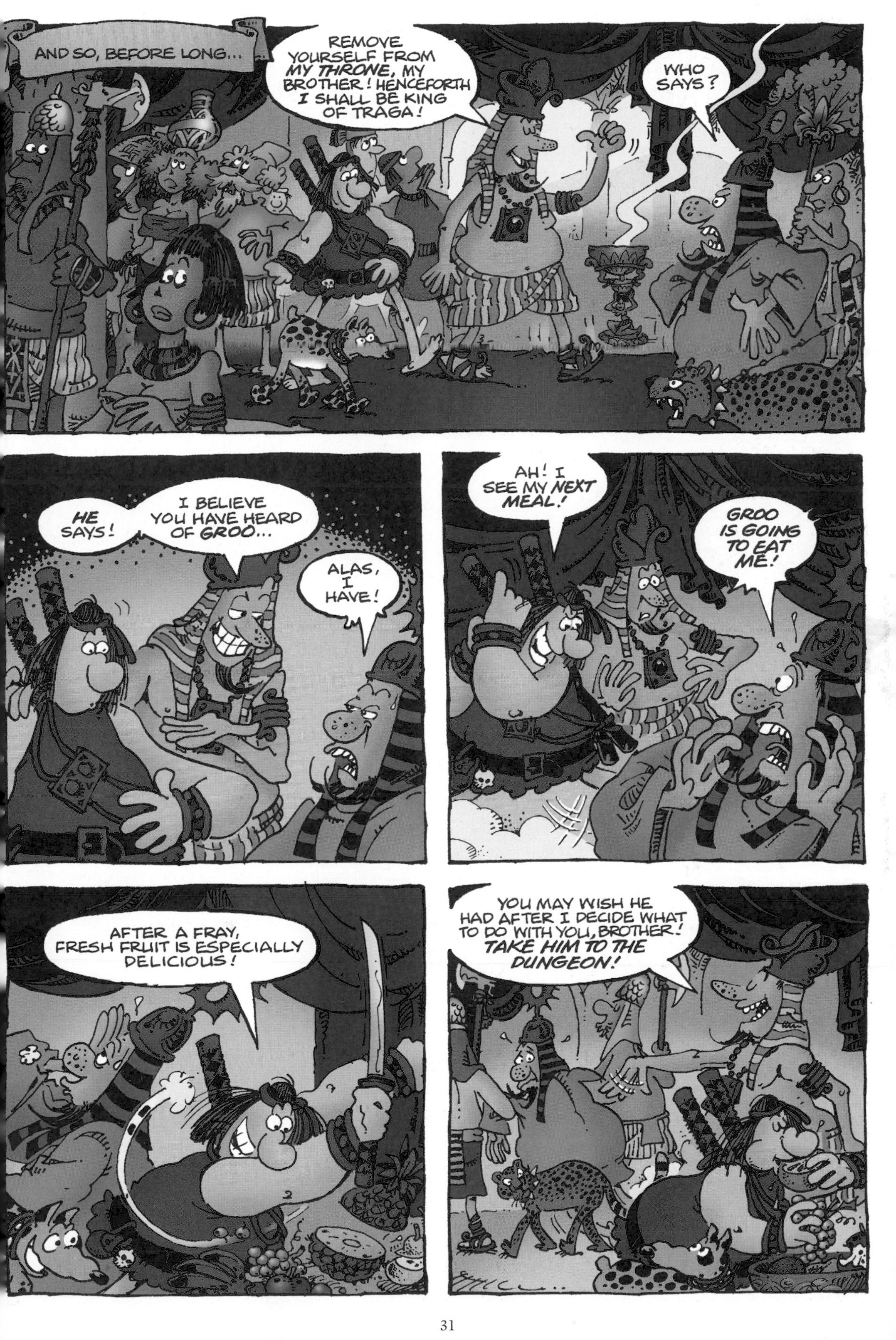
AND SO, BEFORE LONG...
REMOVE YOURSELF FROM MY THRONE, MY BROTHER! HENCEFORTH I SHALL BE KING OF TRAGA!
WHO SAYS?
HE SAYS!
I BELIEVE YOU HAVE HEARD OF GROO...
ALAS, I HAVE!
AH! I SEE MY NEXT MEAL!
GROO IS GOING TO EAT ME!
AFTER A FRAY, FRESH FRUIT IS ESPECIALLY DELICIOUS!
YOU MAY WISH HE HAD AFTER I DECIDE WHAT TO DO WITH YOU, BROTHER! TAKE HIM TO THE DUNGEON!

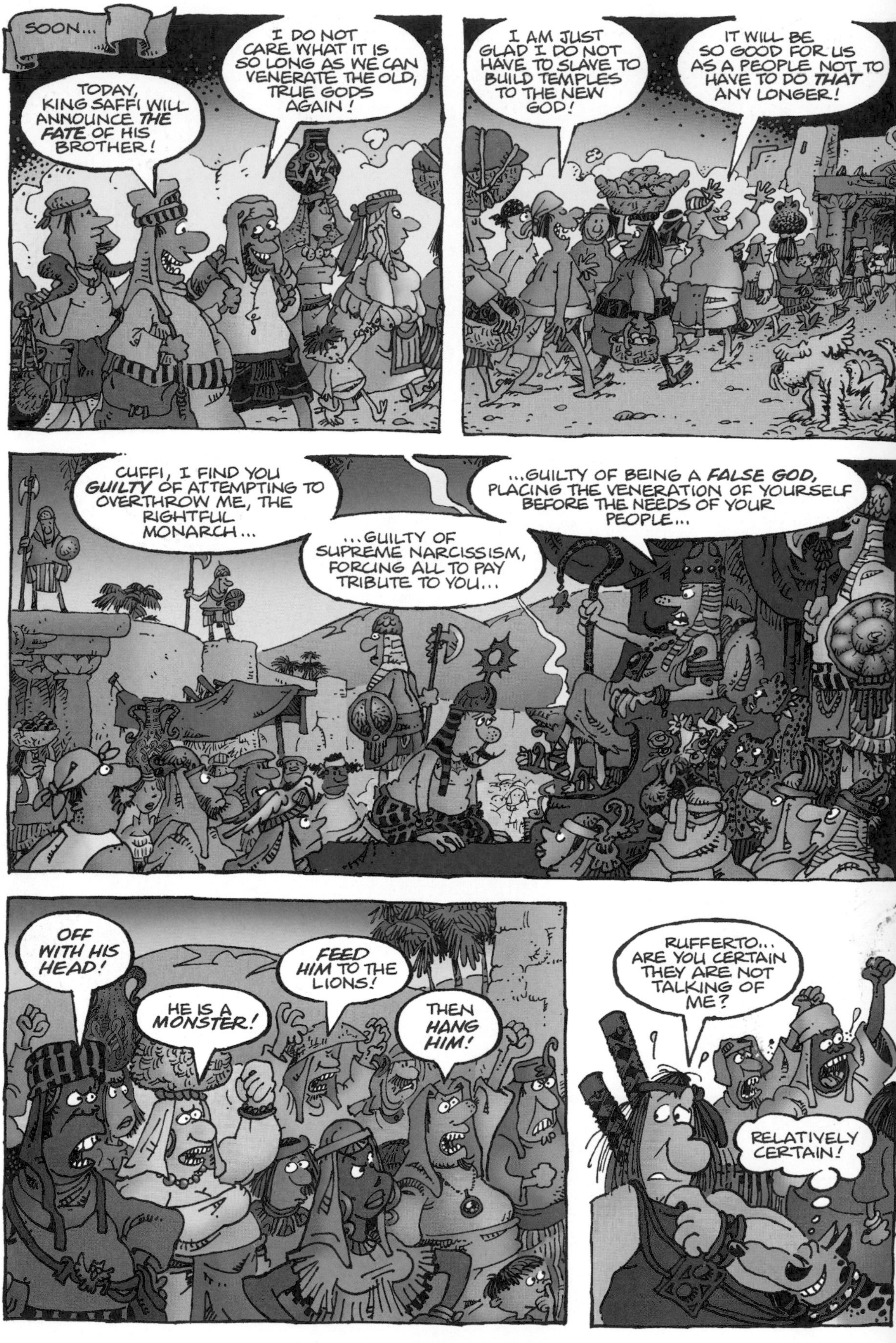
SOON...
TODAY, KING SAFFI WILL ANNOUNCE *THE FATE* OF HIS BROTHER!
I DO NOT CARE WHAT IT IS SO LONG AS WE CAN VENERATE THE OLD, TRUE GODS AGAIN!
I AM JUST GLAD I DO NOT HAVE TO SLAVE TO BUILD TEMPLES TO THE NEW GOD!
IT WILL BE SO GOOD FOR US AS A PEOPLE NOT TO HAVE TO DO *THAT* ANY LONGER!
CUFFI, I FIND YOU *GUILTY* OF ATTEMPTING TO OVERTHROW ME, THE RIGHTFUL MONARCH...
...GUILTY OF SUPREME NARCISSISM, FORCING ALL TO PAY TRIBUTE TO YOU...
...GUILTY OF BEING A *FALSE GOD,* PLACING THE VENERATION OF YOURSELF BEFORE THE NEEDS OF YOUR PEOPLE...
OFF WITH HIS HEAD!
HE IS A *MONSTER!*
FEED HIM TO THE LIONS!
THEN *HANG HIM!*
RUFFERTO... ARE YOU CERTAIN THEY ARE NOT TALKING OF ME?
RELATIVELY CERTAIN!

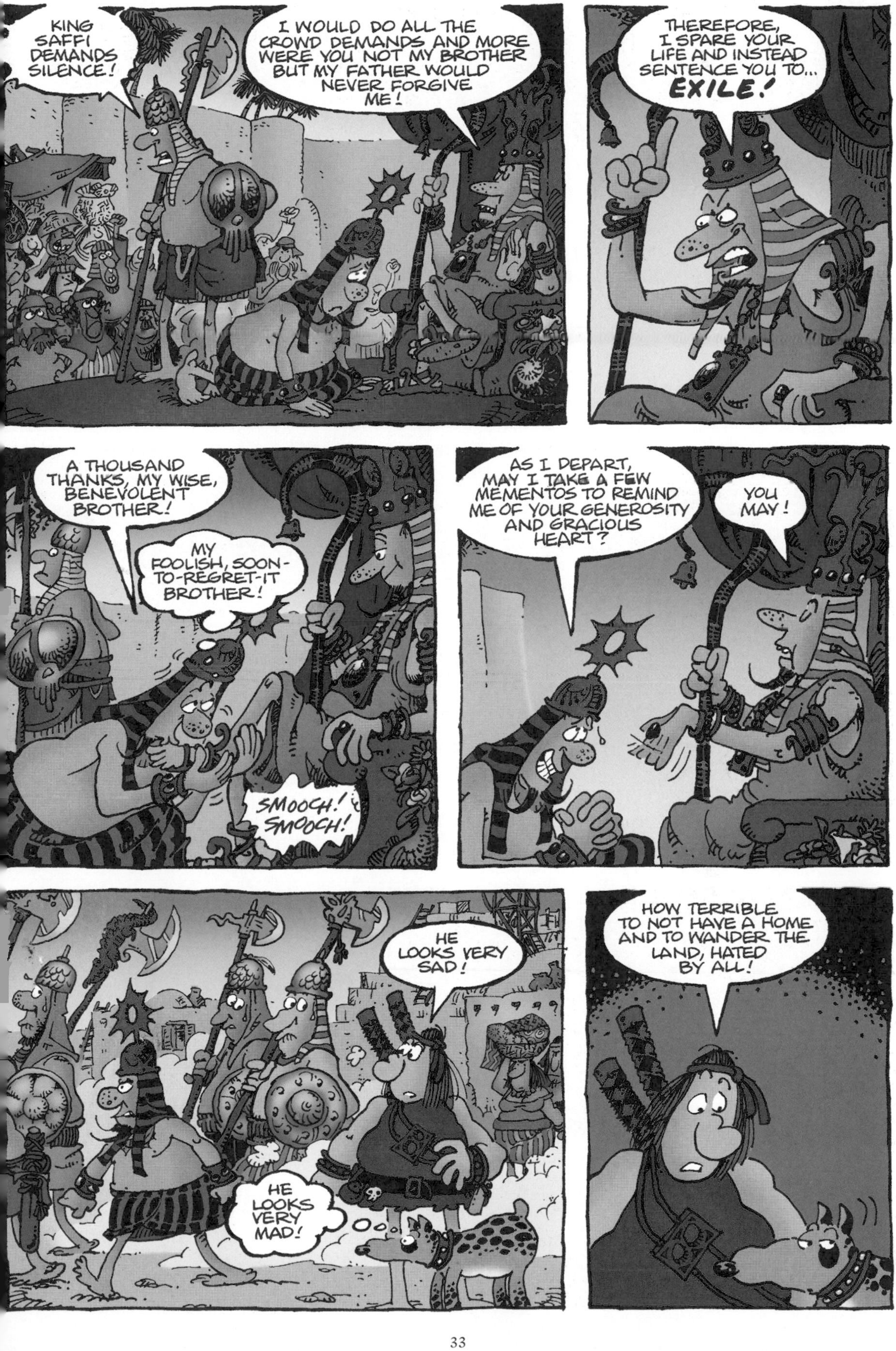
KING SAFFI DEMANDS SILENCE!
I WOULD DO ALL THE CROWD DEMANDS AND MORE WERE YOU NOT MY BROTHER BUT MY FATHER WOULD NEVER FORGIVE ME!
THEREFORE, I SPARE YOUR LIFE AND INSTEAD SENTENCE YOU TO... EXILE!
A THOUSAND THANKS, MY WISE, BENEVOLENT BROTHER!
MY FOOLISH, SOON-TO-REGRET-IT BROTHER!
SMOOCH! SMOOCH!
AS I DEPART, MAY I TAKE A FEW MEMENTOS TO REMIND ME OF YOUR GENEROSITY AND GRACIOUS HEART?
YOU MAY!
HE LOOKS VERY SAD!
HE LOOKS VERY MAD!
HOW TERRIBLE TO NOT HAVE A HOME AND TO WANDER THE LAND, HATED BY ALL!

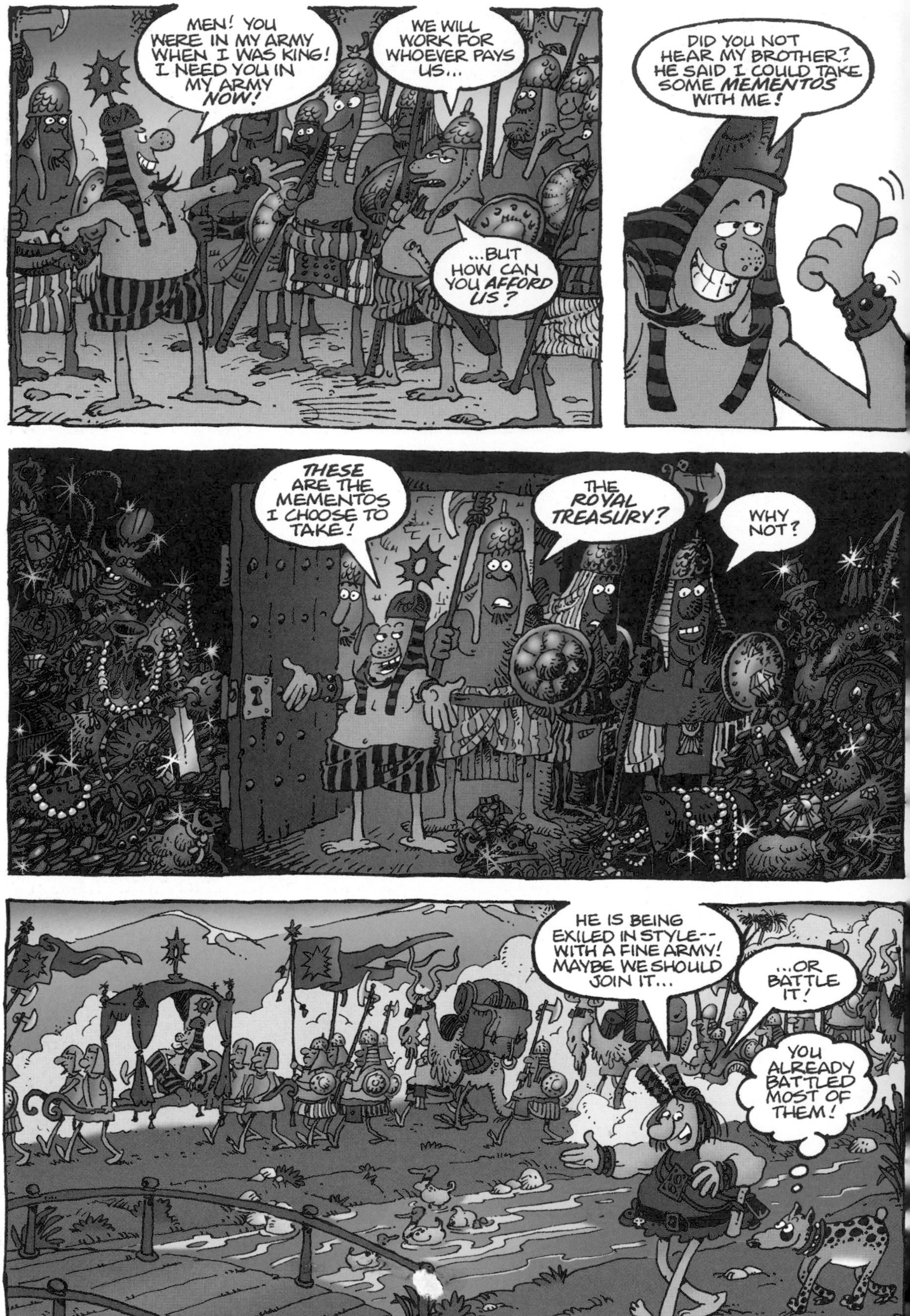

MEN! YOU WERE IN MY ARMY WHEN I WAS KING! I NEED YOU IN MY ARMY NOW!
WE WILL WORK FOR WHOEVER PAYS US...
...BUT HOW CAN YOU AFFORD US?
DID YOU NOT HEAR MY BROTHER? HE SAID I COULD TAKE SOME MEMENTOS WITH ME!
THESE ARE THE MEMENTOS I CHOOSE TO TAKE!
THE ROYAL TREASURY?
WHY NOT?
HE IS BEING EXILED IN STYLE-- WITH A FINE ARMY! MAYBE WE SHOULD JOIN IT...
...OR BATTLE IT!
YOU ALREADY BATTLED MOST OF THEM!

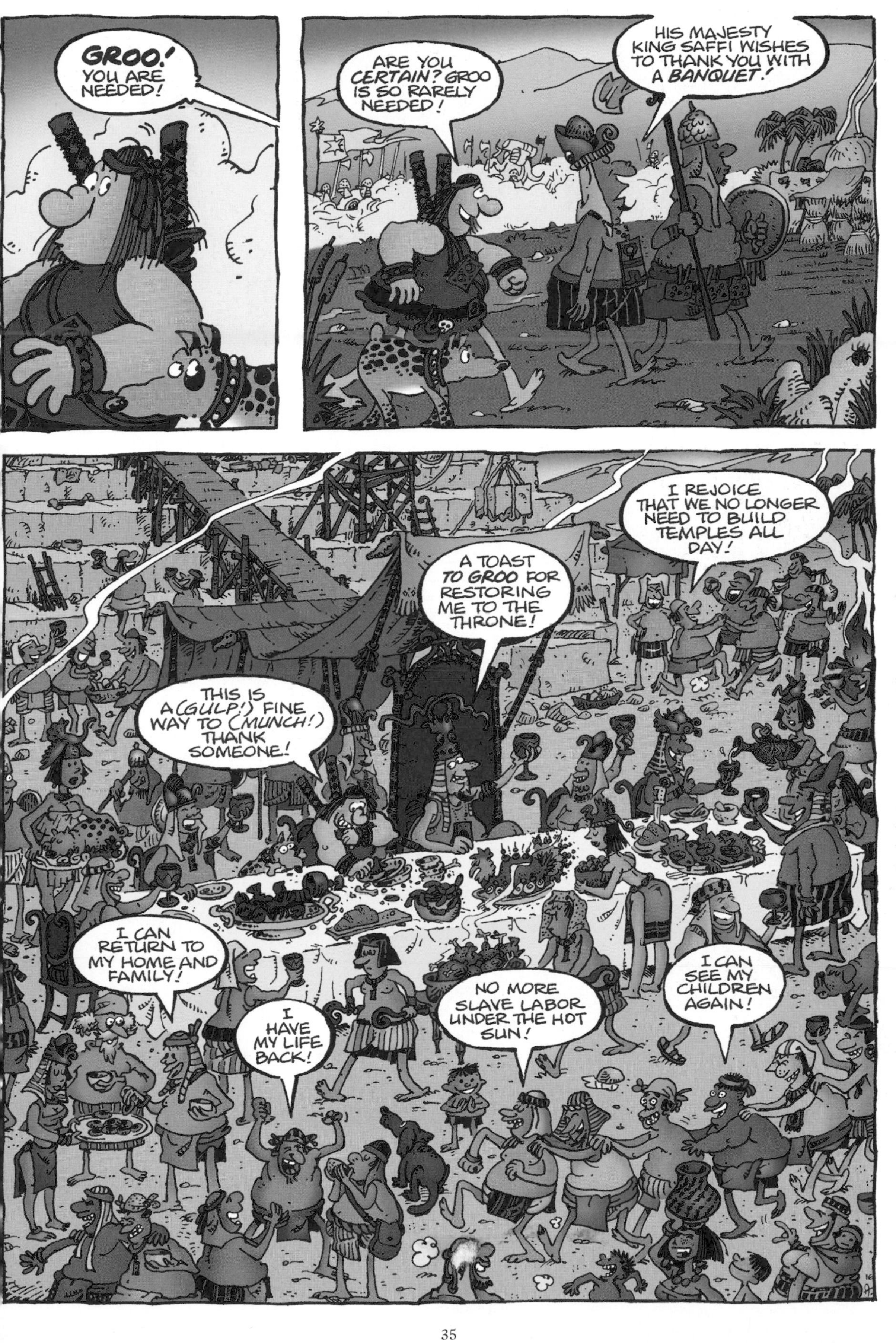
GROO! YOU ARE NEEDED!
ARE YOU CERTAIN? GROO IS SO RARELY NEEDED!
HIS MAJESTY KING SAFFI WISHES TO THANK YOU WITH A BANQUET!
I REJOICE THAT WE NO LONGER NEED TO BUILD TEMPLES ALL DAY!
A TOAST TO GROO FOR RESTORING ME TO THE THRONE!
THIS IS A (GULP!) FINE WAY TO (MUNCH!) THANK SOMEONE!
I CAN RETURN TO MY HOME AND FAMILY!
I HAVE MY LIFE BACK!
NO MORE SLAVE LABOR UNDER THE HOT SUN!
I CAN SEE MY CHILDREN AGAIN!

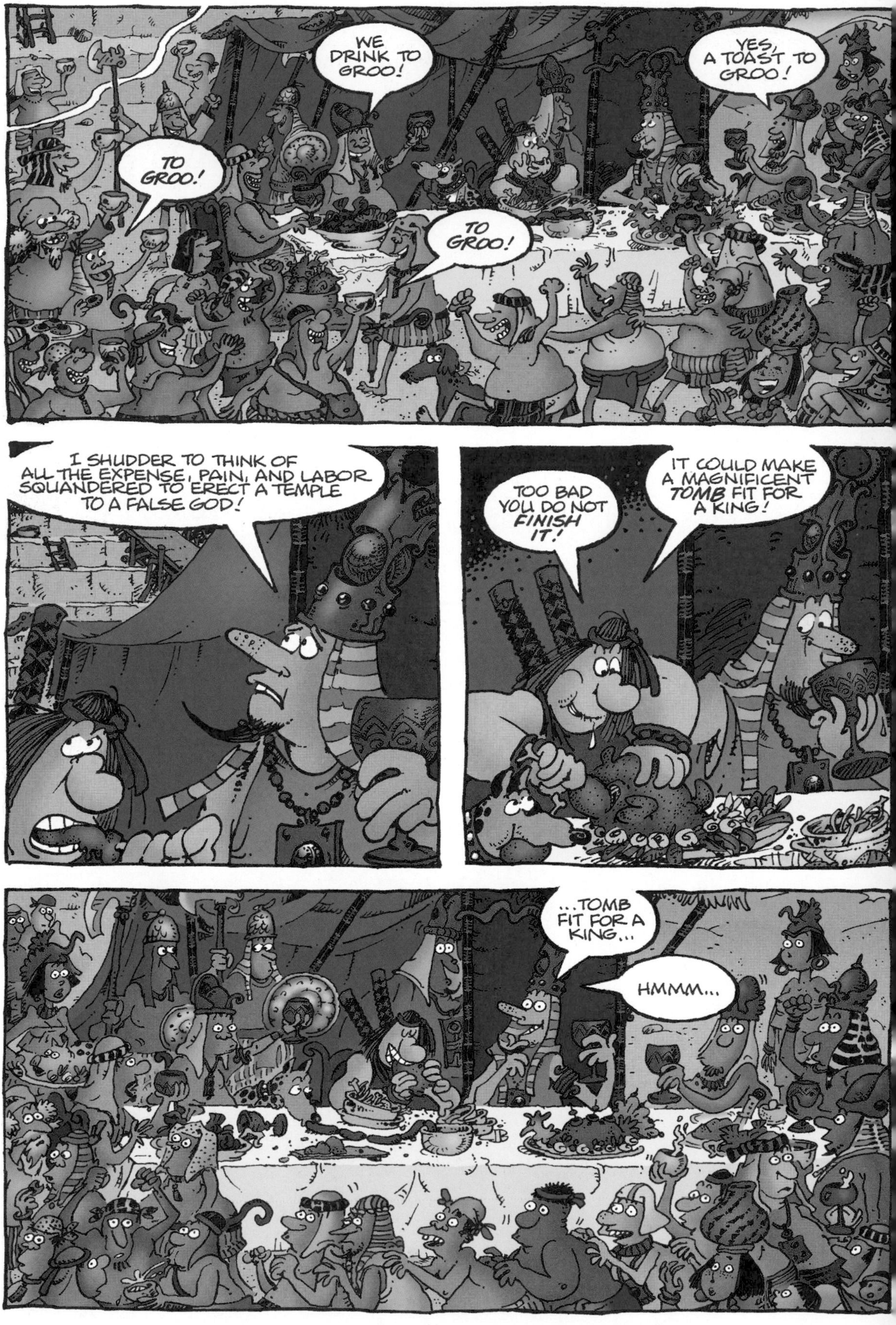
WE DRINK TO GROO!
YES, A TOAST TO GROO!
TO GROO!
TO GROO!
I SHUDDER TO THINK OF ALL THE EXPENSE, PAIN, AND LABOR SQUANDERED TO ERECT A TEMPLE TO A FALSE GOD!
IT COULD MAKE A MAGNIFICENT TOMB FIT FOR A KING!
TOO BAD YOU DO NOT FINISH IT!
...TOMB FIT FOR A KING...
HMMM...

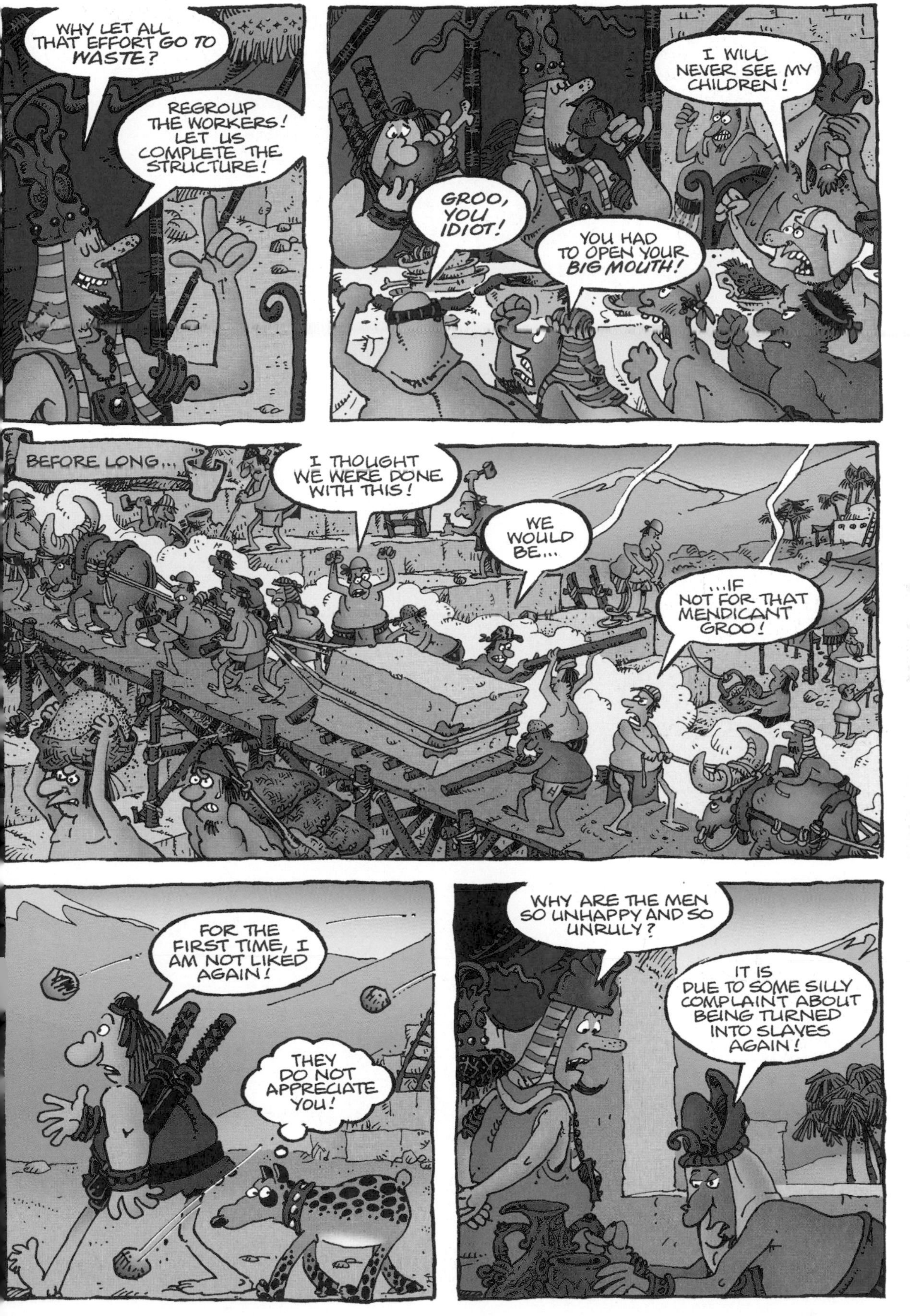
WHY LET ALL THAT EFFORT GO TO WASTE?
REGROUP THE WORKERS! LET US COMPLETE THE STRUCTURE!
I WILL NEVER SEE MY CHILDREN!
GROO, YOU IDIOT!
YOU HAD TO OPEN YOUR BIG MOUTH!
BEFORE LONG...
I THOUGHT WE WERE DONE WITH THIS!
WE WOULD BE...
...IF NOT FOR THAT MENDICANT GROO!
FOR THE FIRST TIME, I AM NOT LIKED AGAIN!
THEY DO NOT APPRECIATE YOU!
WHY ARE THE MEN SO UNHAPPY AND SO UNRULY?
IT IS DUE TO SOME SILLY COMPLAINT ABOUT BEING TURNED INTO SLAVES AGAIN!

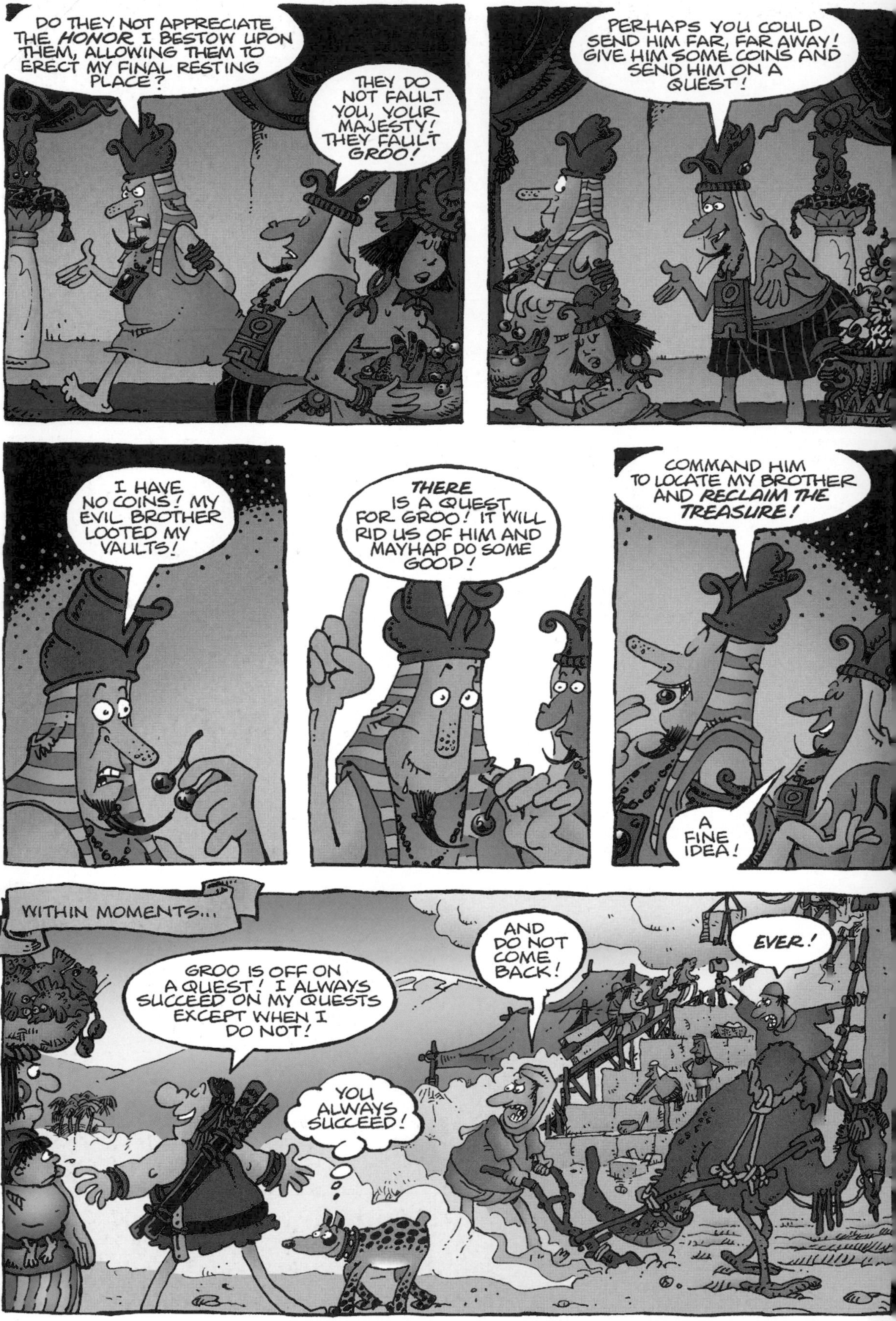
DO THEY NOT APPRECIATE THE *HONOR* I BESTOW UPON THEM, ALLOWING THEM TO ERECT MY FINAL RESTING PLACE?
THEY DO NOT FAULT YOU, YOUR MAJESTY! THEY FAULT *GROO!*
PERHAPS YOU COULD SEND HIM FAR, FAR AWAY! GIVE HIM SOME COINS AND SEND HIM ON A QUEST!
I HAVE NO COINS! MY EVIL BROTHER LOOTED MY VAULTS!
THERE IS A QUEST FOR GROO! IT WILL RID US OF HIM AND MAYHAP DO SOME GOOD!
COMMAND HIM TO LOCATE MY BROTHER AND *RECLAIM THE TREASURE!*
A FINE IDEA!
WITHIN MOMENTS...
GROO IS OFF ON A QUEST! I ALWAYS SUCCEED ON MY QUESTS EXCEPT WHEN I DO NOT!
YOU ALWAYS SUCCEED!
AND DO NOT COME BACK!
EVER!

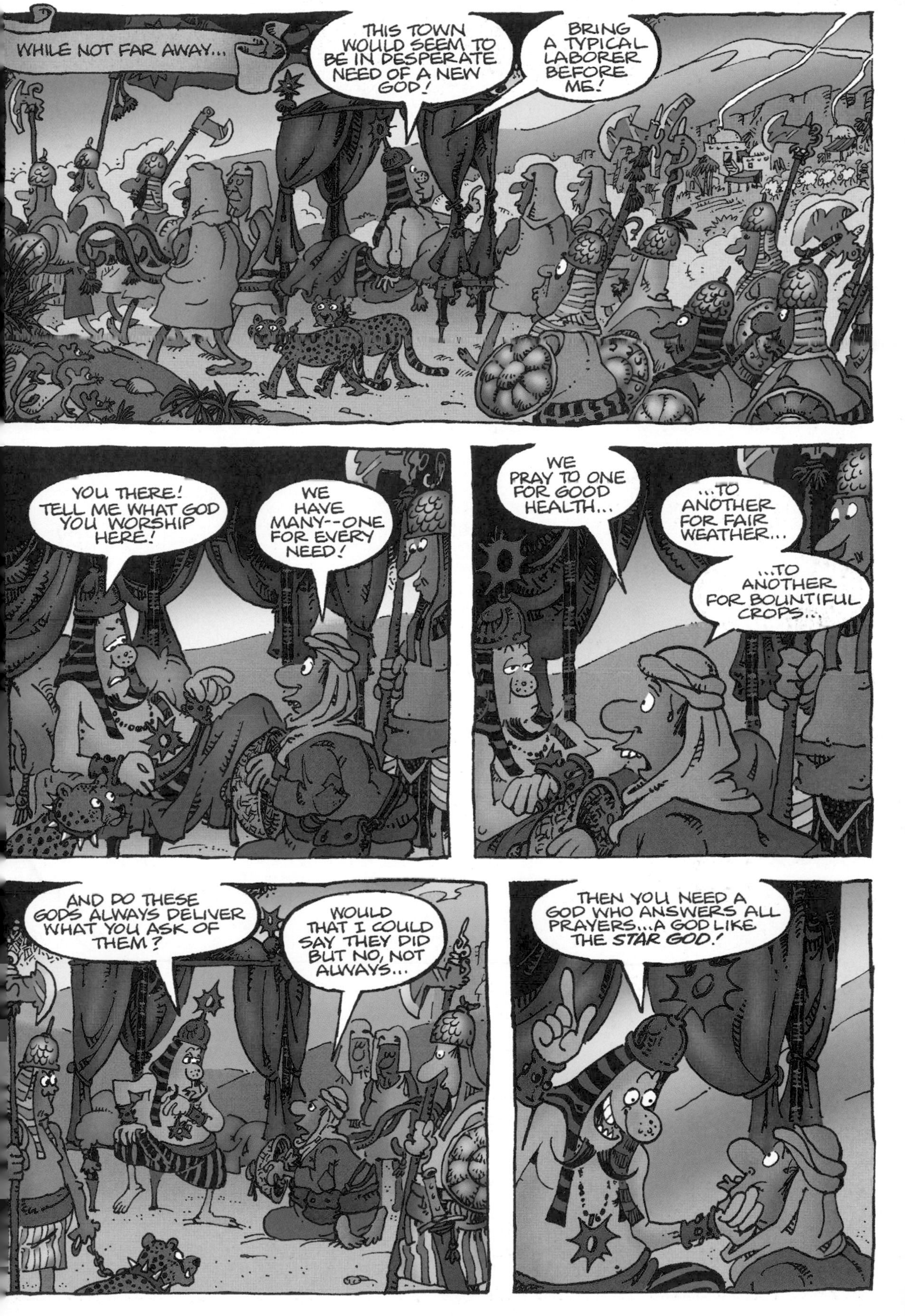
WHILE NOT FAR AWAY...
THIS TOWN WOULD SEEM TO BE IN DESPERATE NEED OF A NEW GOD!
BRING A TYPICAL LABORER BEFORE ME!
YOU THERE! TELL ME WHAT GOD YOU WORSHIP HERE!
WE HAVE MANY--ONE FOR EVERY NEED!
WE PRAY TO ONE FOR GOOD HEALTH...
...TO ANOTHER FOR FAIR WEATHER...
...TO ANOTHER FOR BOUNTIFUL CROPS...
AND DO THESE GODS ALWAYS DELIVER WHAT YOU ASK OF THEM?
WOULD THAT I COULD SAY THEY DID BUT NO, NOT ALWAYS...
THEN YOU NEED A GOD WHO ANSWERS ALL PRAYERS...A GOD LIKE THE STAR GOD!

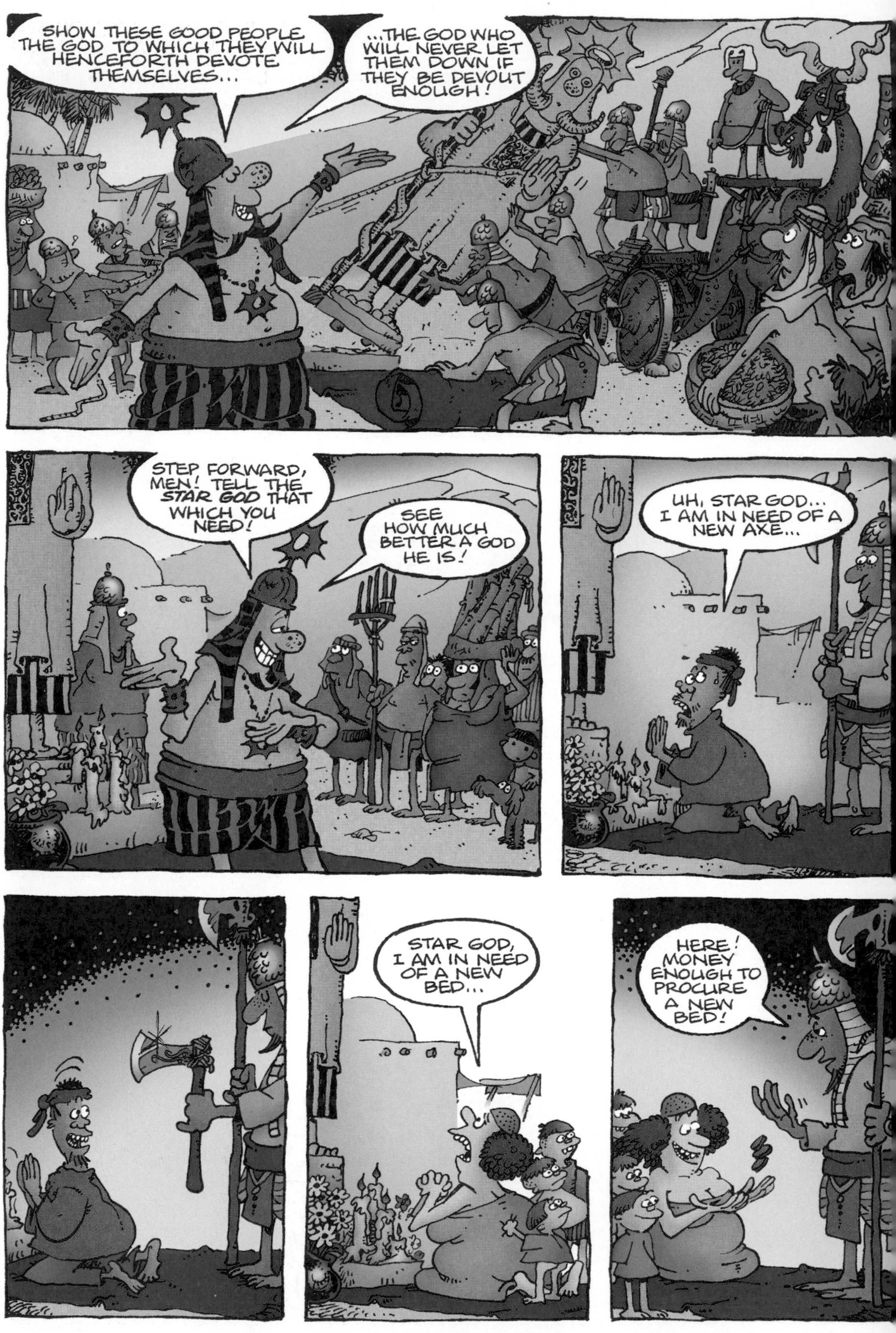
SHOW THESE GOOD PEOPLE THE GOD TO WHICH THEY WILL HENCEFORTH DEVOTE THEMSELVES...
...THE GOD WHO WILL NEVER LET THEM DOWN IF THEY BE DEVOUT ENOUGH!
STEP FORWARD, MEN! TELL THE STAR GOD THAT WHICH YOU NEED!
SEE HOW MUCH BETTER A GOD HE IS!
UH, STAR GOD... I AM IN NEED OF A NEW AXE...
STAR GOD, I AM IN NEED OF A NEW BED...
HERE! MONEY ENOUGH TO PROCURE A NEW BED!

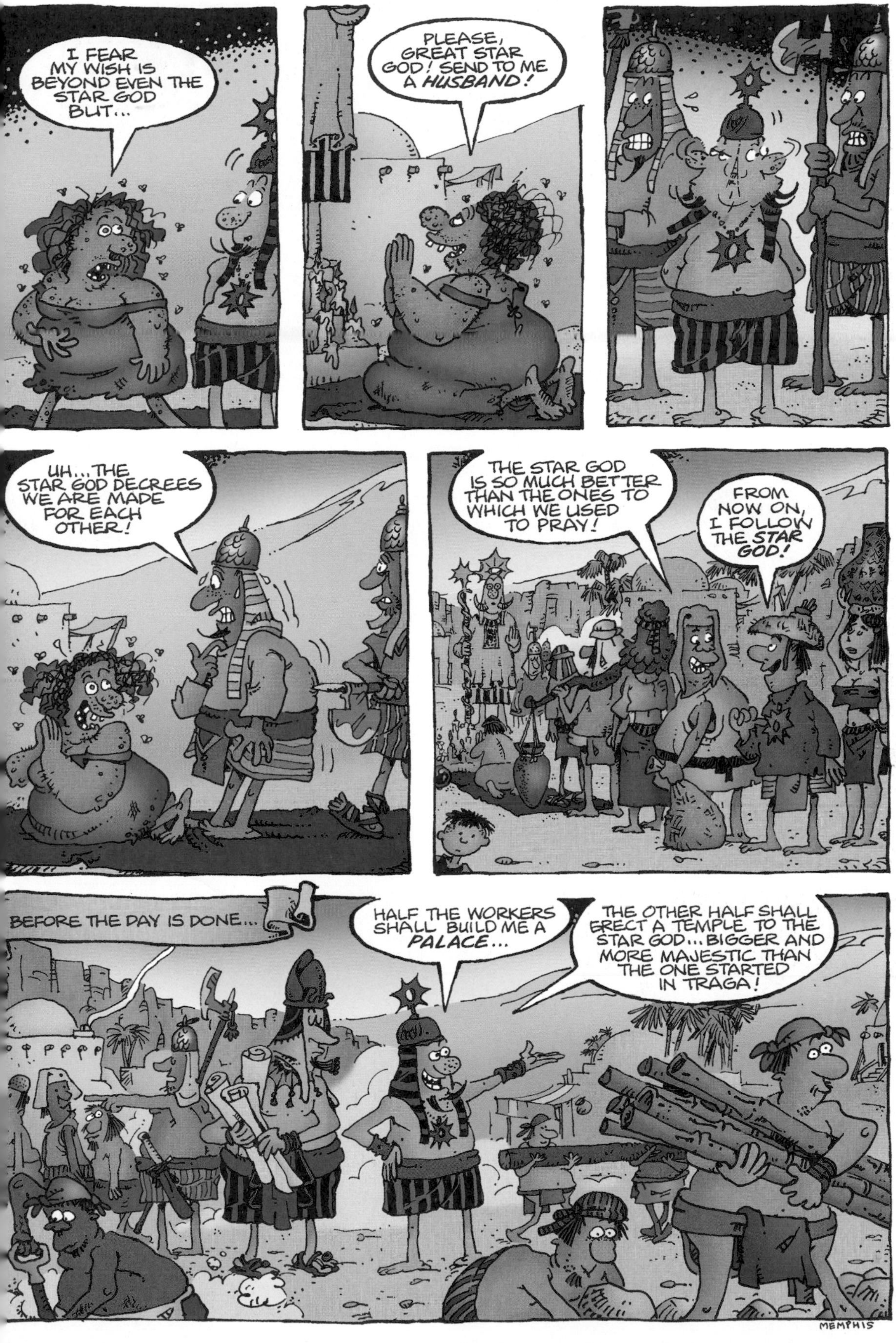
I FEAR MY WISH IS BEYOND EVEN THE STAR GOD BUT...
PLEASE, GREAT STAR GOD! SEND TO ME A *HUSBAND*!
UH... THE STAR GOD DECREES WE ARE MADE FOR EACH OTHER!
THE STAR GOD IS SO MUCH BETTER THAN THE ONES TO WHICH WE USED TO PRAY!
FROM NOW ON, I FOLLOW THE *STAR GOD*!
BEFORE THE DAY IS DONE...
HALF THE WORKERS SHALL BUILD ME A *PALACE*...
THE OTHER HALF SHALL ERECT A TEMPLE TO THE STAR GOD... BIGGER AND MORE MAJESTIC THAN THE ONE STARTED IN TRAGA!
MEMPHIS

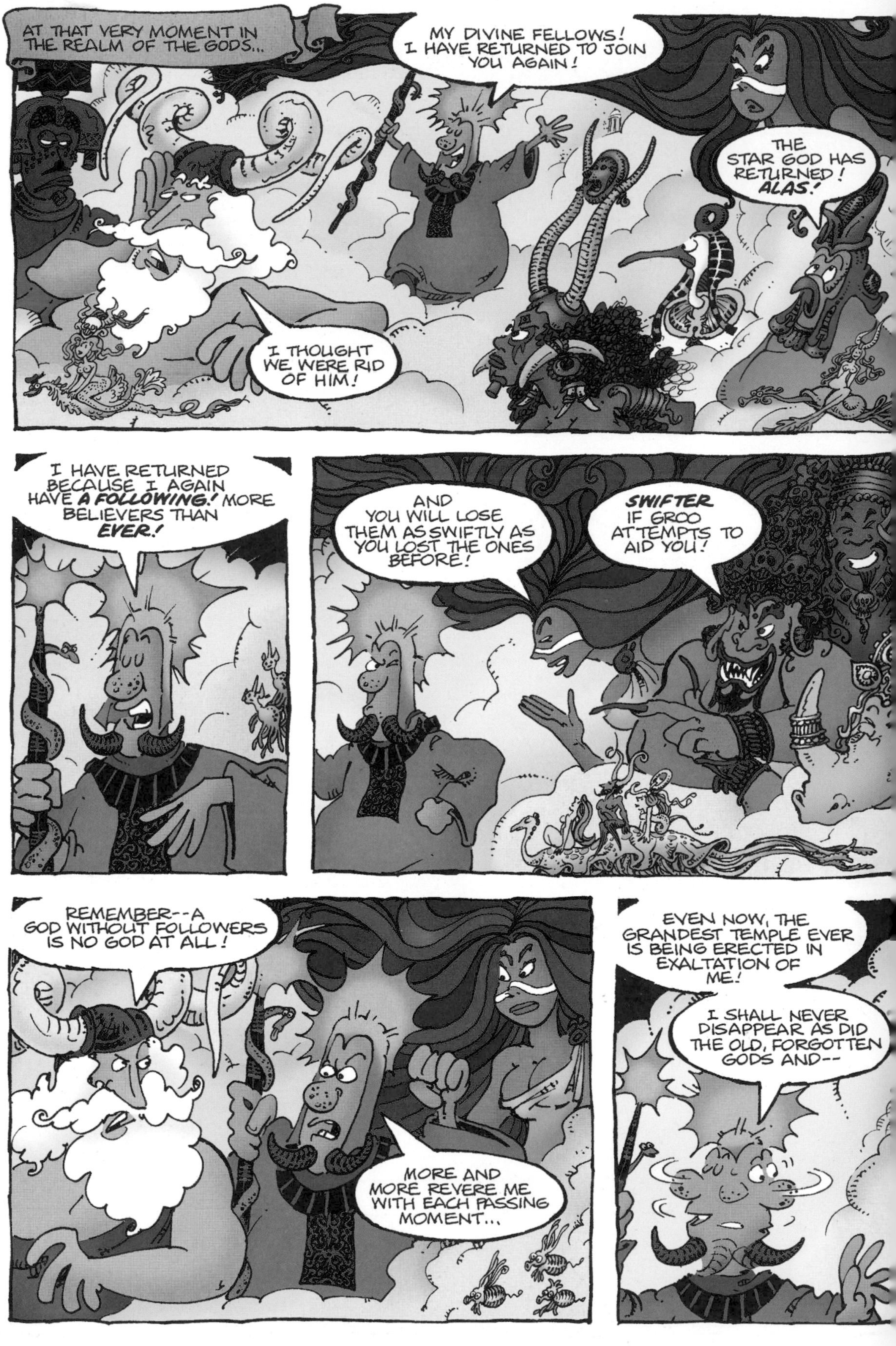
AT THAT VERY MOMENT IN THE REALM OF THE GODS...
MY DIVINE FELLOWS! I HAVE RETURNED TO JOIN YOU AGAIN!
THE STAR GOD HAS RETURNED! ALAS!
I THOUGHT WE WERE RID OF HIM!
I HAVE RETURNED BECAUSE I AGAIN HAVE A FOLLOWING! MORE BELIEVERS THAN EVER!
AND YOU WILL LOSE THEM AS SWIFTLY AS YOU LOST THE ONES BEFORE!
SWIFTER IF GROO ATTEMPTS TO AID YOU!
REMEMBER--A GOD WITHOUT FOLLOWERS IS NO GOD AT ALL!
MORE AND MORE REVERE ME WITH EACH PASSING MOMENT...
EVEN NOW, THE GRANDEST TEMPLE EVER IS BEING ERECTED IN EXALTATION OF ME!
I SHALL NEVER DISAPPEAR AS DID THE OLD, FORGOTTEN GODS AND--

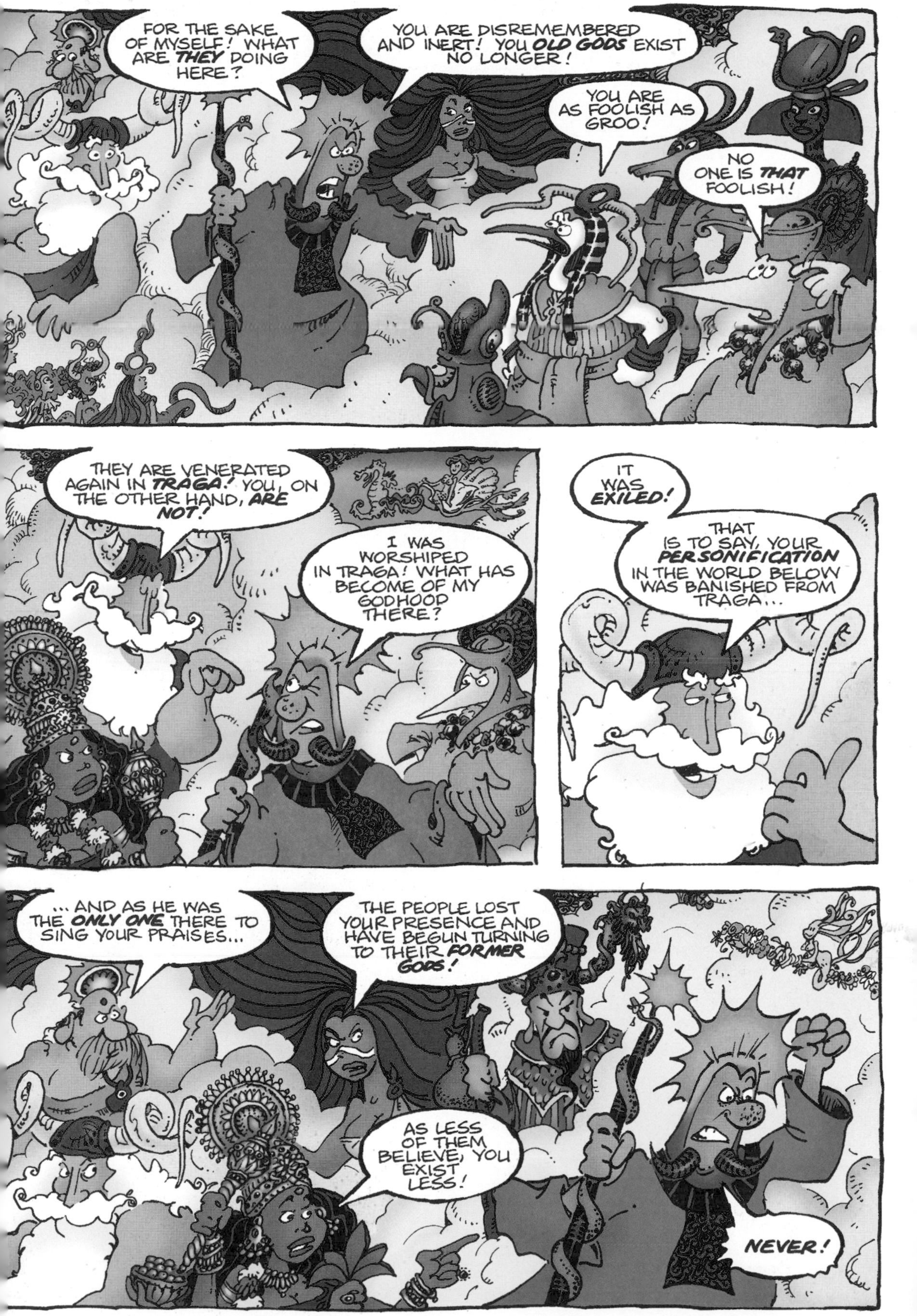
FOR THE SAKE OF MYSELF! WHAT ARE THEY DOING HERE?
YOU ARE DISREMEMBERED AND INERT! YOU OLD GODS EXIST NO LONGER!
YOU ARE AS FOOLISH AS GROO!
NO ONE IS THAT FOOLISH!
THEY ARE VENERATED AGAIN IN TRAGA! YOU, ON THE OTHER HAND, ARE NOT!
I WAS WORSHIPED IN TRAGA! WHAT HAS BECOME OF MY GODHOOD THERE?
IT WAS EXILED!
THAT IS TO SAY, YOUR PERSONIFICATION IN THE WORLD BELOW WAS BANISHED FROM TRAGA...
...AND AS HE WAS THE ONLY ONE THERE TO SING YOUR PRAISES...
THE PEOPLE LOST YOUR PRESENCE AND HAVE BEGUN TURNING TO THEIR FORMER GODS!
AS LESS OF THEM BELIEVE, YOU EXIST LESS!
NEVER!

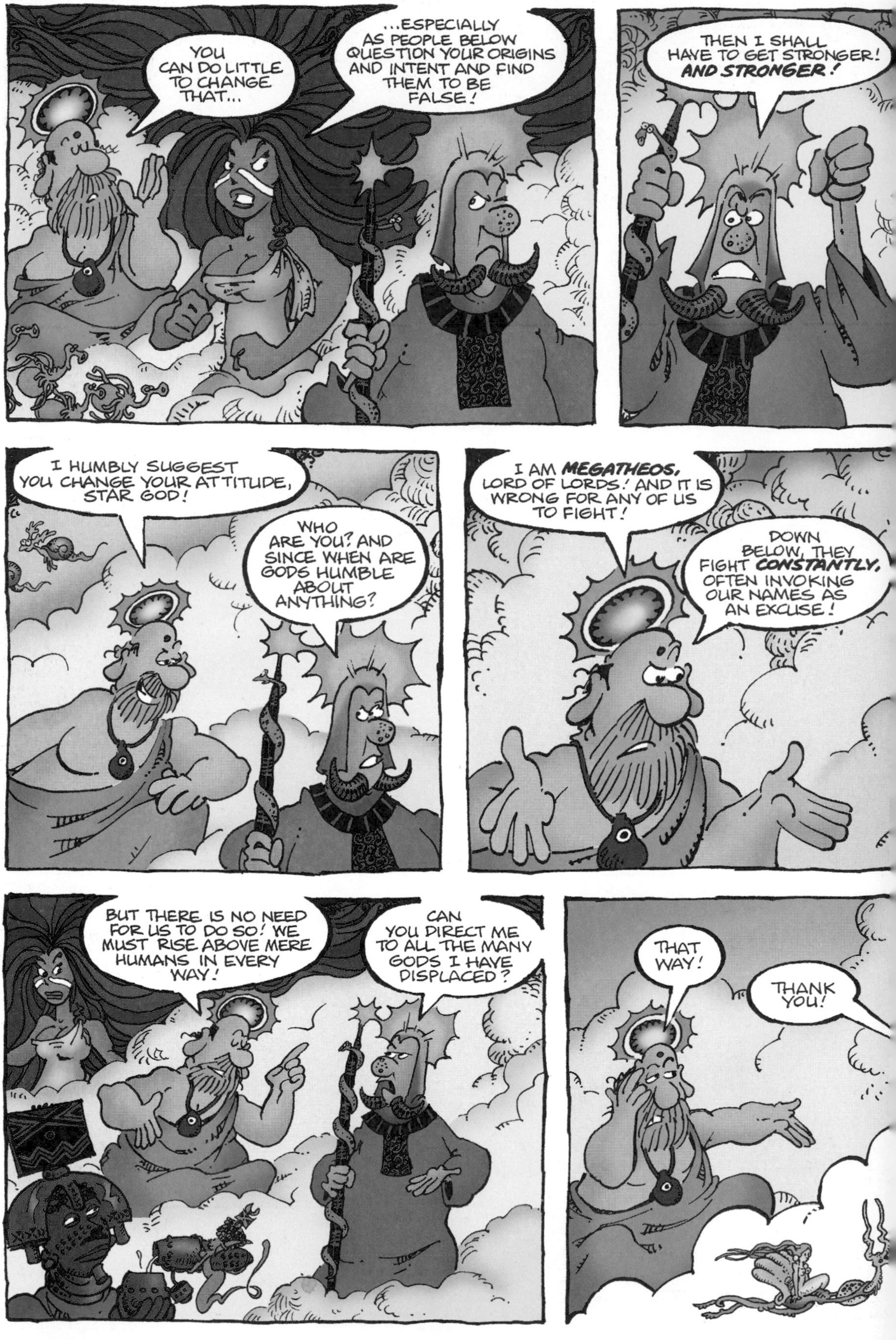
YOU CAN DO LITTLE TO CHANGE THAT...
...ESPECIALLY AS PEOPLE BELOW QUESTION YOUR ORIGINS AND INTENT AND FIND THEM TO BE FALSE!
THEN I SHALL HAVE TO GET STRONGER! AND STRONGER!
I HUMBLY SUGGEST YOU CHANGE YOUR ATTITUDE, STAR GOD!
WHO ARE YOU? AND SINCE WHEN ARE GODS HUMBLE ABOUT ANYTHING?
I AM MEGATHEOS, LORD OF LORDS! AND IT IS WRONG FOR ANY OF US TO FIGHT!
DOWN BELOW, THEY FIGHT CONSTANTLY, OFTEN INVOKING OUR NAMES AS AN EXCUSE!
BUT THERE IS NO NEED FOR US TO DO SO! WE MUST RISE ABOVE MERE HUMANS IN EVERY WAY!
CAN YOU DIRECT ME TO ALL THE MANY GODS I HAVE DISPLACED?
THAT WAY!
THANK YOU!

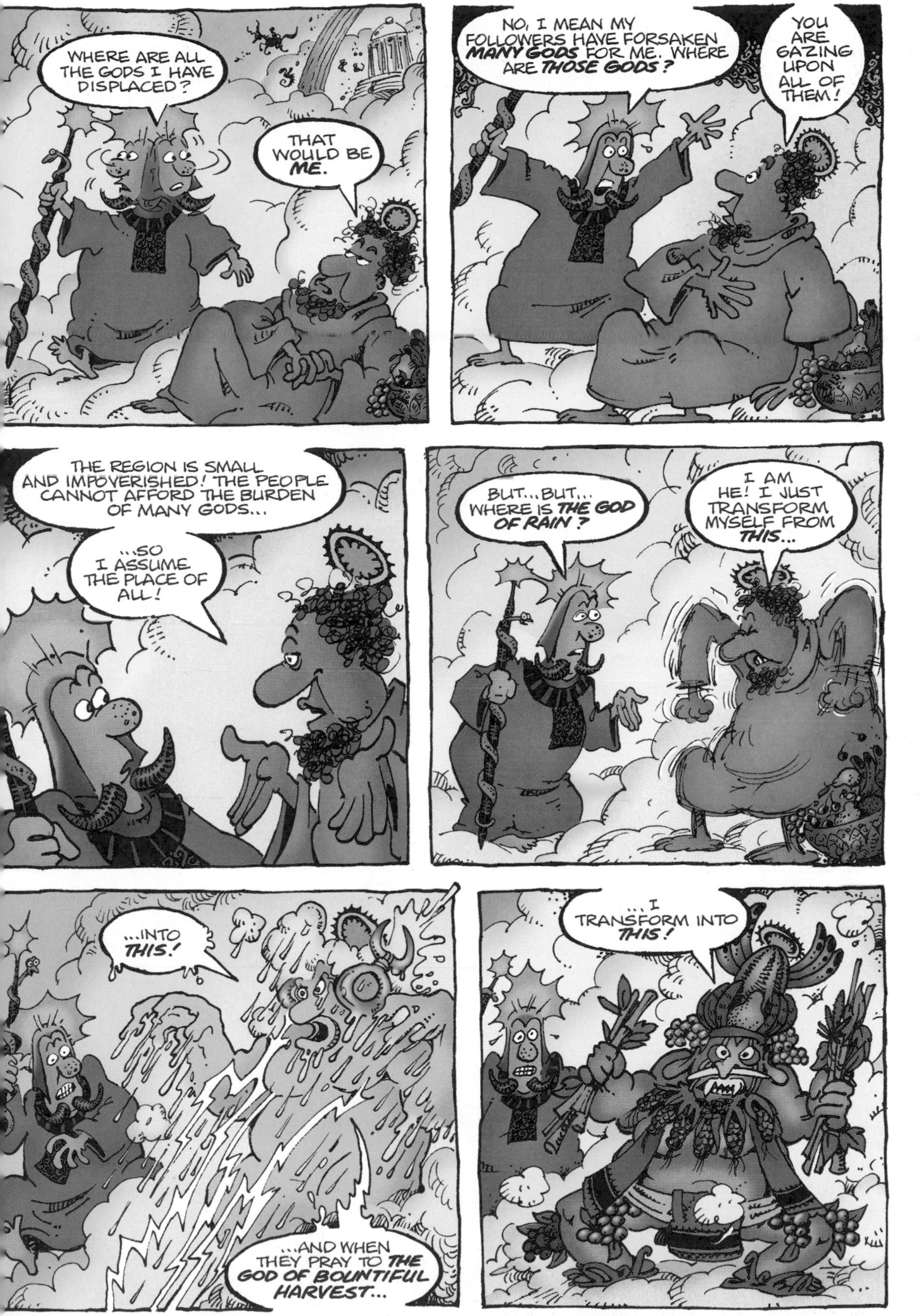

WHERE ARE ALL THE GODS I HAVE DISPLACED?
THAT WOULD BE **ME.**
NO, I MEAN MY FOLLOWERS HAVE FORSAKEN **MANY GODS** FOR ME. WHERE ARE **THOSE GODS?**
YOU ARE GAZING UPON ALL OF THEM!
THE REGION IS SMALL AND IMPOVERISHED! THE PEOPLE CANNOT AFFORD THE BURDEN OF MANY GODS...
...SO I ASSUME THE PLACE OF ALL!
BUT...BUT... WHERE IS **THE GOD OF RAIN?**
I AM HE! I JUST TRANSFORM MYSELF FROM **THIS...**
...INTO **THIS!**
...AND WHEN THEY PRAY TO **THE GOD OF BOUNTIFUL HARVEST...**
...I TRANSFORM INTO **THIS!**

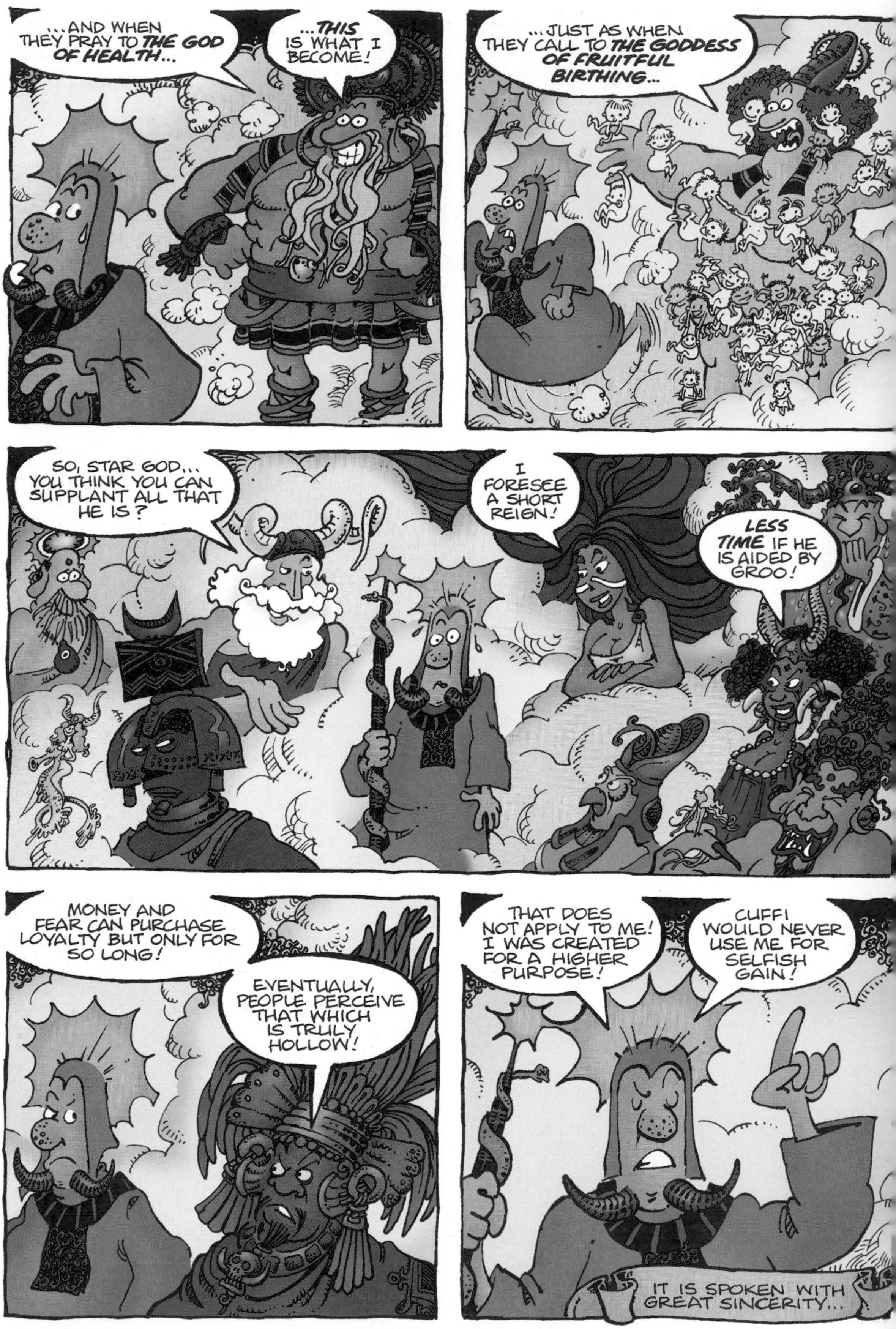
...AND WHEN THEY PRAY TO THE GOD OF HEALTH...
...THIS IS WHAT I BECOME!
...JUST AS WHEN THEY CALL TO THE GODDESS OF FRUITFUL BIRTHING...
SO, STAR GOD... YOU THINK YOU CAN SUPPLANT ALL THAT HE IS?
I FORESEE A SHORT REIGN!
LESS TIME IF HE IS AIDED BY GROO!
MONEY AND FEAR CAN PURCHASE LOYALTY BUT ONLY FOR SO LONG!
EVENTUALLY, PEOPLE PERCEIVE THAT WHICH IS TRULY HOLLOW!
THAT DOES NOT APPLY TO ME! I WAS CREATED FOR A HIGHER PURPOSE!
CUFFI WOULD NEVER USE ME FOR SELFISH GAIN!
IT IS SPOKEN WITH GREAT SINCERITY...

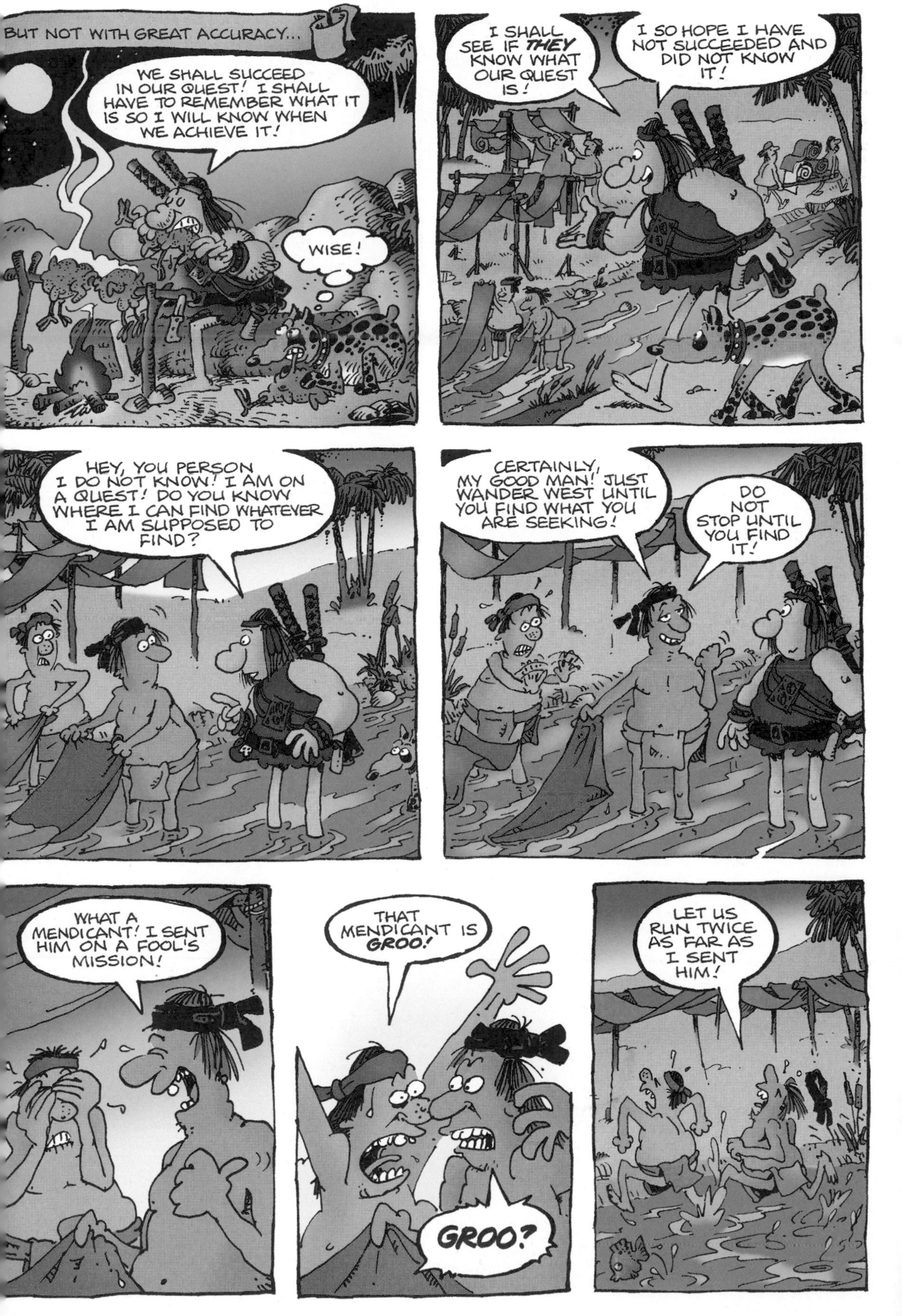
BUT NOT WITH GREAT ACCURACY...
WE SHALL SUCCEED IN OUR QUEST! I SHALL HAVE TO REMEMBER WHAT IT IS SO I WILL KNOW WHEN WE ACHIEVE IT!
WISE!
I SHALL SEE IF THEY KNOW WHAT OUR QUEST IS!
I SO HOPE I HAVE NOT SUCCEEDED AND DID NOT KNOW IT!
HEY, YOU PERSON I DO NOT KNOW! I AM ON A QUEST! DO YOU KNOW WHERE I CAN FIND WHATEVER I AM SUPPOSED TO FIND?
CERTAINLY, MY GOOD MAN! JUST WANDER WEST UNTIL YOU FIND WHAT YOU ARE SEEKING!
DO NOT STOP UNTIL YOU FIND IT!
WHAT A MENDICANT! I SENT HIM ON A FOOL'S MISSION!
THAT MENDICANT IS GROO!
GROO?
LET US RUN TWICE AS FAR AS I SENT HIM!

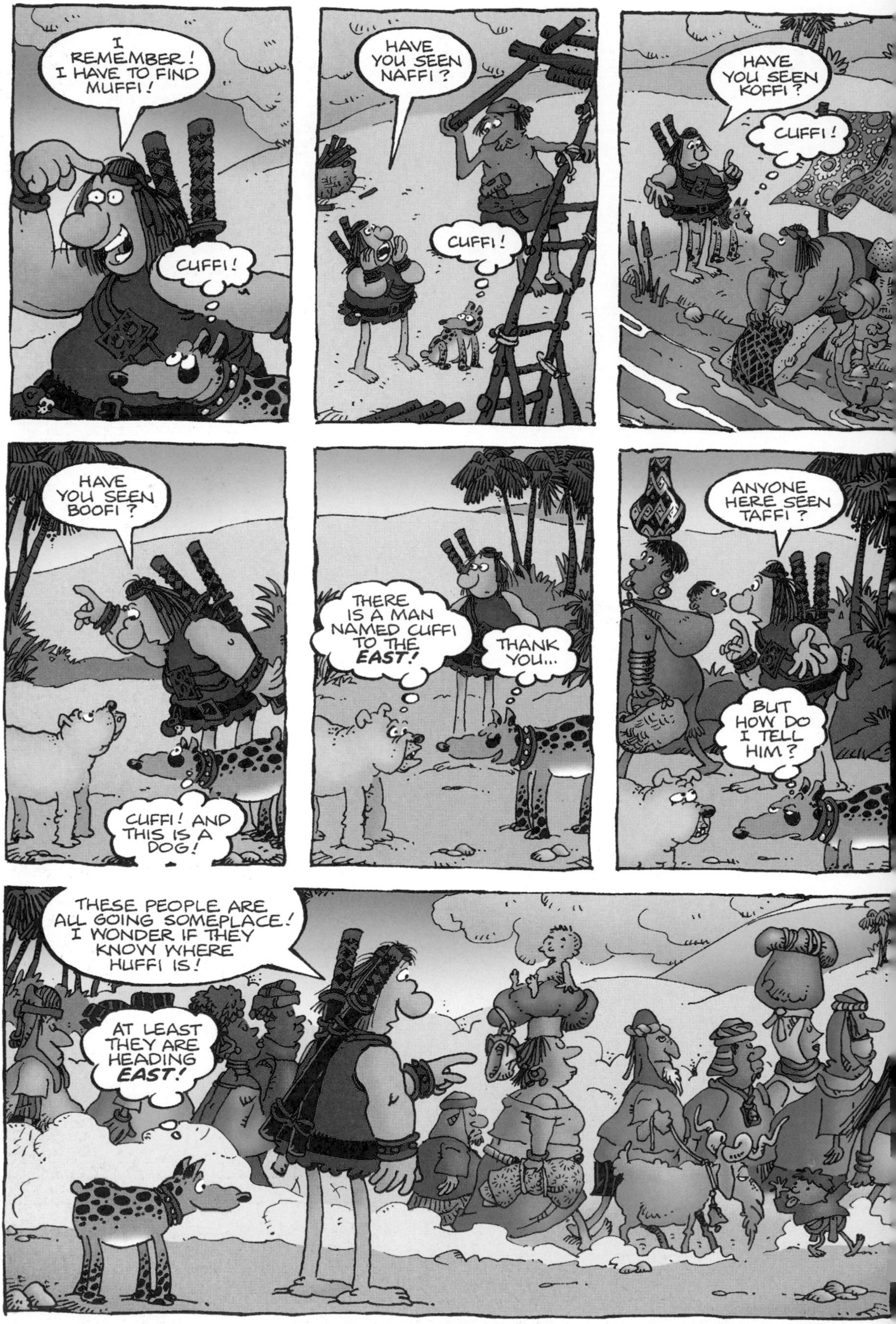

I REMEMBER! I HAVE TO FIND MUFFI!
CUFFI!
HAVE YOU SEEN NAFFI?
CUFFI!
HAVE YOU SEEN KOFFI?
CUFFI!
HAVE YOU SEEN BOOFI?
CUFFI! AND THIS IS A DOG!
THERE IS A MAN NAMED CUFFI TO THE EAST!
THANK YOU...
ANYONE HERE SEEN TAFFI?
BUT HOW DO I TELL HIM?
THESE PEOPLE ARE ALL GOING SOMEPLACE! I WONDER IF THEY KNOW WHERE HUFFI IS!
AT LEAST THEY ARE HEADING EAST!

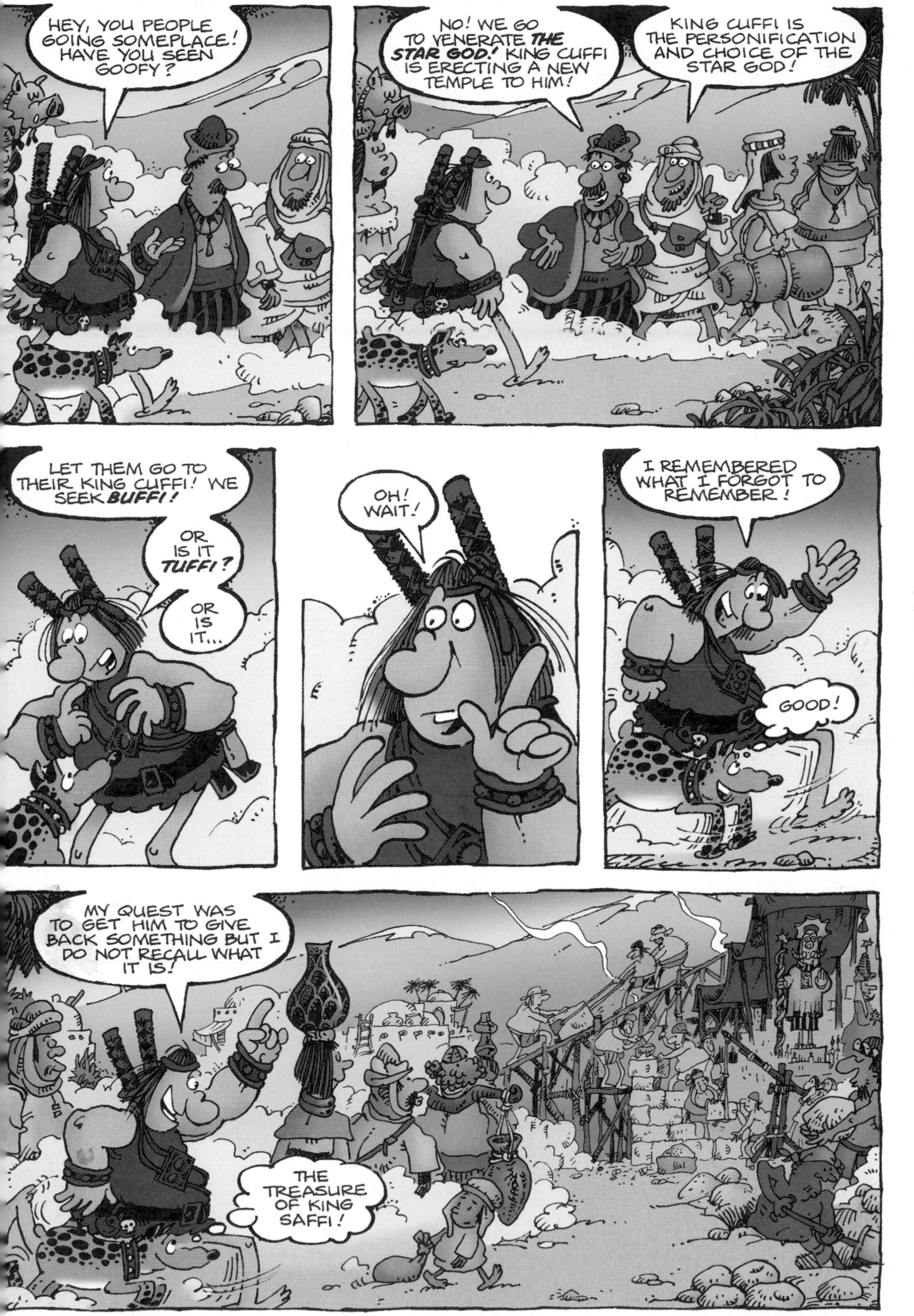
HEY, YOU PEOPLE GOING SOMEPLACE! HAVE YOU SEEN GOOFY?
NO! WE GO TO VENERATE THE STAR GOD! KING CUFFI IS ERECTING A NEW TEMPLE TO HIM!
KING CUFFI IS THE PERSONIFICATION AND CHOICE OF THE STAR GOD!
LET THEM GO TO THEIR KING CUFFI! WE SEEK BUFFI!
OR IS IT TUFFI?
OR IS IT...
OH! WAIT!
I REMEMBERED WHAT I FORGOT TO REMEMBER!
GOOD!
MY QUEST WAS TO GET HIM TO GIVE BACK SOMETHING BUT I DO NOT RECALL WHAT IT IS!
THE TREASURE OF KING SAFFI!

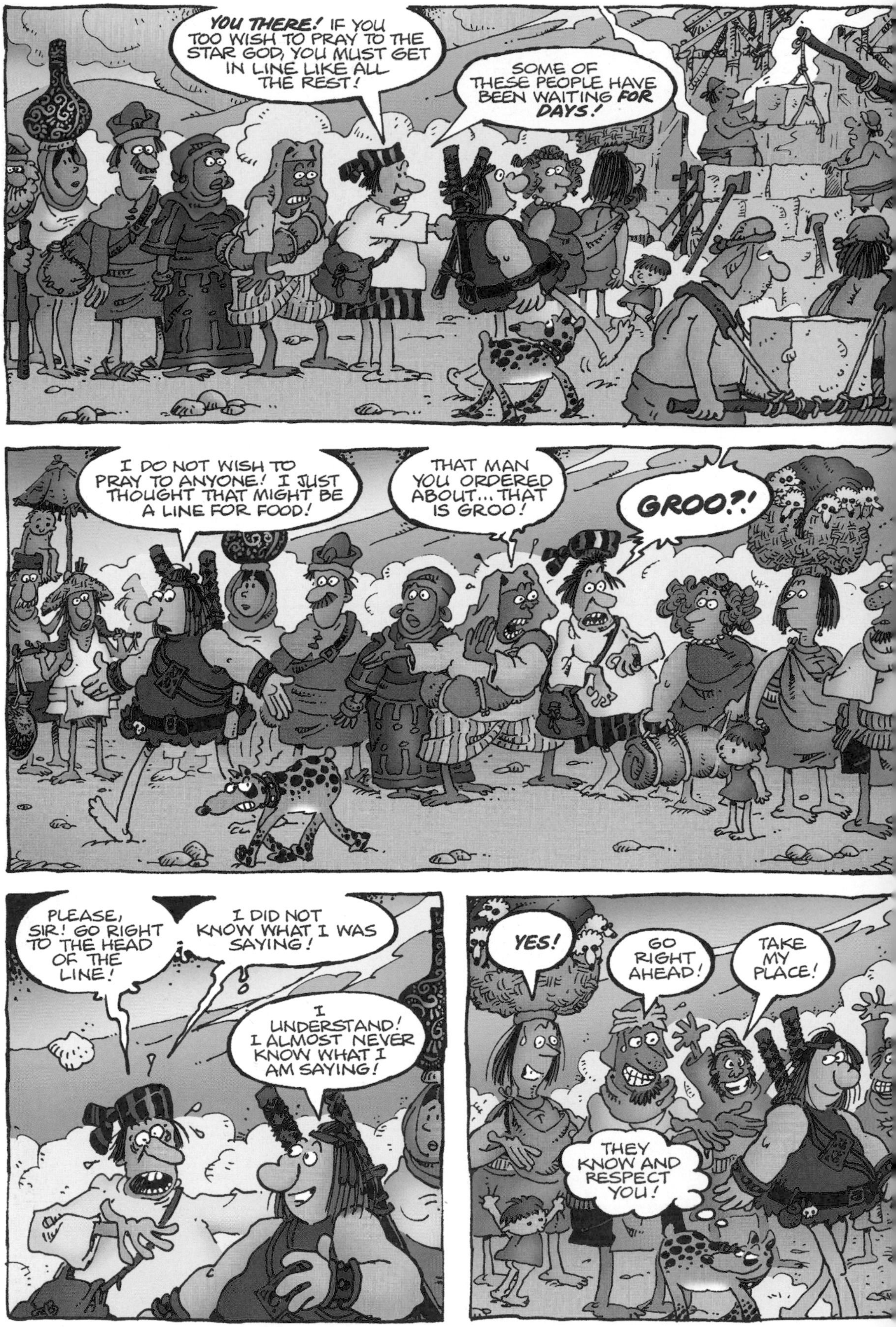

YOU THERE! IF YOU TOO WISH TO PRAY TO THE STAR GOD, YOU MUST GET IN LINE LIKE ALL THE REST!
SOME OF THESE PEOPLE HAVE BEEN WAITING FOR DAYS!
I DO NOT WISH TO PRAY TO ANYONE! I JUST THOUGHT THAT MIGHT BE A LINE FOR FOOD!
THAT MAN YOU ORDERED ABOUT... THAT IS GROO!
GROO?!
PLEASE, SIR! GO RIGHT TO THE HEAD OF THE LINE!
I DID NOT KNOW WHAT I WAS SAYING!
I UNDERSTAND! I ALMOST NEVER KNOW WHAT I AM SAYING!
YES!
GO RIGHT AHEAD!
TAKE MY PLACE!
THEY KNOW AND RESPECT YOU!

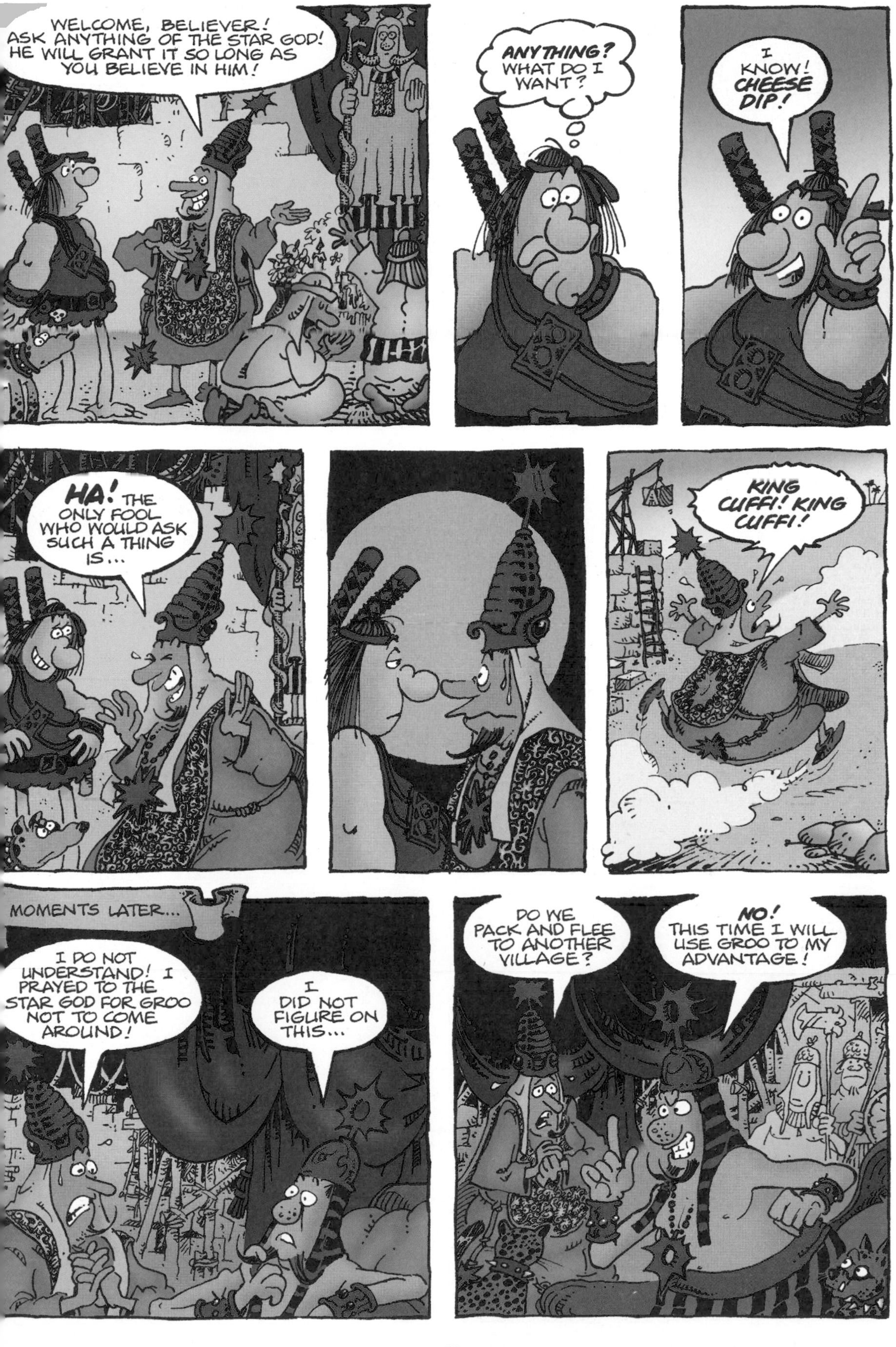
WELCOME, BELIEVER! ASK ANYTHING OF THE STAR GOD! HE WILL GRANT IT SO LONG AS YOU BELIEVE IN HIM!
ANYTHING? WHAT DO I WANT?
I KNOW! CHEESE DIP!
HA! THE ONLY FOOL WHO WOULD ASK SUCH A THING IS...
KING CUFFI! KING CUFFI!
MOMENTS LATER...
I DO NOT UNDERSTAND! I PRAYED TO THE STAR GOD FOR GROO NOT TO COME AROUND!
I DID NOT FIGURE ON THIS...
DO WE PACK AND FLEE TO ANOTHER VILLAGE?
NO! THIS TIME I WILL USE GROO TO MY ADVANTAGE!

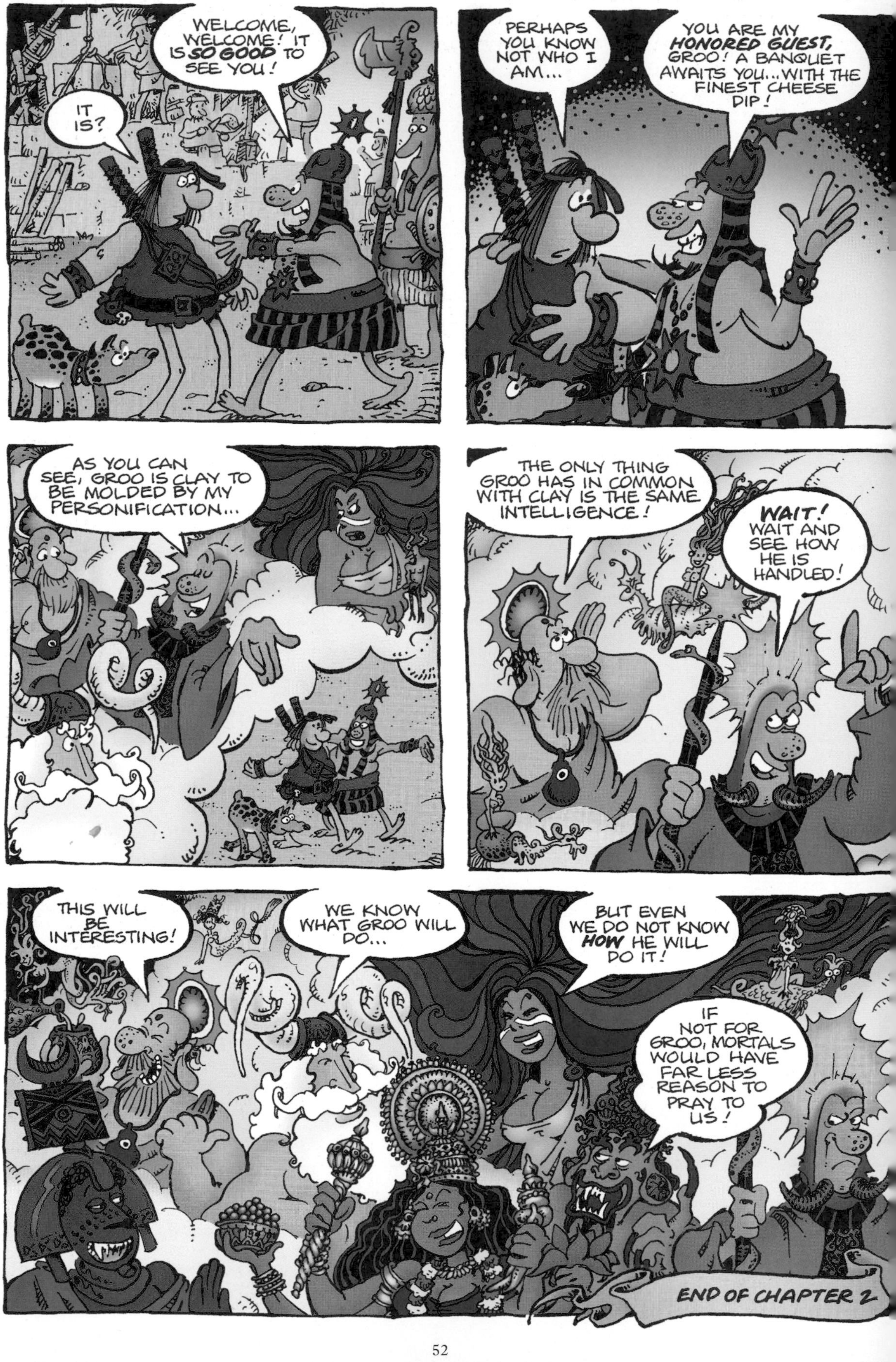
WELCOME, WELCOME! IT IS SO GOOD TO SEE YOU!
IT IS?
PERHAPS YOU KNOW NOT WHO I AM...
YOU ARE MY HONORED GUEST, GROO! A BANQUET AWAITS YOU...WITH THE FINEST CHEESE DIP!
AS YOU CAN SEE, GROO IS CLAY TO BE MOLDED BY MY PERSONIFICATION...
THE ONLY THING GROO HAS IN COMMON WITH CLAY IS THE SAME INTELLIGENCE!
WAIT! WAIT AND SEE HOW HE IS HANDLED!
THIS WILL BE INTERESTING!
WE KNOW WHAT GROO WILL DO...
BUT EVEN WE DO NOT KNOW HOW HE WILL DO IT!
IF NOT FOR GROO, MORTALS WOULD HAVE FAR LESS REASON TO PRAY TO US!
END OF CHAPTER 2

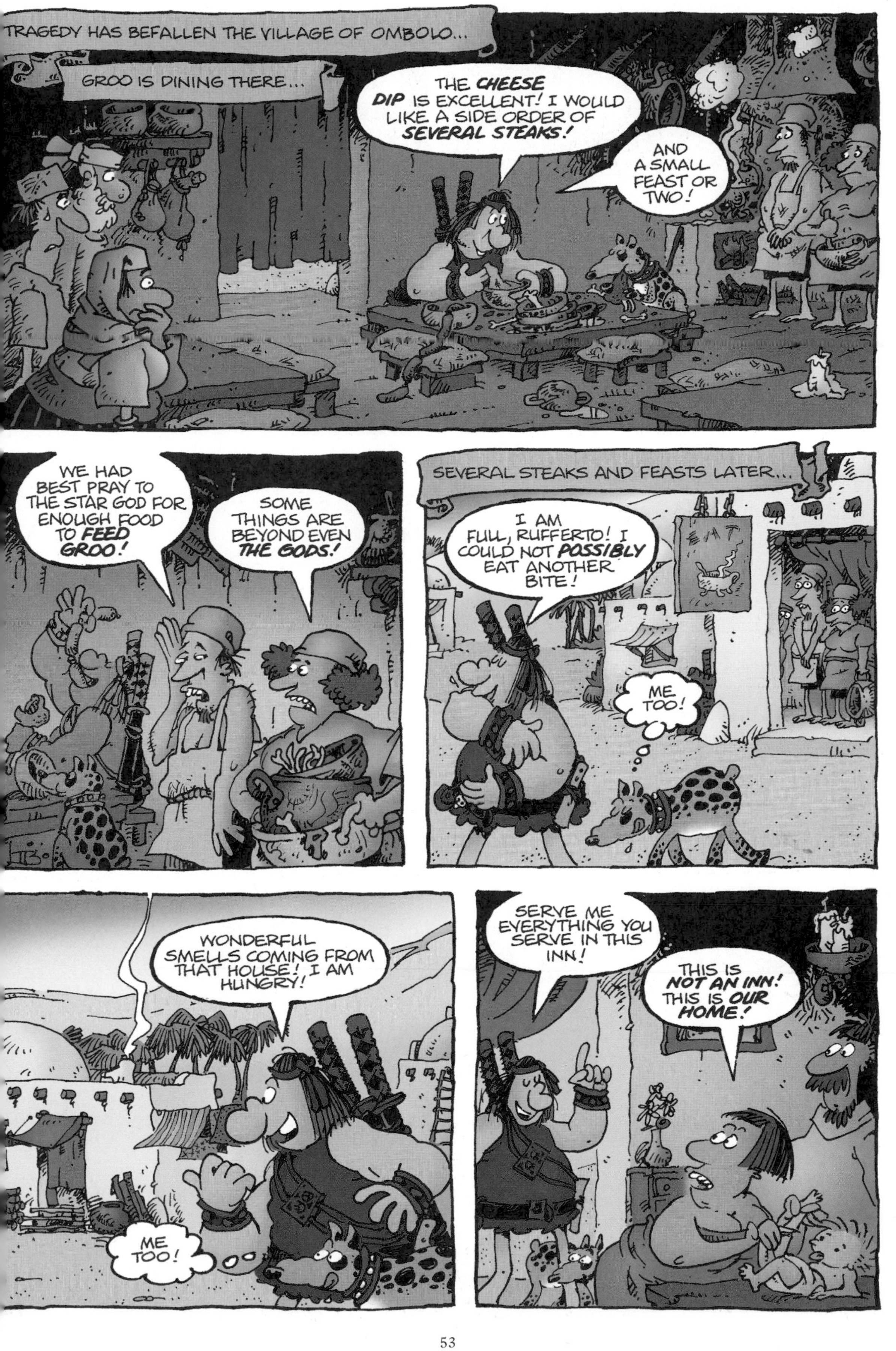
TRAGEDY HAS BEFALLEN THE VILLAGE OF OMBOLO...
GROO IS DINING THERE...
THE **CHEESE DIP** IS EXCELLENT! I WOULD LIKE A SIDE ORDER OF **SEVERAL STEAKS!**
AND A SMALL FEAST OR TWO!
WE HAD BEST PRAY TO THE STAR GOD FOR ENOUGH FOOD TO **FEED GROO!**
SOME THINGS ARE BEYOND EVEN **THE GODS!**
SEVERAL STEAKS AND FEASTS LATER...
I AM FULL, RUFFERTO! I COULD NOT **POSSIBLY** EAT ANOTHER BITE!
EAT
ME TOO!
WONDERFUL SMELLS COMING FROM THAT HOUSE! I AM HUNGRY!
ME TOO!
SERVE ME EVERYTHING YOU SERVE IN THIS INN!
THIS IS **NOT AN INN!** THIS IS **OUR HOME!**

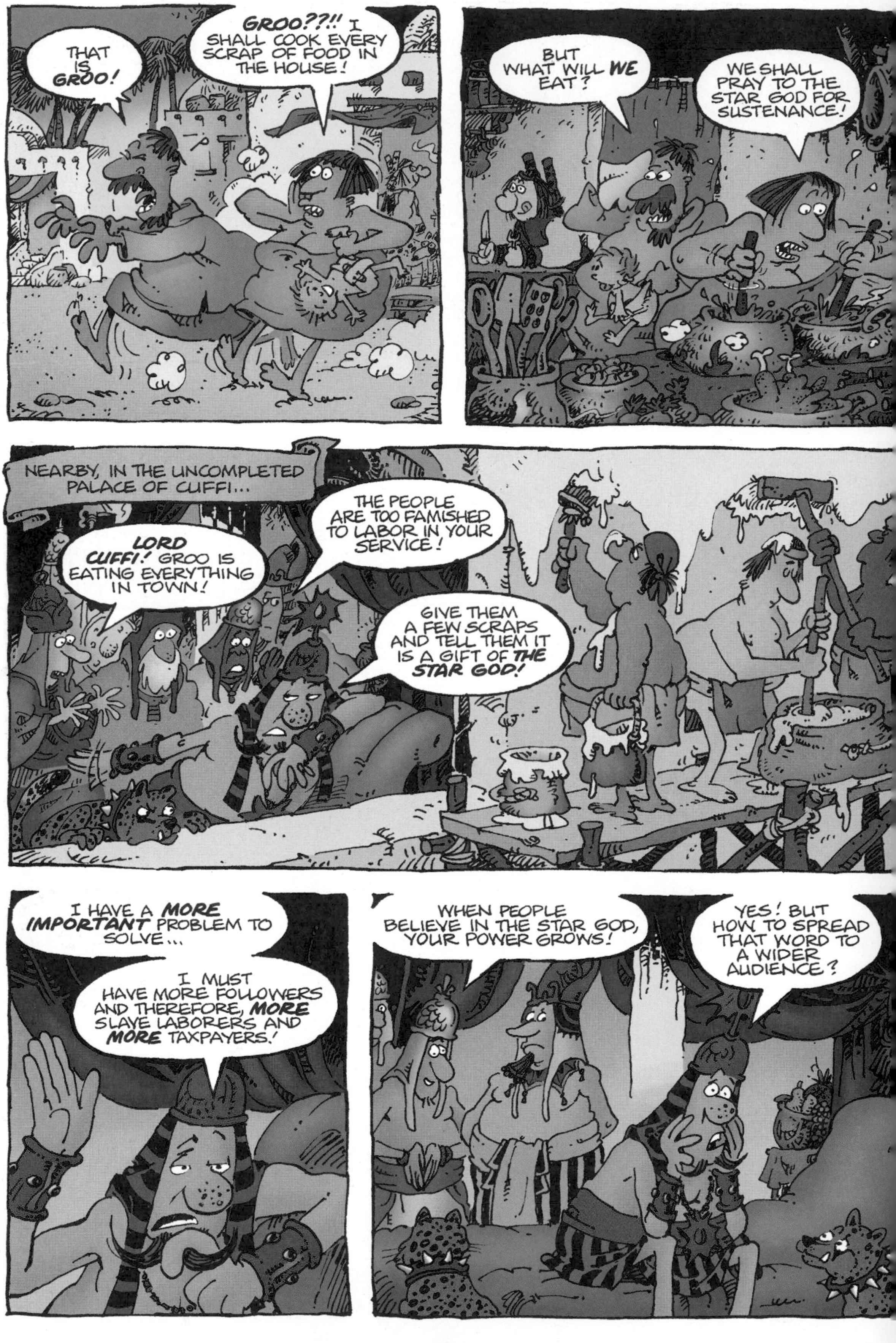

THAT IS GROO!
GROO??!! I SHALL COOK EVERY SCRAP OF FOOD IN THE HOUSE!
BUT WHAT WILL WE EAT?
WE SHALL PRAY TO THE STAR GOD FOR SUSTENANCE!
NEARBY, IN THE UNCOMPLETED PALACE OF CUFFI...
LORD CUFFI! GROO IS EATING EVERYTHING IN TOWN!
THE PEOPLE ARE TOO FAMISHED TO LABOR IN YOUR SERVICE!
GIVE THEM A FEW SCRAPS AND TELL THEM IT IS A GIFT OF THE STAR GOD!
I HAVE A MORE IMPORTANT PROBLEM TO SOLVE...
I MUST HAVE MORE FOLLOWERS AND THEREFORE, MORE SLAVE LABORERS AND MORE TAXPAYERS!
WHEN PEOPLE BELIEVE IN THE STAR GOD, YOUR POWER GROWS!
YES! BUT HOW TO SPREAD THAT WORD TO A WIDER AUDIENCE?

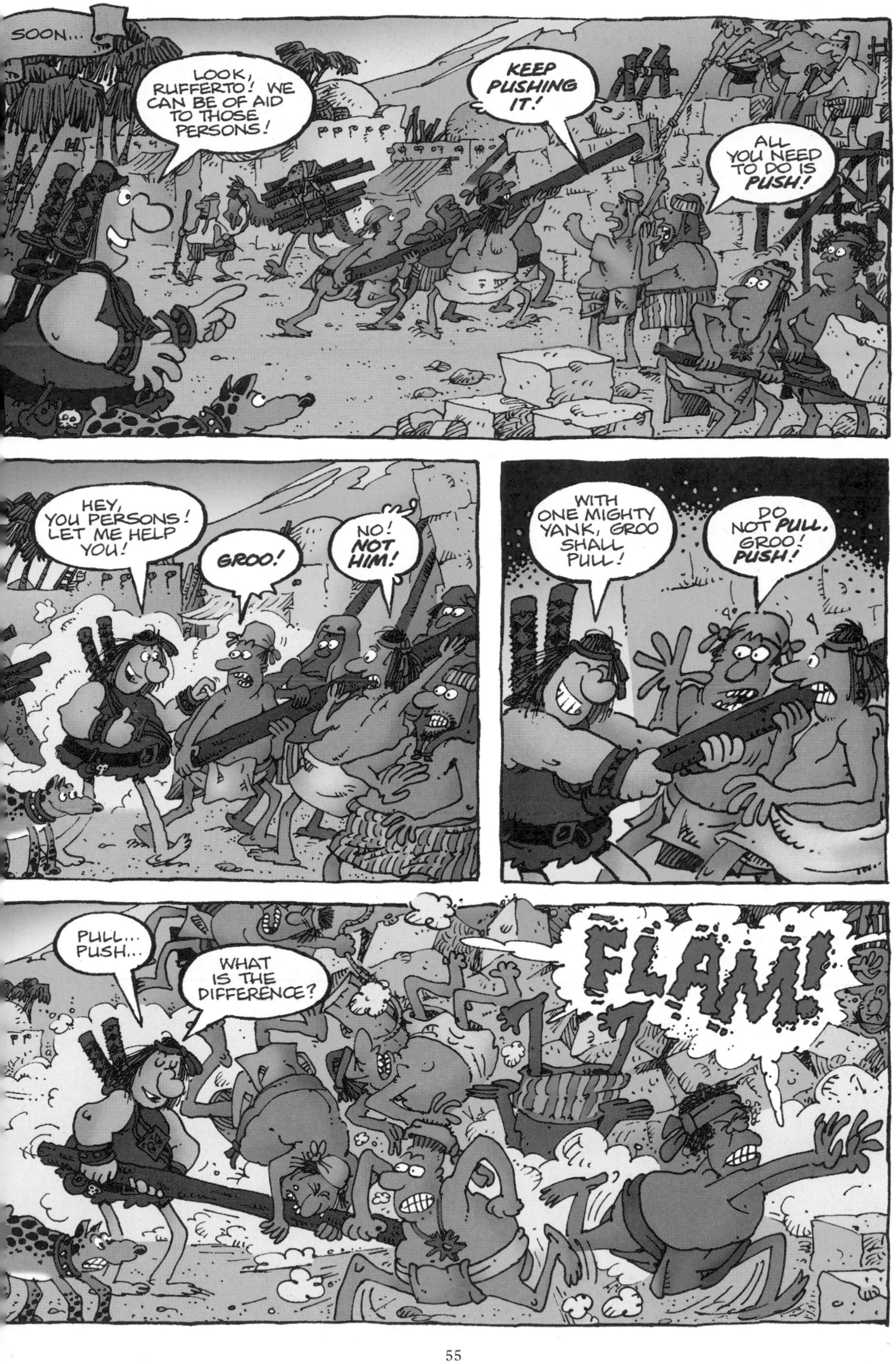
SOON...
LOOK, RUFFERTO! WE CAN BE OF AID TO THOSE PERSONS!
KEEP PUSHING IT!
ALL YOU NEED TO DO IS PUSH!
HEY, YOU PERSONS! LET ME HELP YOU!
GROO!
NO! NOT HIM!
WITH ONE MIGHTY YANK, GROO SHALL PULL!
DO NOT PULL, GROO! PUSH!
PULL... PUSH...
WHAT IS THE DIFFERENCE?
FLAM!

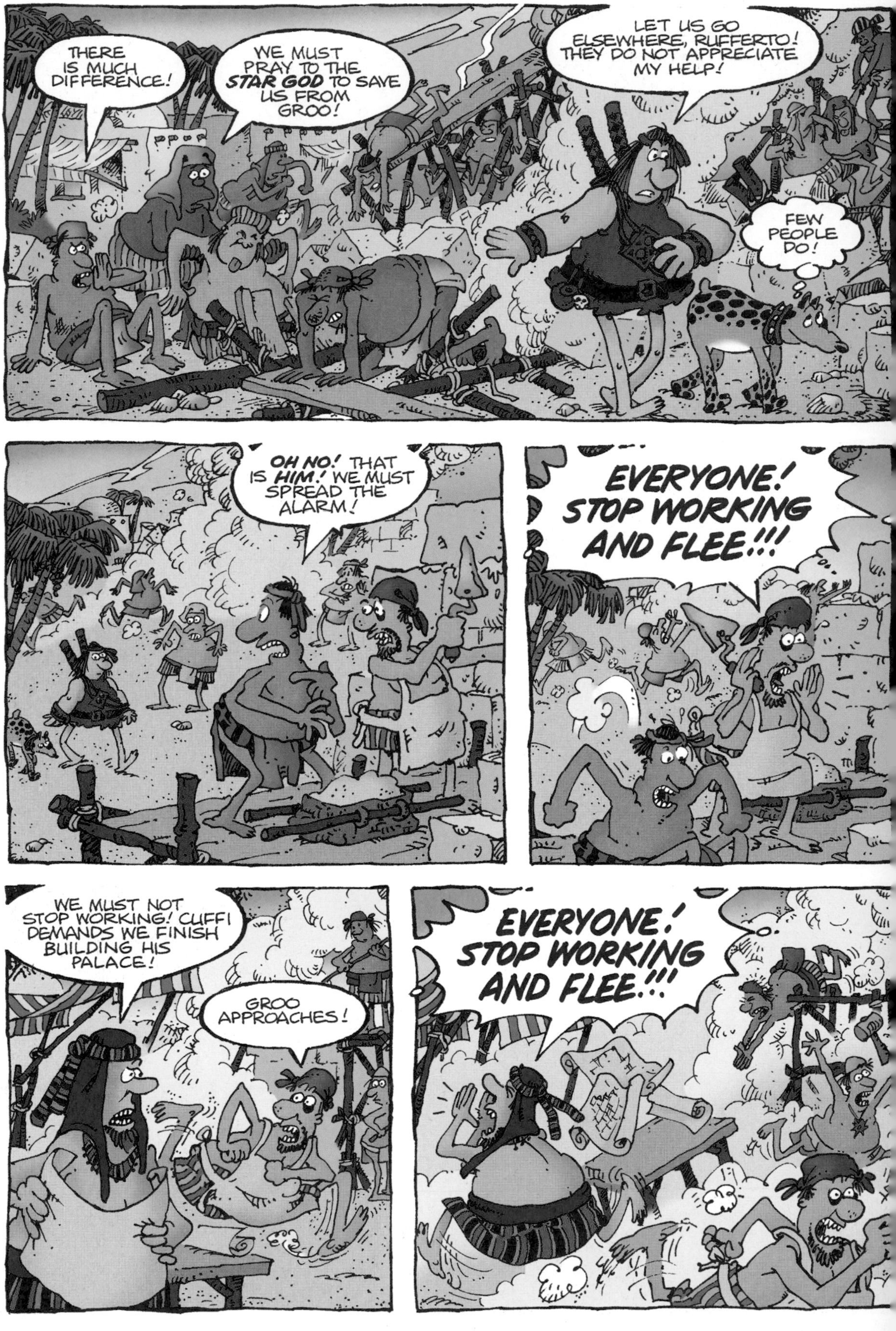

THERE IS MUCH DIFFERENCE!
WE MUST PRAY TO THE STAR GOD TO SAVE US FROM GROO!
LET US GO ELSEWHERE, RUFFERTO! THEY DO NOT APPRECIATE MY HELP!
FEW PEOPLE DO!
OH NO! THAT IS HIM! WE MUST SPREAD THE ALARM!
EVERYONE! STOP WORKING AND FLEE!!!
WE MUST NOT STOP WORKING! CUFFI DEMANDS WE FINISH BUILDING HIS PALACE!
GROO APPROACHES!
EVERYONE! STOP WORKING AND FLEE!!!

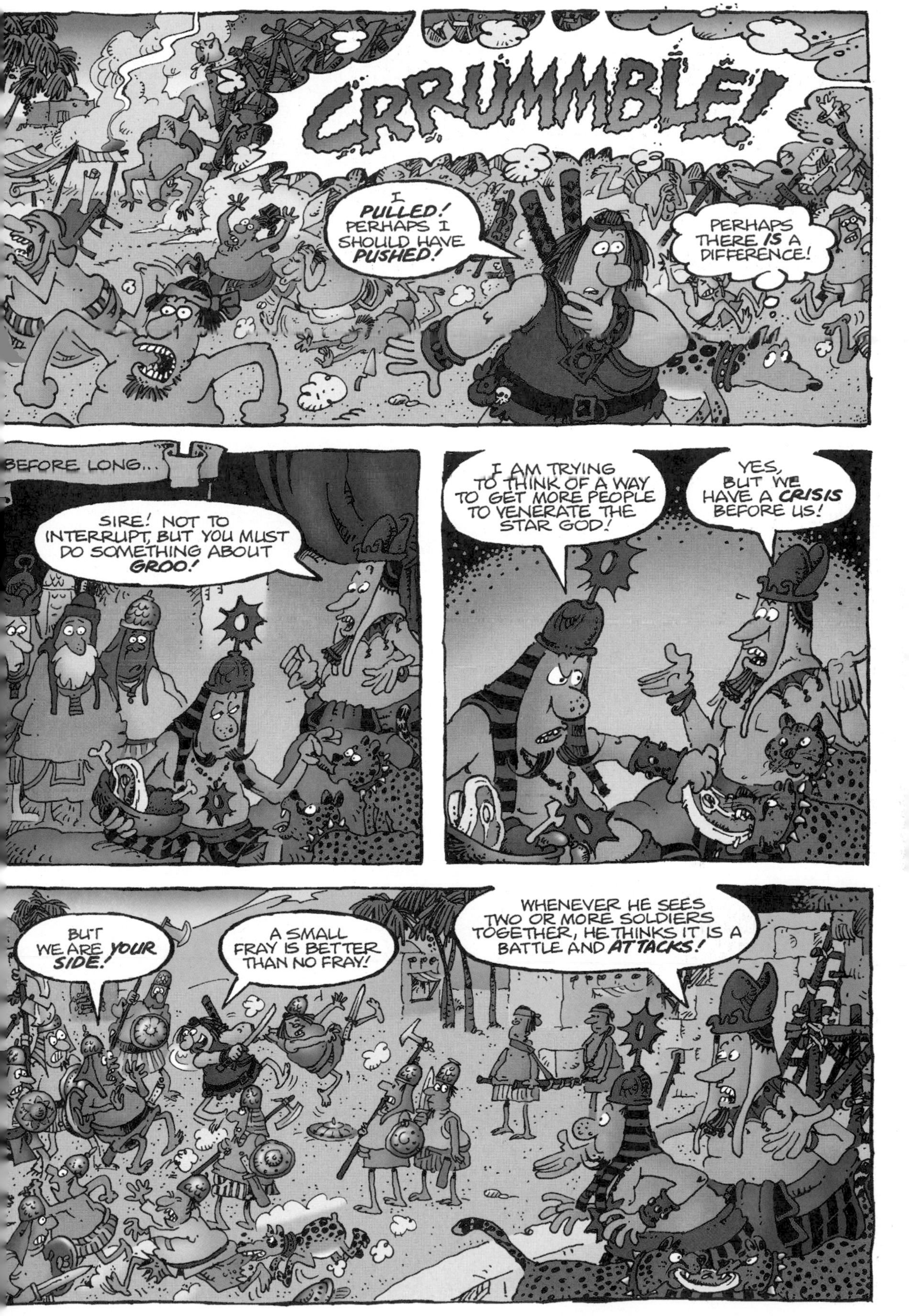
CRRUMMBLE!
I PULLED! PERHAPS I SHOULD HAVE PUSHED!
PERHAPS THERE IS A DIFFERENCE!
BEFORE LONG...
SIRE! NOT TO INTERRUPT, BUT YOU MUST DO SOMETHING ABOUT GROO!
I AM TRYING TO THINK OF A WAY TO GET MORE PEOPLE TO VENERATE THE STAR GOD!
YES, BUT WE HAVE A CRISIS BEFORE US!
WHENEVER HE SEES TWO OR MORE SOLDIERS TOGETHER, HE THINKS IT IS A BATTLE AND ATTACKS!
BUT WE ARE YOUR SIDE!
A SMALL FRAY IS BETTER THAN NO FRAY!

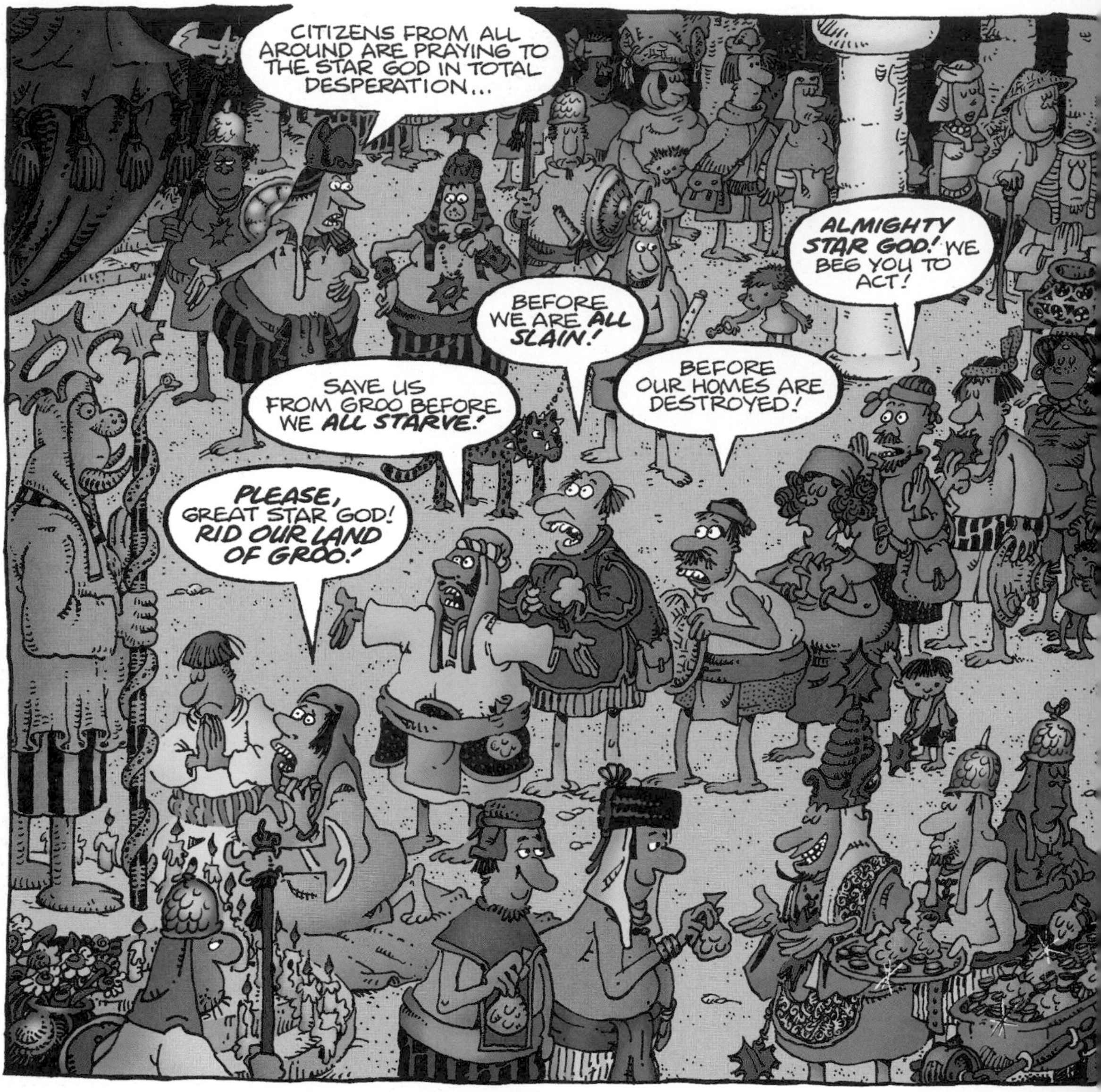
CITIZENS FROM ALL AROUND ARE PRAYING TO THE STAR GOD IN TOTAL DESPERATION...
ALMIGHTY STAR GOD! WE BEG YOU TO ACT!
BEFORE WE ARE ALL SLAIN!
BEFORE OUR HOMES ARE DESTROYED!
SAVE US FROM GROO BEFORE WE ALL STARVE!
PLEASE, GREAT STAR GOD! RID OUR LAND OF GROO!

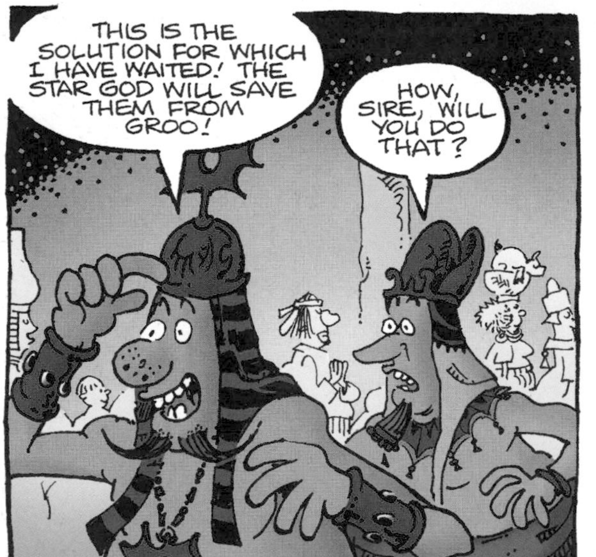
THIS IS THE SOLUTION FOR WHICH I HAVE WAITED! THE STAR GOD WILL SAVE THEM FROM GROO!
HOW, SIRE, WILL YOU DO THAT?

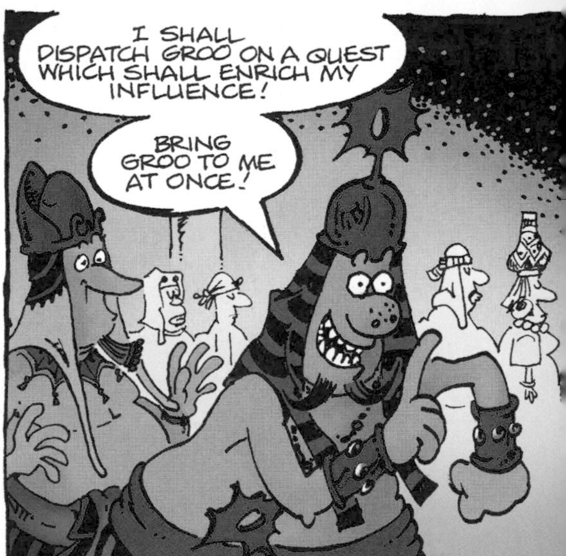
I SHALL DISPATCH GROO ON A QUEST WHICH SHALL ENRICH MY INFLUENCE!
BRING GROO TO ME AT ONCE!

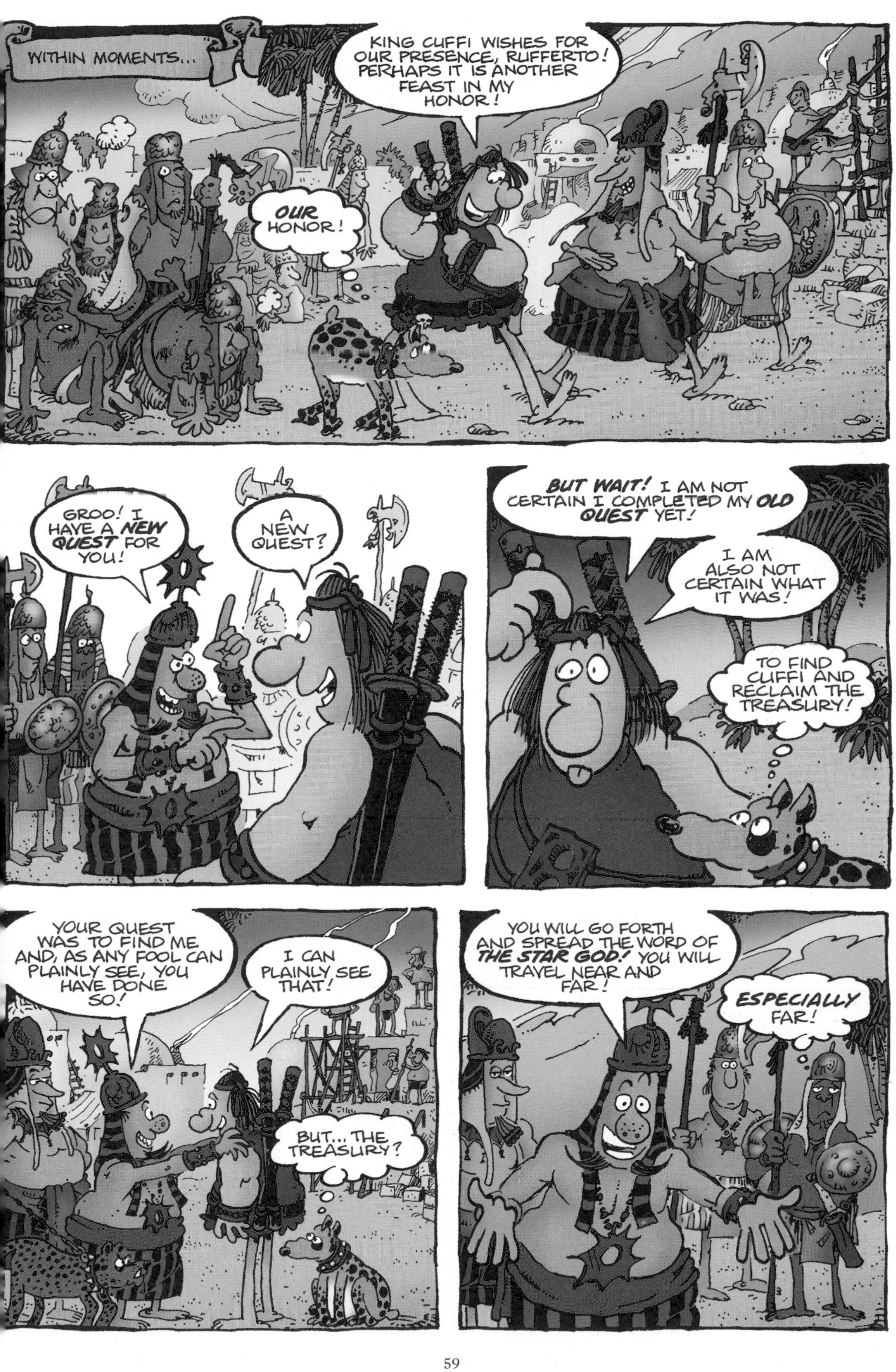
WITHIN MOMENTS...
KING CUFFI WISHES FOR OUR PRESENCE, RUFFERTO! PERHAPS IT IS ANOTHER FEAST IN MY HONOR!
OUR HONOR!
GROO! I HAVE A NEW QUEST FOR YOU!
A NEW QUEST?
BUT WAIT! I AM NOT CERTAIN I COMPLETED MY OLD QUEST YET!
I AM ALSO NOT CERTAIN WHAT IT WAS!
TO FIND CUFFI AND RECLAIM THE TREASURY!
YOUR QUEST WAS TO FIND ME AND, AS ANY FOOL CAN PLAINLY SEE, YOU HAVE DONE SO!
I CAN PLAINLY SEE THAT!
BUT... THE TREASURY?
YOU WILL GO FORTH AND SPREAD THE WORD OF THE STAR GOD! YOU WILL TRAVEL NEAR AND FAR!
ESPECIALLY FAR!

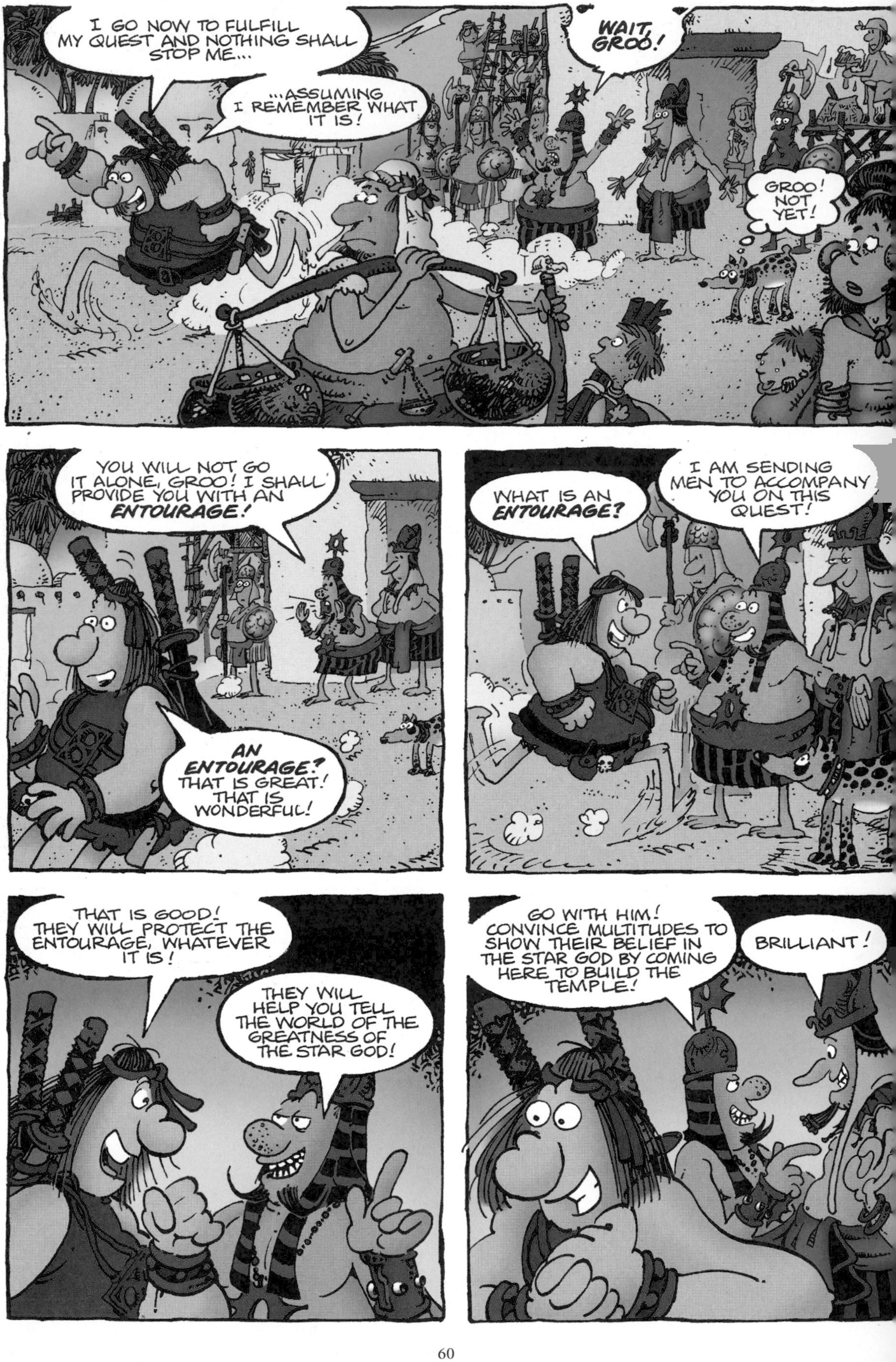

I GO NOW TO FULFILL MY QUEST AND NOTHING SHALL STOP ME...
...ASSUMING I REMEMBER WHAT IT IS!
WAIT, GROO!
GROO! NOT YET!
YOU WILL NOT GO IT ALONE, GROO! I SHALL PROVIDE YOU WITH AN ENTOURAGE!
AN ENTOURAGE? THAT IS GREAT! THAT IS WONDERFUL!
WHAT IS AN ENTOURAGE?
I AM SENDING MEN TO ACCOMPANY YOU ON THIS QUEST!
THAT IS GOOD! THEY WILL PROTECT THE ENTOURAGE, WHATEVER IT IS!
THEY WILL HELP YOU TELL THE WORLD OF THE GREATNESS OF THE STAR GOD!
GO WITH HIM! CONVINCE MULTITUDES TO SHOW THEIR BELIEF IN THE STAR GOD BY COMING HERE TO BUILD THE TEMPLE!
BRILLIANT!

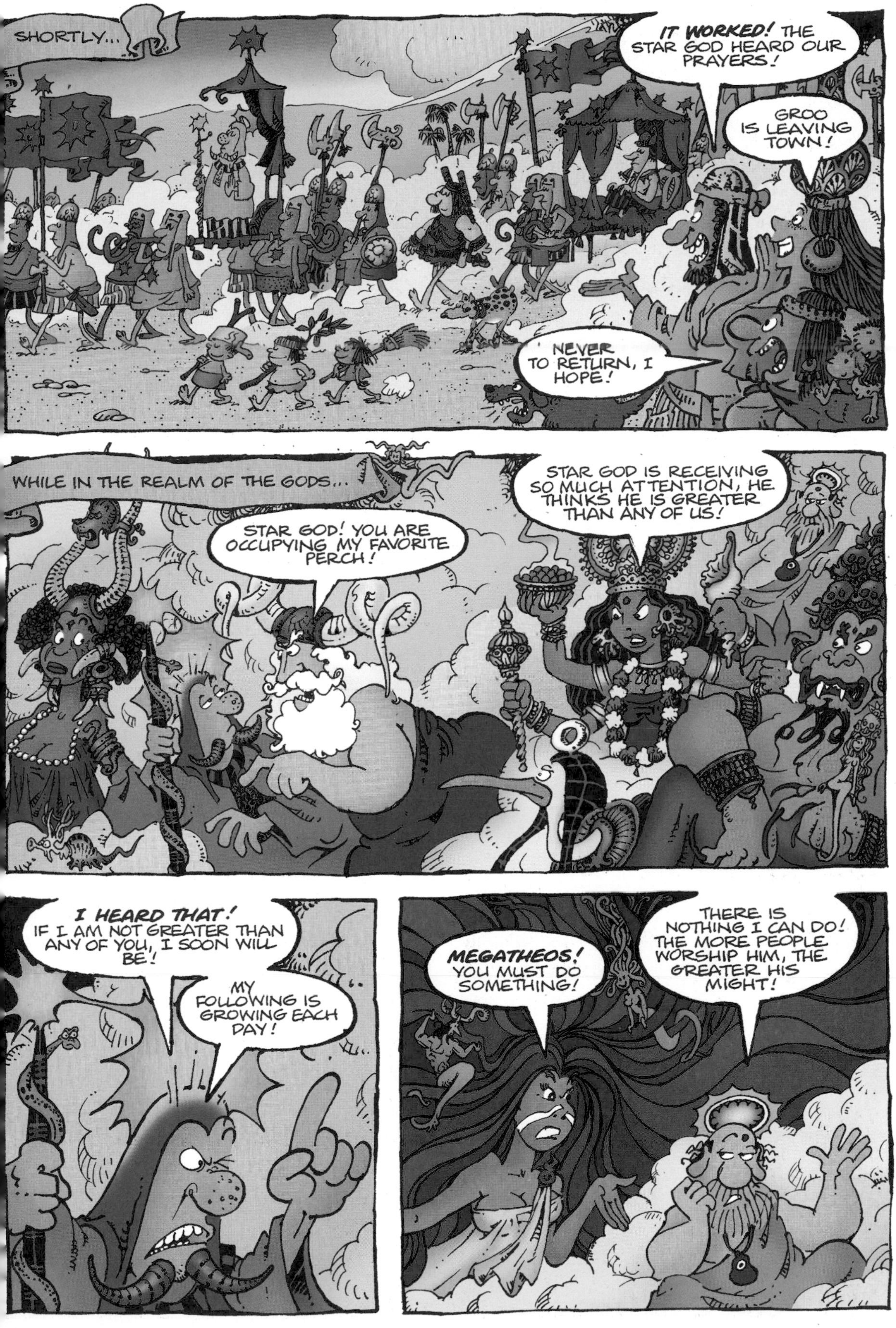

SHORTLY...
IT WORKED! THE STAR GOD HEARD OUR PRAYERS!
GROO IS LEAVING TOWN!
NEVER TO RETURN, I HOPE!
WHILE IN THE REALM OF THE GODS...
STAR GOD! YOU ARE OCCUPYING MY FAVORITE PERCH!
STAR GOD IS RECEIVING SO MUCH ATTENTION, HE THINKS HE IS GREATER THAN ANY OF US!
I HEARD THAT! IF I AM NOT GREATER THAN ANY OF YOU, I SOON WILL BE!
MY FOLLOWING IS GROWING EACH DAY!
MEGATHEOS! YOU MUST DO SOMETHING!
THERE IS NOTHING I CAN DO! THE MORE PEOPLE WORSHIP HIM, THE GREATER HIS MIGHT!

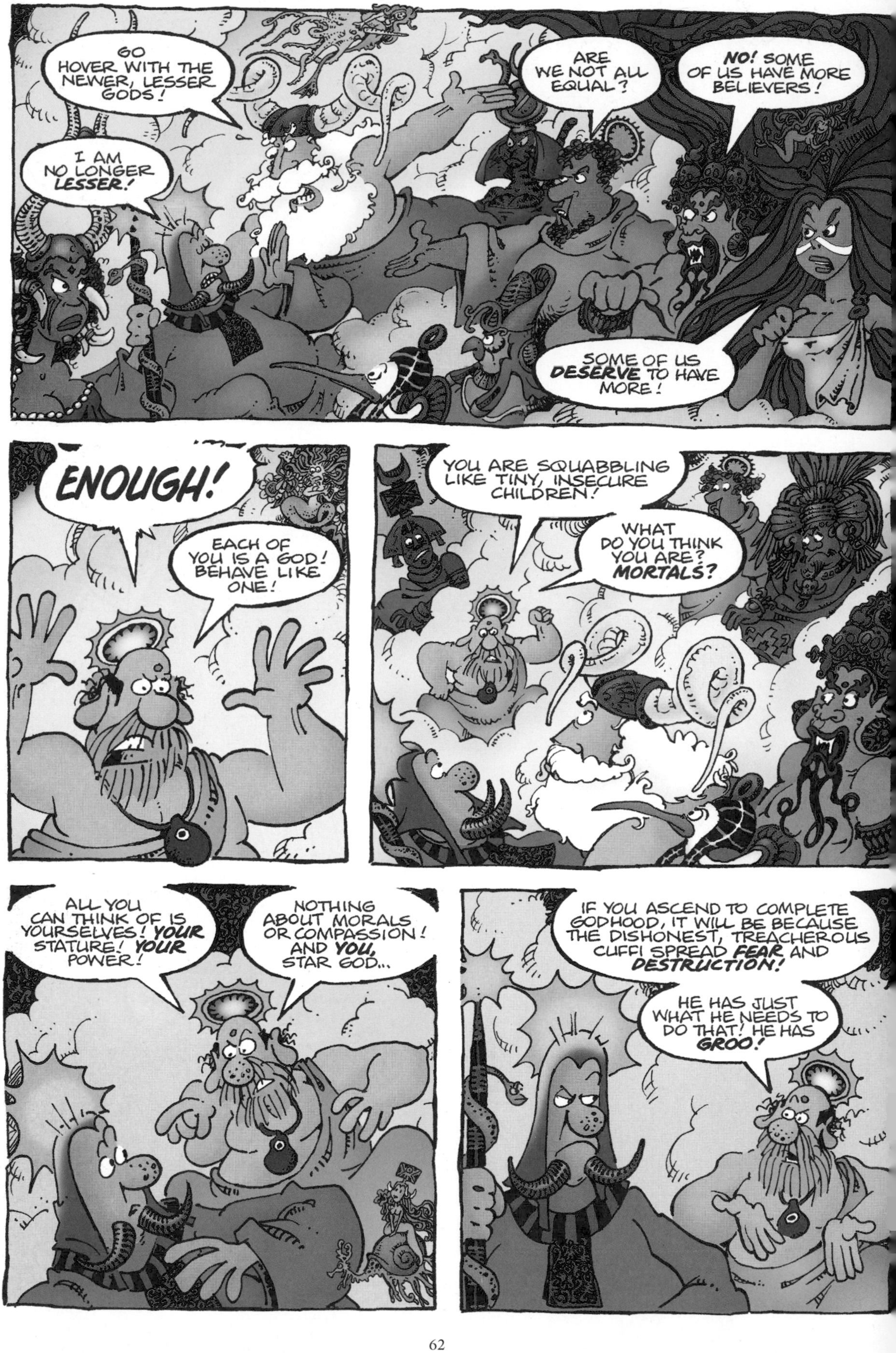
GO HOVER WITH THE NEWER, LESSER GODS!
I AM NO LONGER LESSER!
ARE WE NOT ALL EQUAL?
NO! SOME OF US HAVE MORE BELIEVERS!
SOME OF US DESERVE TO HAVE MORE!
ENOUGH!
EACH OF YOU IS A GOD! BEHAVE LIKE ONE!
YOU ARE SQUABBLING LIKE TINY, INSECURE CHILDREN!
WHAT DO YOU THINK YOU ARE? MORTALS?
ALL YOU CAN THINK OF IS YOURSELVES! YOUR STATURE! YOUR POWER!
NOTHING ABOUT MORALS OR COMPASSION! AND YOU, STAR GOD...
IF YOU ASCEND TO COMPLETE GODHOOD, IT WILL BE BECAUSE THE DISHONEST, TREACHEROUS CUFFI SPREAD FEAR AND DESTRUCTION!
HE HAS JUST WHAT HE NEEDS TO DO THAT! HE HAS GROO!

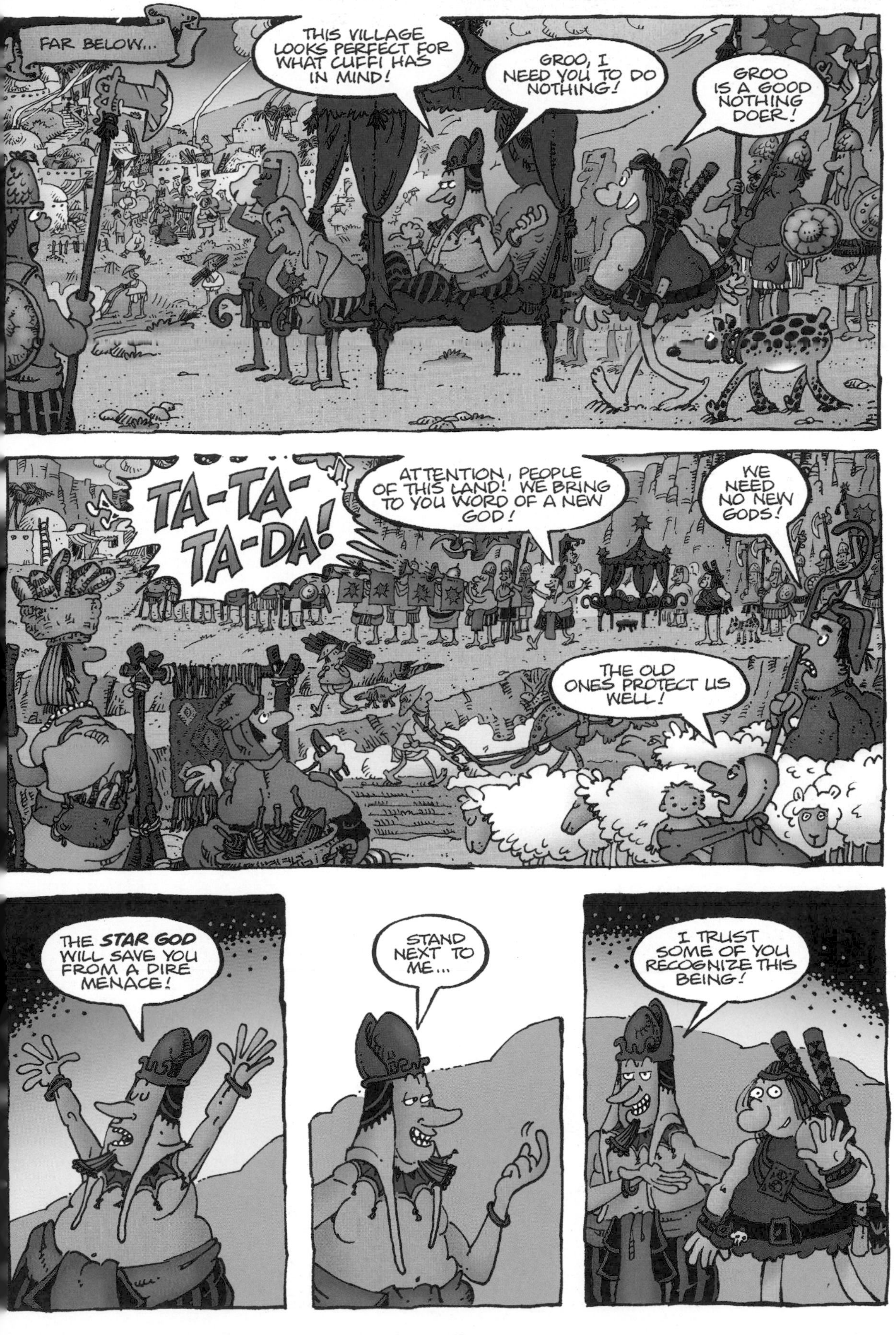
FAR BELOW...
THIS VILLAGE LOOKS PERFECT FOR WHAT CUFFI HAS IN MIND!
GROO, I NEED YOU TO DO NOTHING!
GROO IS A GOOD NOTHING DOER!
TA-TA-TA-DA!
ATTENTION, PEOPLE OF THIS LAND! WE BRING TO YOU WORD OF A NEW GOD!
WE NEED NO NEW GODS!
THE OLD ONES PROTECT US WELL!
THE STAR GOD WILL SAVE YOU FROM A DIRE MENACE!
STAND NEXT TO ME...
I TRUST SOME OF YOU RECOGNIZE THIS BEING!

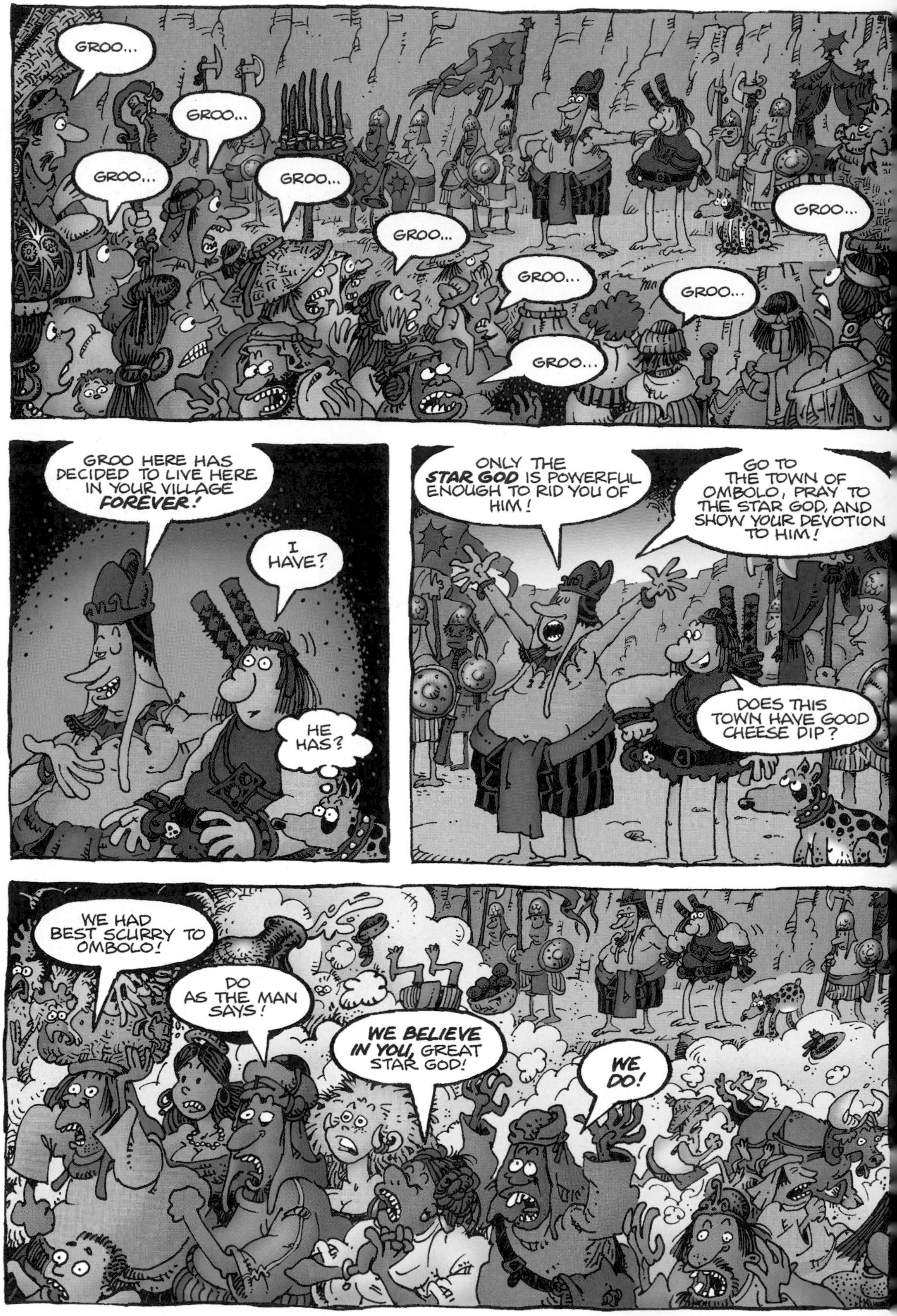
GROO...
GROO...
GROO...
GROO...
GROO...
GROO...
GROO...
GROO...
GROO...
GROO HERE HAS DECIDED TO LIVE HERE IN YOUR VILLAGE **FOREVER!**
I HAVE?
HE HAS?
ONLY THE **STAR GOD** IS POWERFUL ENOUGH TO RID YOU OF HIM!
GO TO THE TOWN OF OMBOLO, PRAY TO THE STAR GOD, AND SHOW YOUR DEVOTION TO HIM!
DOES THIS TOWN HAVE GOOD CHEESE DIP?
WE HAD BEST SCURRY TO OMBOLO!
DO AS THE MAN SAYS!
WE BELIEVE IN YOU, GREAT STAR GOD!
WE DO!

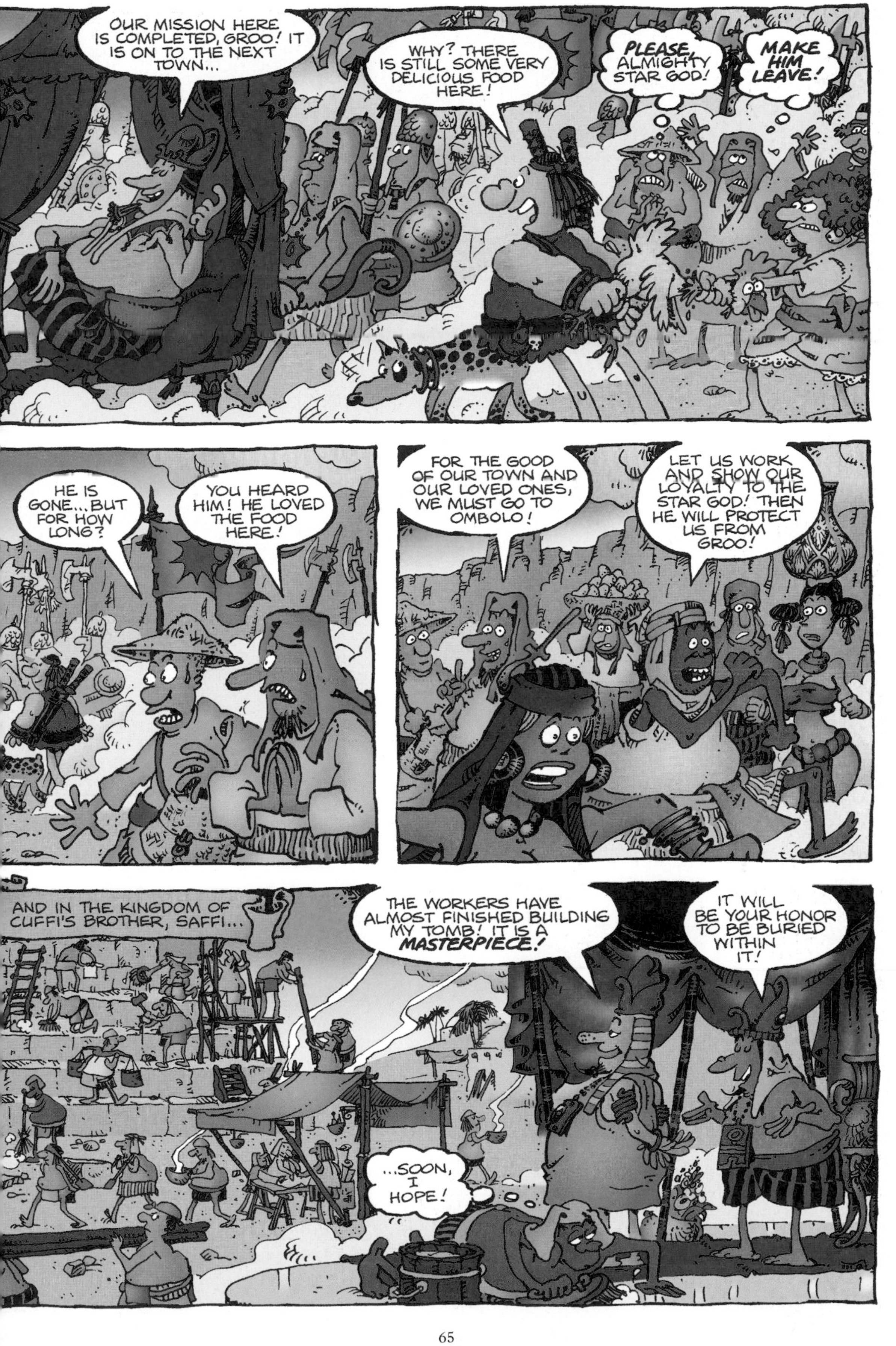
OUR MISSION HERE IS COMPLETED, GROO! IT IS ON TO THE NEXT TOWN...
WHY? THERE IS STILL SOME VERY DELICIOUS FOOD HERE!
PLEASE, ALMIGHTY STAR GOD!
MAKE HIM LEAVE!
HE IS GONE... BUT FOR HOW LONG?
YOU HEARD HIM! HE LOVED THE FOOD HERE!
FOR THE GOOD OF OUR TOWN AND OUR LOVED ONES, WE MUST GO TO OMBOLO!
LET US WORK AND SHOW OUR LOYALTY TO THE STAR GOD! THEN HE WILL PROTECT US FROM GROO!
AND IN THE KINGDOM OF CUFFI'S BROTHER, SAFFI...
THE WORKERS HAVE ALMOST FINISHED BUILDING MY TOMB! IT IS A MASTERPIECE!
IT WILL BE YOUR HONOR TO BE BURIED WITHIN IT!
...SOON, I HOPE!

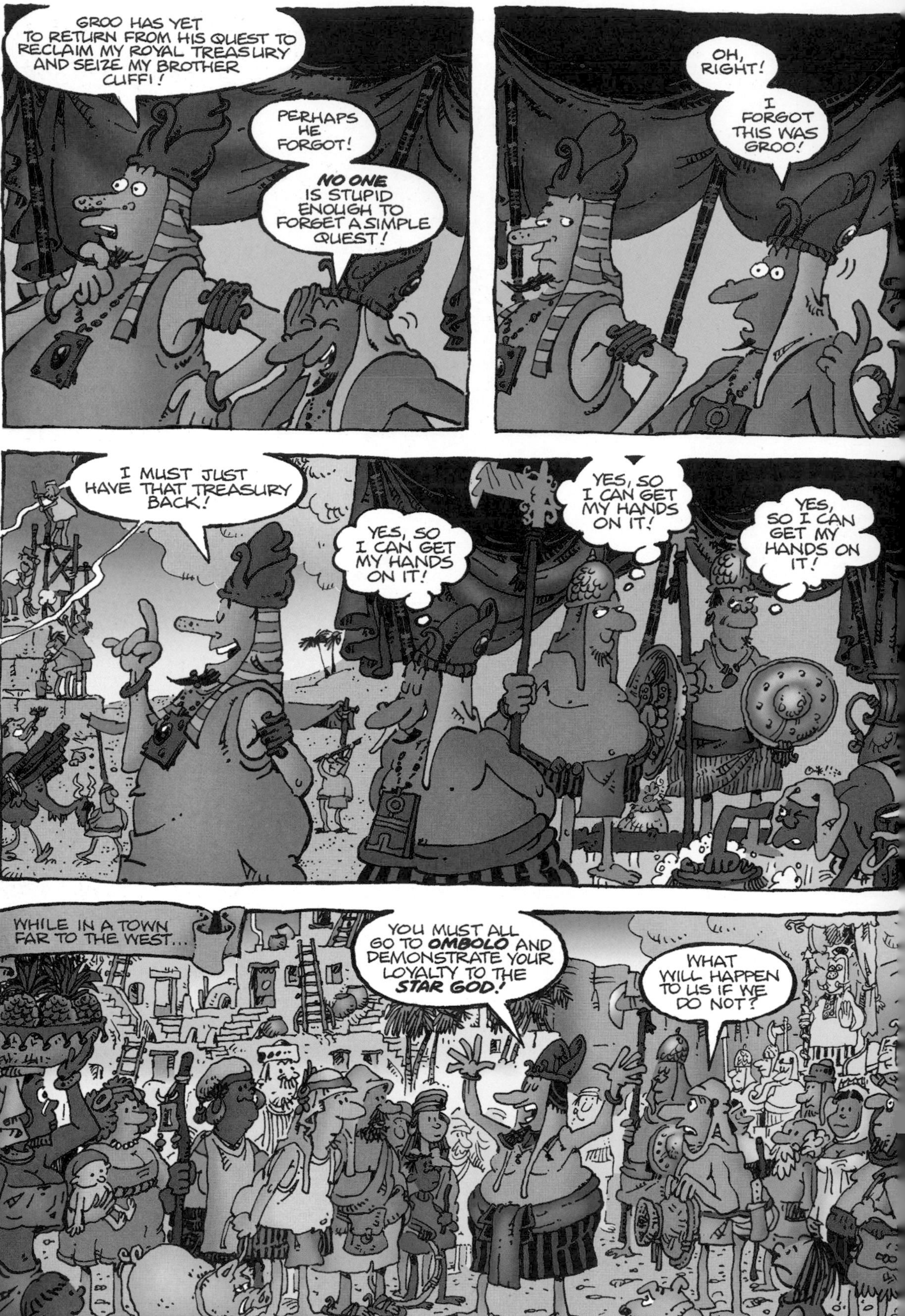
GROO HAS YET TO RETURN FROM HIS QUEST TO RECLAIM MY ROYAL TREASURY AND SEIZE MY BROTHER CUFFI!
PERHAPS HE FORGOT!
NO ONE IS STUPID ENOUGH TO FORGET A SIMPLE QUEST!
OH, RIGHT!
I FORGOT THIS WAS GROO!
I MUST JUST HAVE THAT TREASURY BACK!
YES, SO I CAN GET MY HANDS ON IT!
YES, SO I CAN GET MY HANDS ON IT!
YES, SO I CAN GET MY HANDS ON IT!
WHILE IN A TOWN FAR TO THE WEST...
YOU MUST ALL GO TO **OMBOLO** AND DEMONSTRATE YOUR LOYALTY TO THE **STAR GOD!**
WHAT WILL HAPPEN TO US IF WE DO NOT?

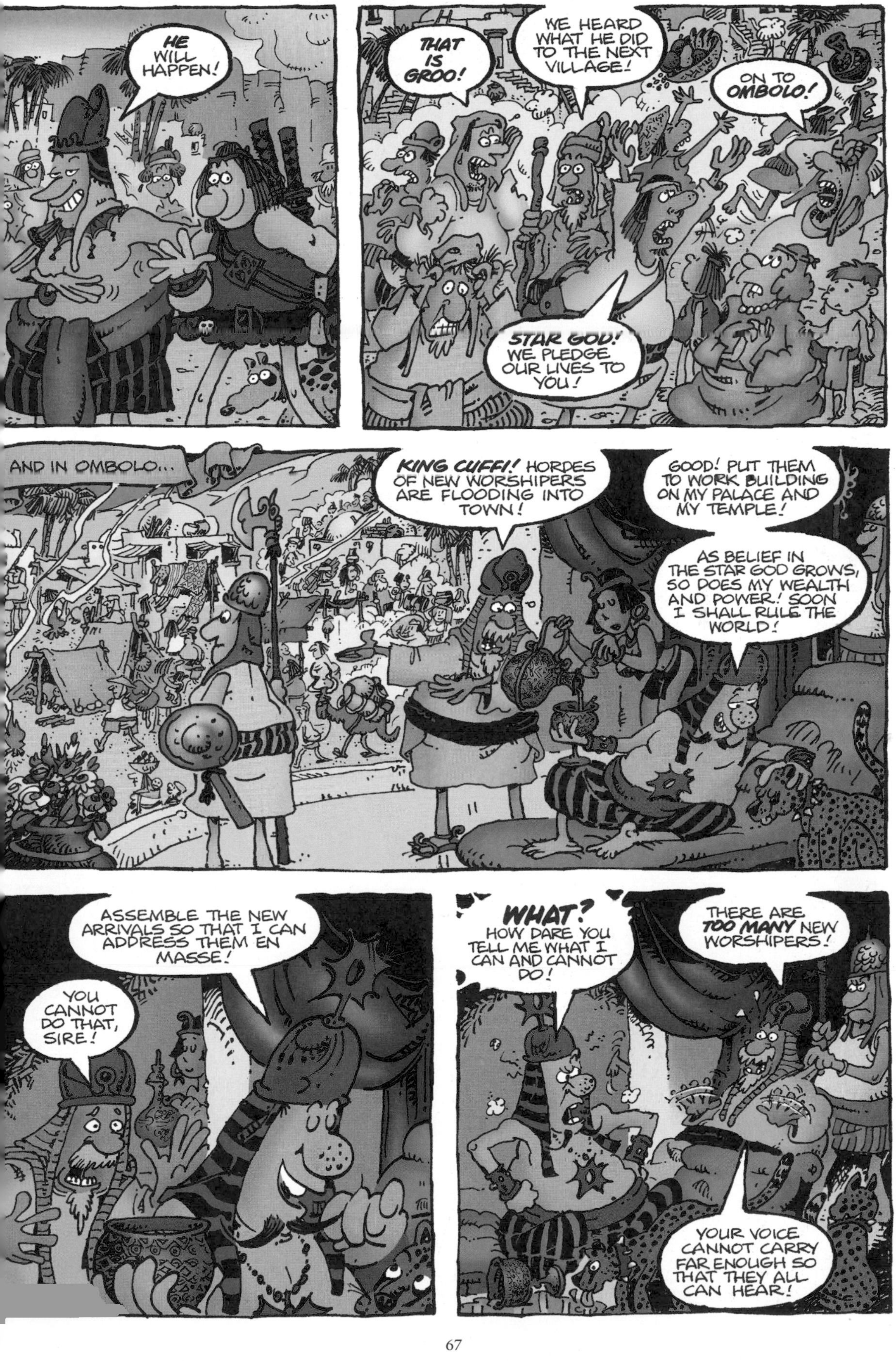

HE WILL HAPPEN!
THAT IS GROO!
WE HEARD WHAT HE DID TO THE NEXT VILLAGE!
ON TO OMBOLO!
STAR GOD! WE PLEDGE OUR LIVES TO YOU!
AND IN OMBOLO...
KING CUFFI! HORDES OF NEW WORSHIPERS ARE FLOODING INTO TOWN!
GOOD! PUT THEM TO WORK BUILDING ON MY PALACE AND MY TEMPLE!
AS BELIEF IN THE STAR GOD GROWS, SO DOES MY WEALTH AND POWER! SOON I SHALL RULE THE WORLD!
ASSEMBLE THE NEW ARRIVALS SO THAT I CAN ADDRESS THEM EN MASSE!
YOU CANNOT DO THAT, SIRE!
WHAT? HOW DARE YOU TELL ME WHAT I CAN AND CANNOT DO!
THERE ARE TOO MANY NEW WORSHIPERS!
YOUR VOICE CANNOT CARRY FAR ENOUGH SO THAT THEY ALL CAN HEAR!

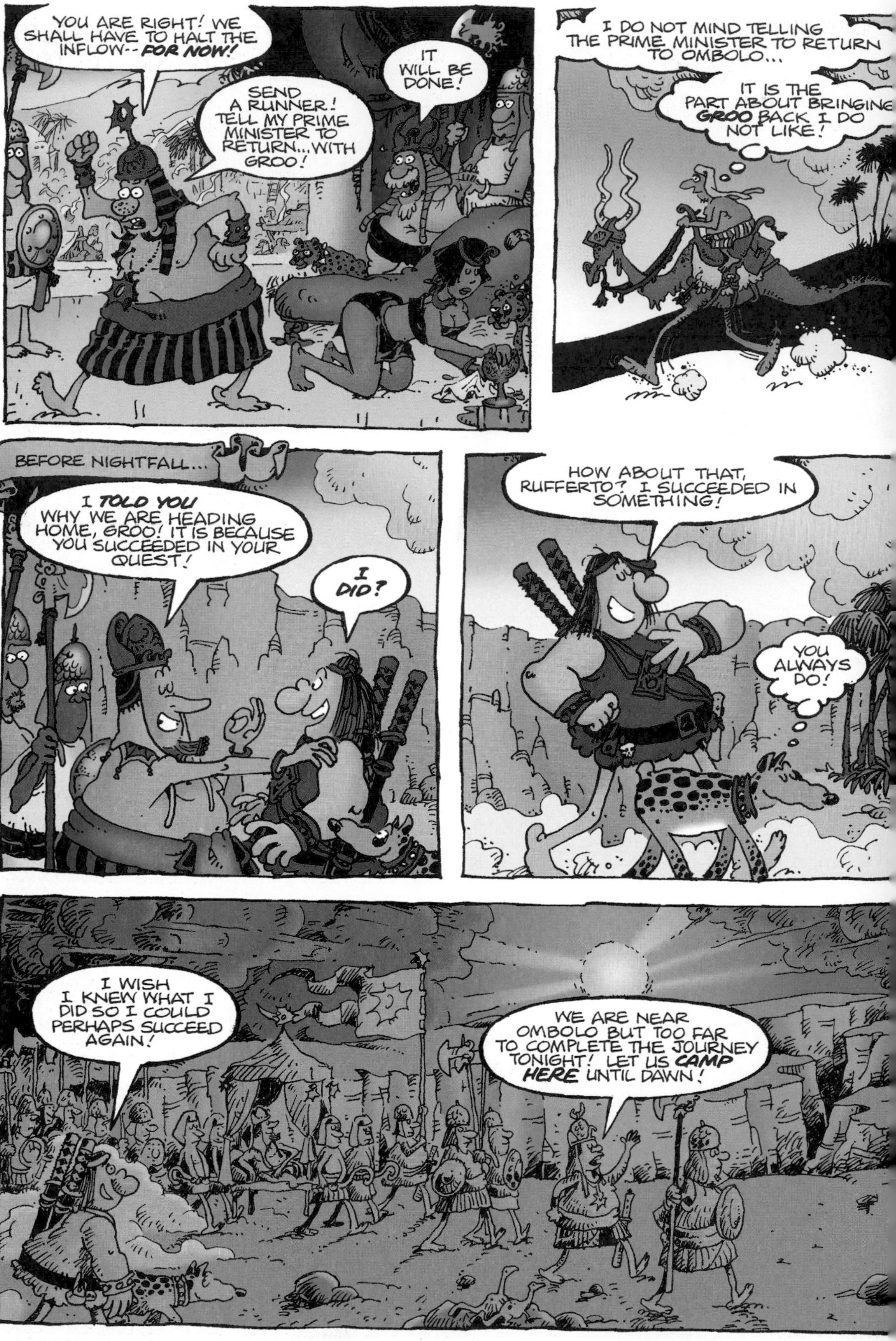

YOU ARE RIGHT! WE SHALL HAVE TO HALT THE INFLOW-- FOR NOW!
SEND A RUNNER! TELL MY PRIME MINISTER TO RETURN... WITH GROO!
IT WILL BE DONE!
I DO NOT MIND TELLING THE PRIME MINISTER TO RETURN TO OMBOLO...
IT IS THE PART ABOUT BRINGING GROO BACK I DO NOT LIKE!
BEFORE NIGHTFALL...
I TOLD YOU WHY WE ARE HEADING HOME, GROO! IT IS BECAUSE YOU SUCCEEDED IN YOUR QUEST!
I DID?
HOW ABOUT THAT, RUFFERTO? I SUCCEEDED IN SOMETHING!
YOU ALWAYS DO!
I WISH I KNEW WHAT I DID SO I COULD PERHAPS SUCCEED AGAIN!
WE ARE NEAR OMBOLO BUT TOO FAR TO COMPLETE THE JOURNEY TONIGHT! LET US CAMP HERE UNTIL DAWN!

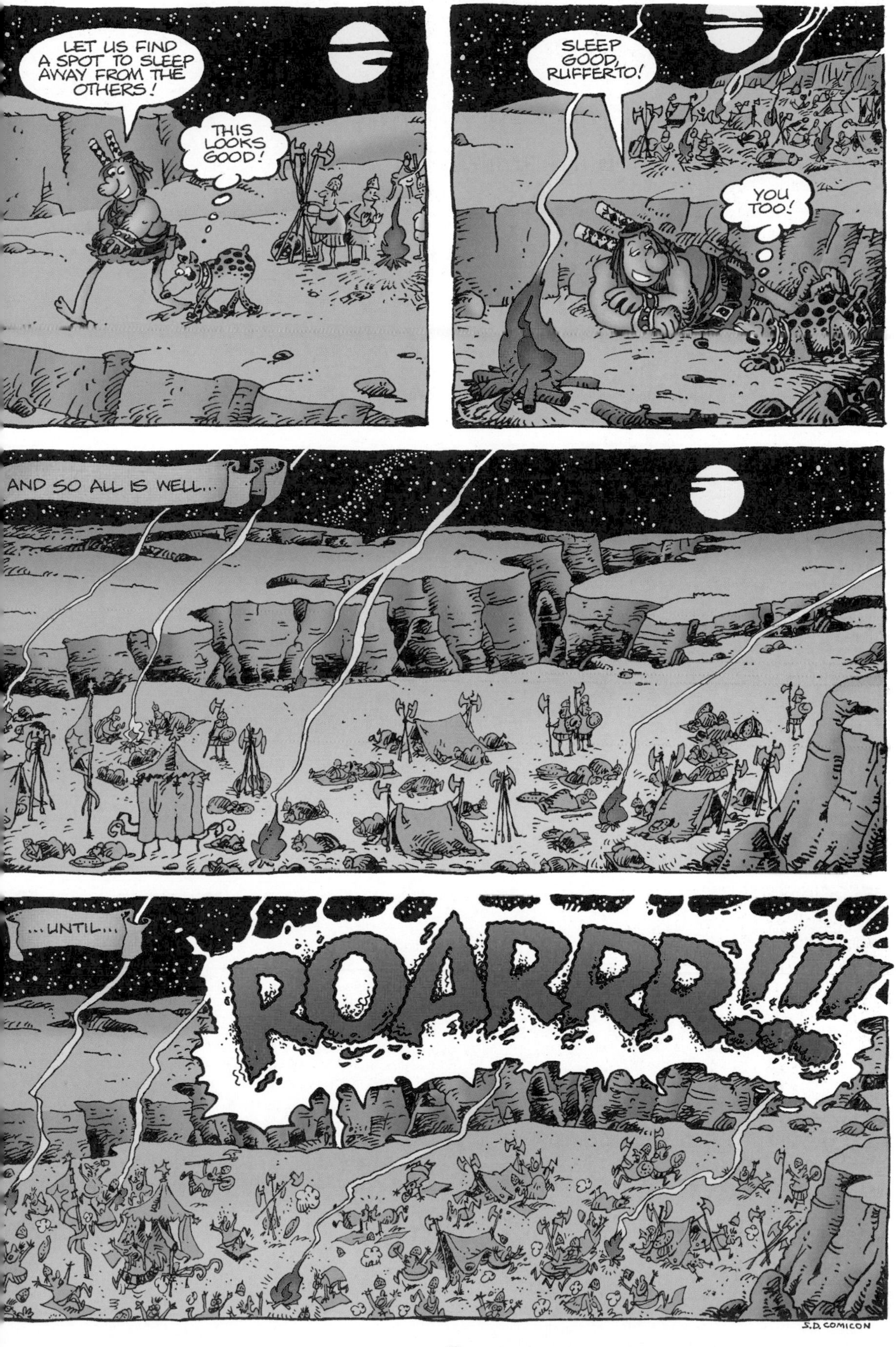
LET US FIND A SPOT TO SLEEP AWAY FROM THE OTHERS!
THIS LOOKS GOOD!
SLEEP GOOD, RUFFERTO!
YOU TOO!
AND SO ALL IS WELL...
...UNTIL...
ROARRR!!!
S.D. COMICON

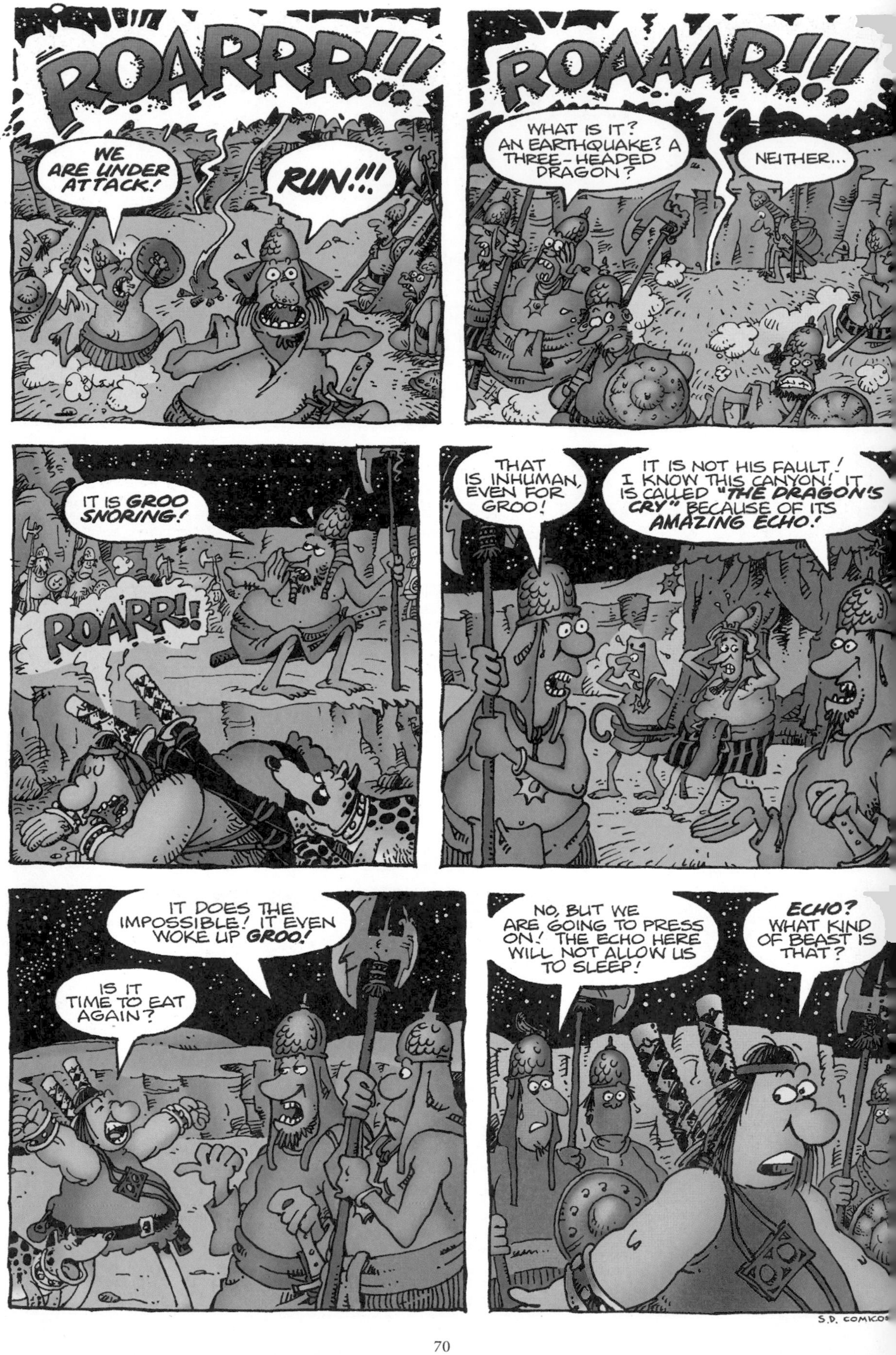
ROARRR!!!
WE ARE UNDER ATTACK!
RUN!!!
ROAAAR!!!
WHAT IS IT? AN EARTHQUAKE? A THREE-HEADED DRAGON?
NEITHER...
IT IS GROO SNORING!
ROARR!
THAT IS INHUMAN, EVEN FOR GROO!
IT IS NOT HIS FAULT! I KNOW THIS CANYON! IT IS CALLED "THE DRAGON'S CRY" BECAUSE OF ITS AMAZING ECHO!
IT DOES THE IMPOSSIBLE! IT EVEN WOKE UP GROO!
IS IT TIME TO EAT AGAIN?
NO, BUT WE ARE GOING TO PRESS ON! THE ECHO HERE WILL NOT ALLOW US TO SLEEP!
ECHO? WHAT KIND OF BEAST IS THAT?
S.D. COMKO

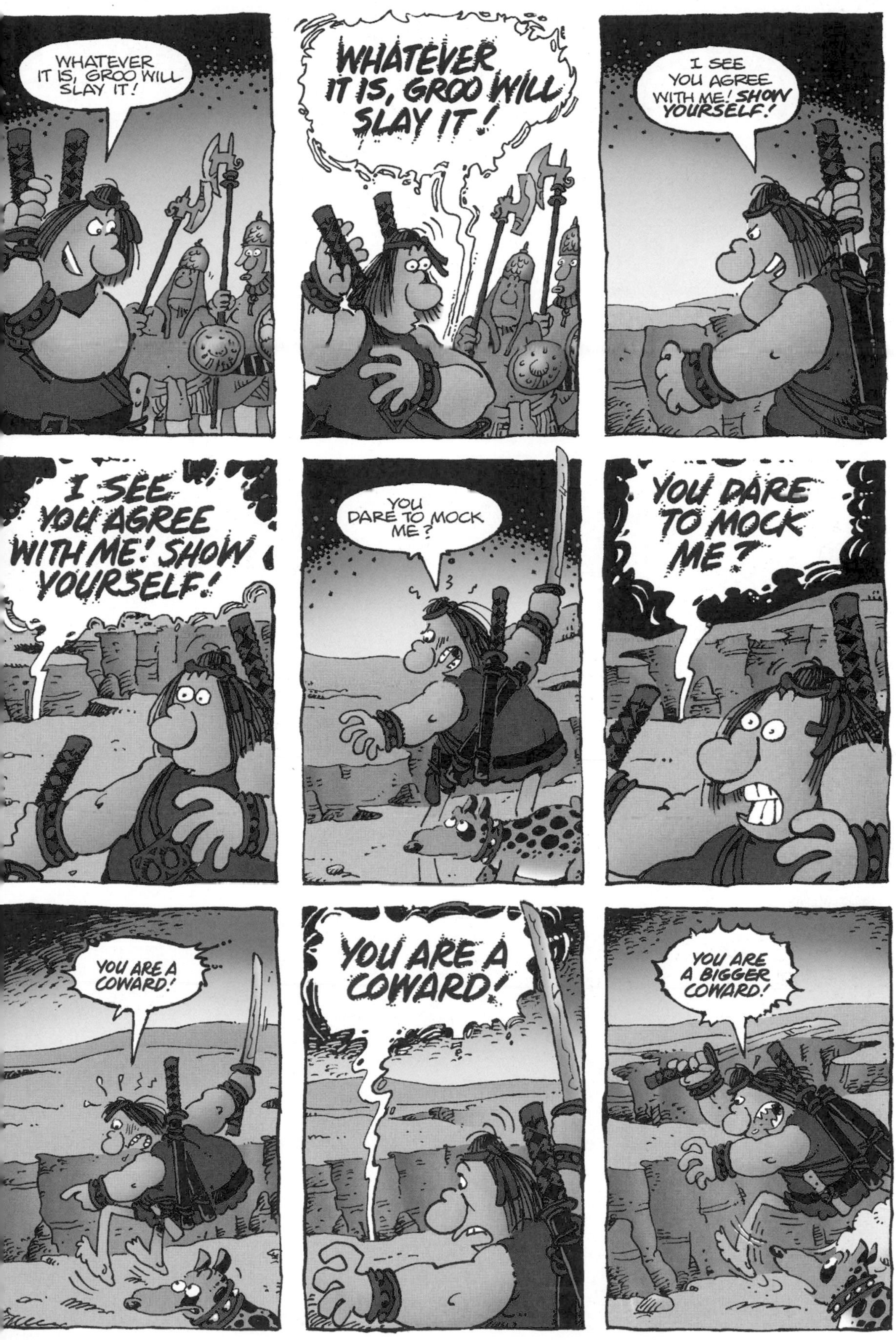
WHATEVER IT IS, GROO WILL SLAY IT!
WHATEVER IT IS, GROO WILL SLAY IT!
I SEE YOU AGREE WITH ME! SHOW YOURSELF!
I SEE YOU AGREE WITH ME! SHOW YOURSELF!
YOU DARE TO MOCK ME?
YOU DARE TO MOCK ME?
YOU ARE A COWARD!
YOU ARE A COWARD!
YOU ARE A BIGGER COWARD!

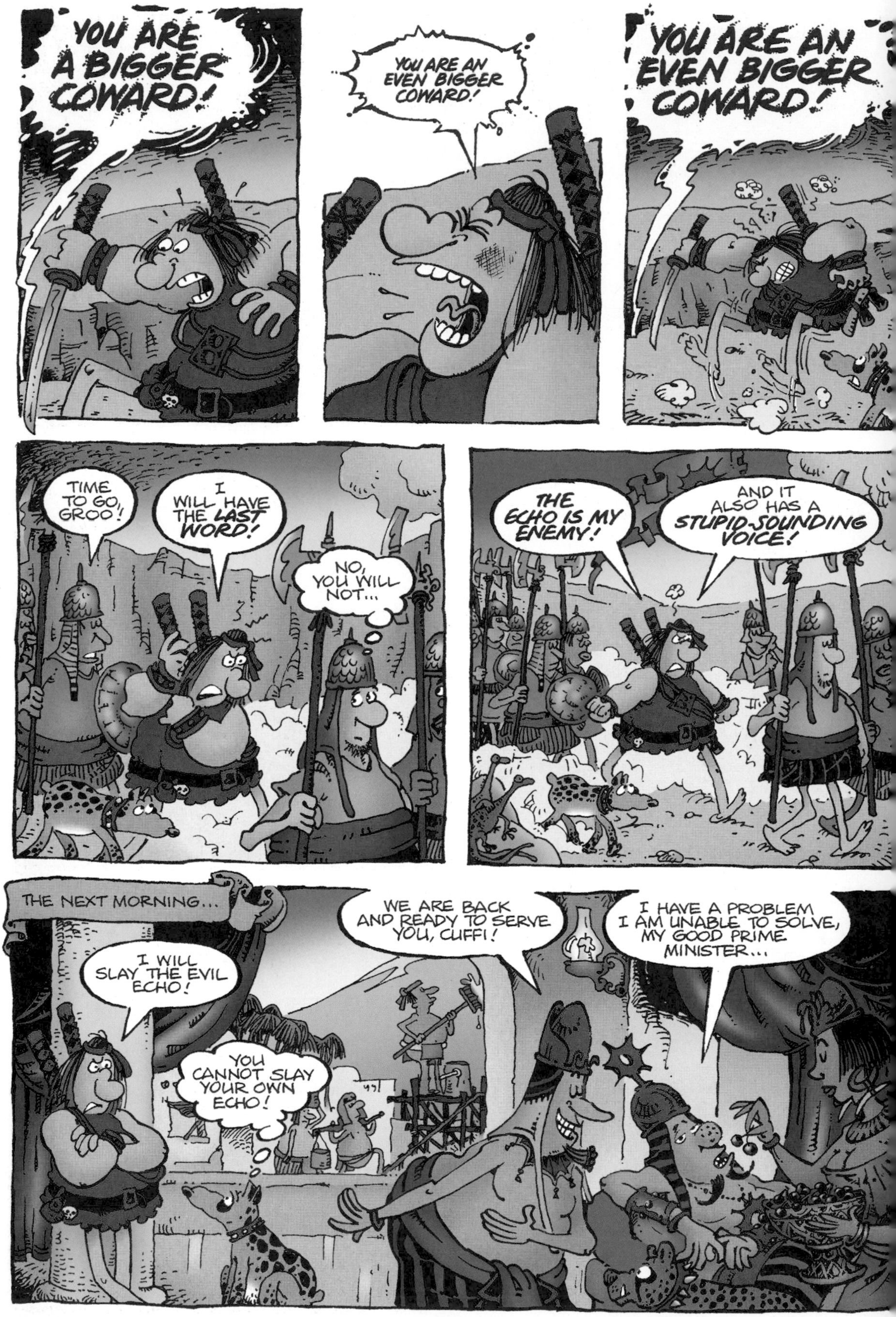

YOU ARE A BIGGER COWARD!
YOU ARE AN EVEN BIGGER COWARD!
YOU ARE AN EVEN BIGGER COWARD!
TIME TO GO, GROO!
I WILL HAVE THE LAST WORD!
NO, YOU WILL NOT...
THE ECHO IS MY ENEMY!
AND IT ALSO HAS A STUPID-SOUNDING VOICE!
THE NEXT MORNING...
I WILL SLAY THE EVIL ECHO!
YOU CANNOT SLAY YOUR OWN ECHO!
WE ARE BACK AND READY TO SERVE YOU, CUFFI!
I HAVE A PROBLEM I AM UNABLE TO SOLVE, MY GOOD PRIME MINISTER...

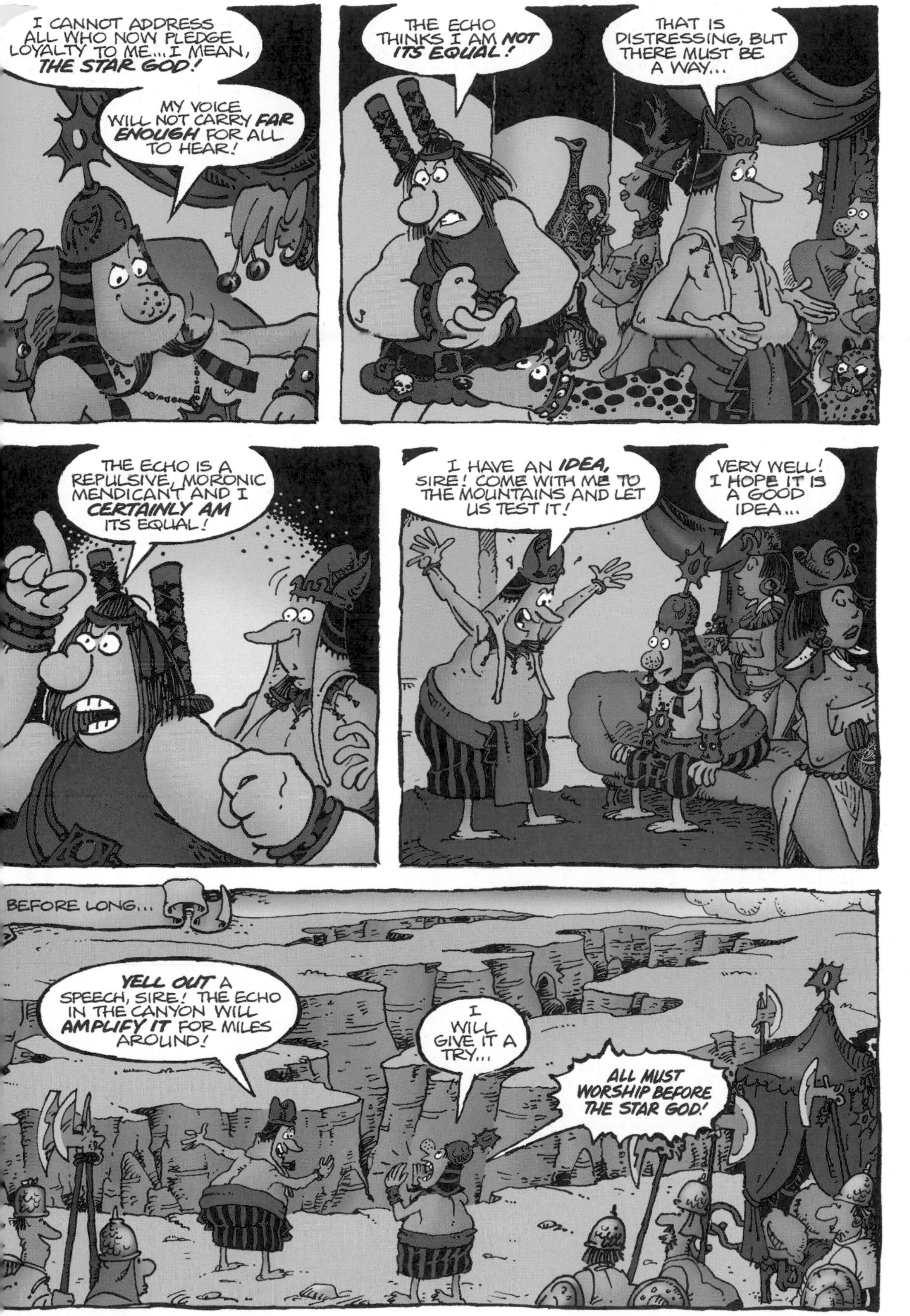
I CANNOT ADDRESS ALL WHO NOW PLEDGE LOYALTY TO ME... I MEAN, THE STAR GOD!
MY VOICE WILL NOT CARRY FAR ENOUGH FOR ALL TO HEAR!
THE ECHO THINKS I AM NOT ITS EQUAL!
THAT IS DISTRESSING, BUT THERE MUST BE A WAY...
THE ECHO IS A REPULSIVE, MORONIC MENDICANT AND I CERTAINLY AM ITS EQUAL!
I HAVE AN IDEA, SIRE! COME WITH ME TO THE MOUNTAINS AND LET US TEST IT!
VERY WELL! I HOPE IT IS A GOOD IDEA...
BEFORE LONG...
YELL OUT A SPEECH, SIRE! THE ECHO IN THE CANYON WILL AMPLIFY IT FOR MILES AROUND!
I WILL GIVE IT A TRY...
ALL MUST WORSHIP BEFORE THE STAR GOD!

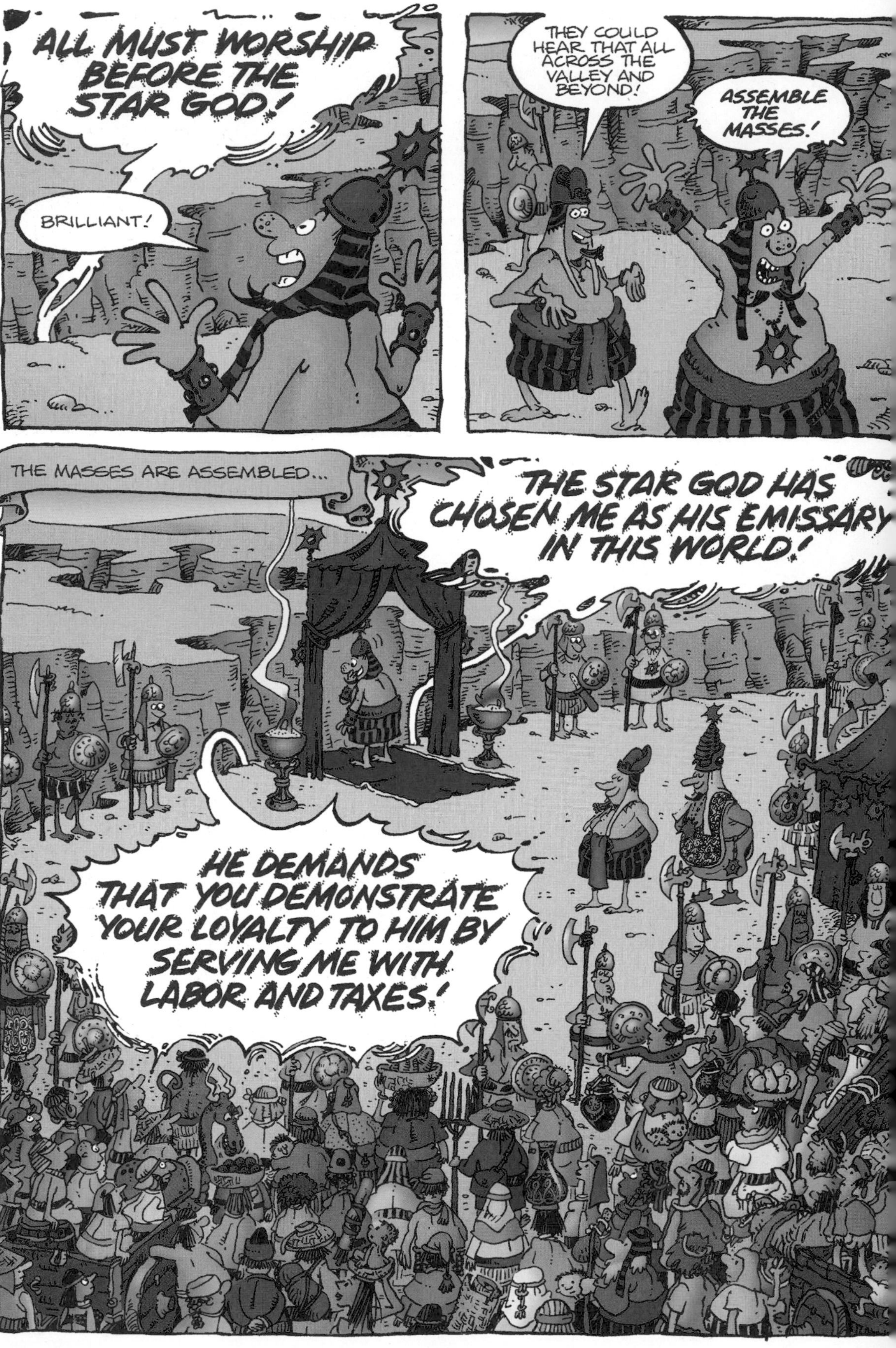
ALL MUST WORSHIP BEFORE THE STAR GOD!
BRILLIANT!
THEY COULD HEAR THAT ALL ACROSS THE VALLEY AND BEYOND!
ASSEMBLE THE MASSES!
THE MASSES ARE ASSEMBLED...
THE STAR GOD HAS CHOSEN ME AS HIS EMISSARY IN THIS WORLD!
HE DEMANDS THAT YOU DEMONSTRATE YOUR LOYALTY TO HIM BY SERVING ME WITH LABOR AND TAXES!

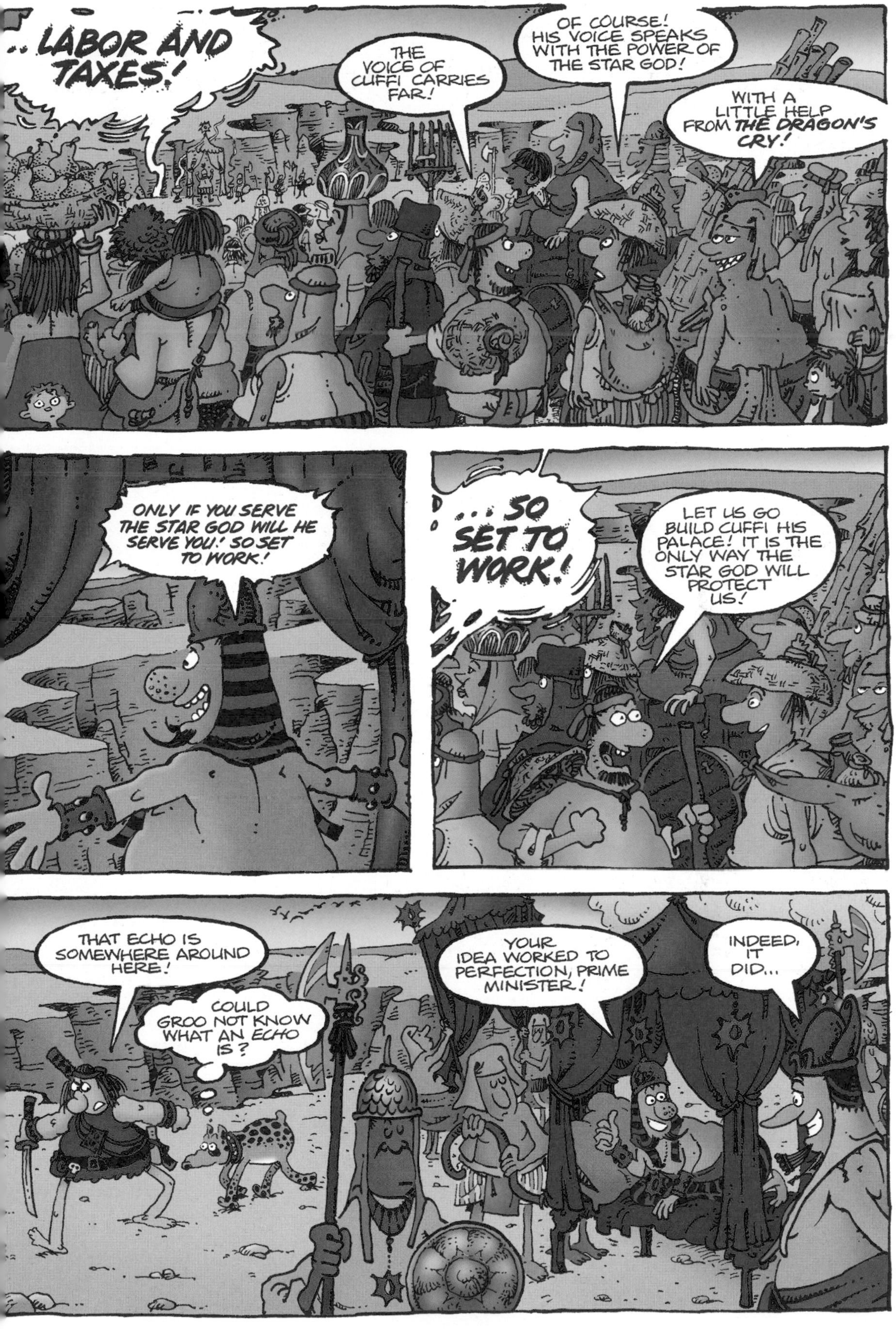

...LABOR AND TAXES!
THE VOICE OF CUFFI CARRIES FAR!
OF COURSE! HIS VOICE SPEAKS WITH THE POWER OF THE STAR GOD!
WITH A LITTLE HELP FROM THE DRAGON'S CRY!
ONLY IF YOU SERVE THE STAR GOD WILL HE SERVE YOU! SO SET TO WORK!
...SO SET TO WORK!
LET US GO BUILD CUFFI HIS PALACE! IT IS THE ONLY WAY THE STAR GOD WILL PROTECT US!
THAT ECHO IS SOMEWHERE AROUND HERE!
COULD GROO NOT KNOW WHAT AN ECHO IS?
YOUR IDEA WORKED TO PERFECTION, PRIME MINISTER!
INDEED, IT DID...

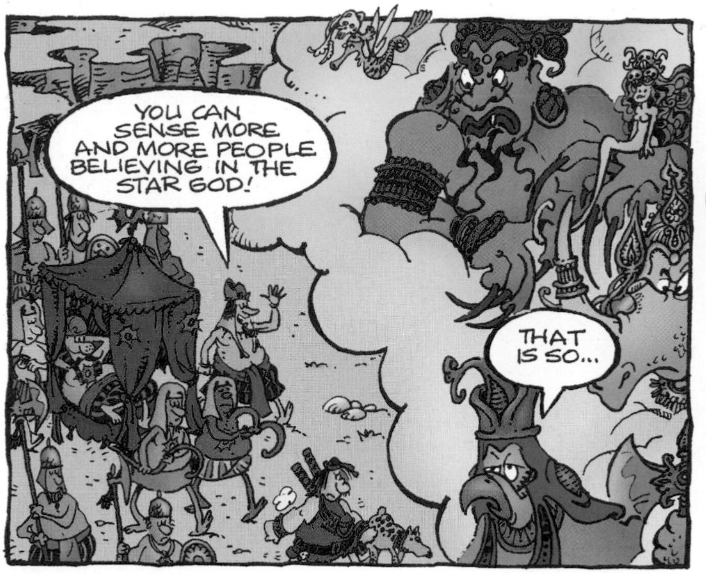
YOU CAN SENSE MORE AND MORE PEOPLE BELIEVING IN THE STAR GOD!
THAT IS SO...

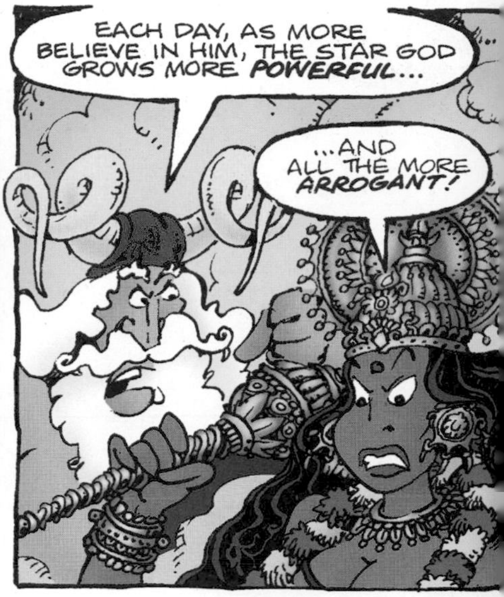
EACH DAY, AS MORE BELIEVE IN HIM, THE STAR GOD GROWS MORE POWERFUL...
...AND ALL THE MORE ARROGANT!

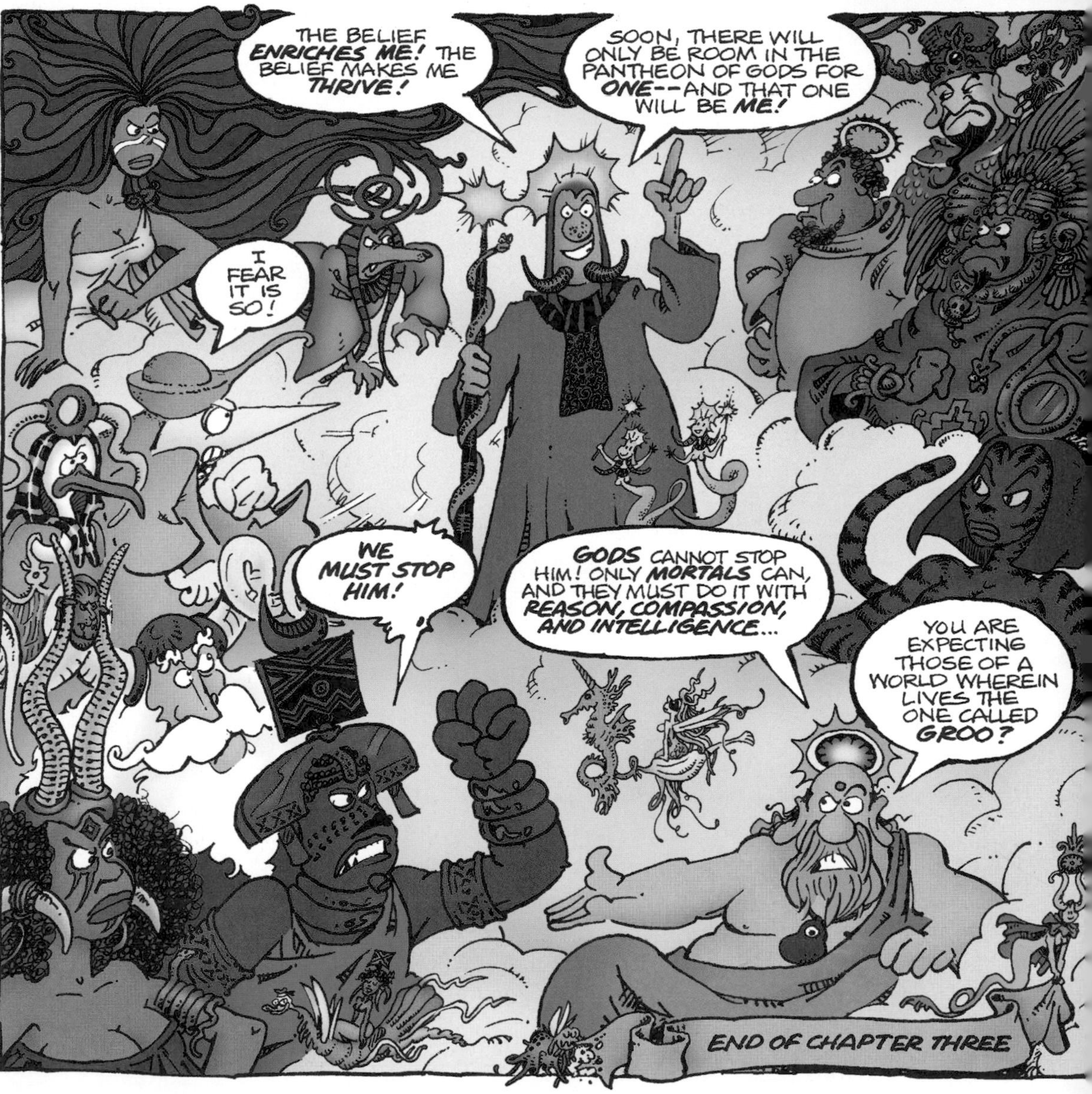
THE BELIEF ENRICHES ME! THE BELIEF MAKES ME THRIVE!
SOON, THERE WILL ONLY BE ROOM IN THE PANTHEON OF GODS FOR ONE--AND THAT ONE WILL BE ME!
I FEAR IT IS SO!
WE MUST STOP HIM!
GODS CANNOT STOP HIM! ONLY MORTALS CAN, AND THEY MUST DO IT WITH REASON, COMPASSION, AND INTELLIGENCE...
YOU ARE EXPECTING THOSE OF A WORLD WHEREIN LIVES THE ONE CALLED GROO?
END OF CHAPTER THREE

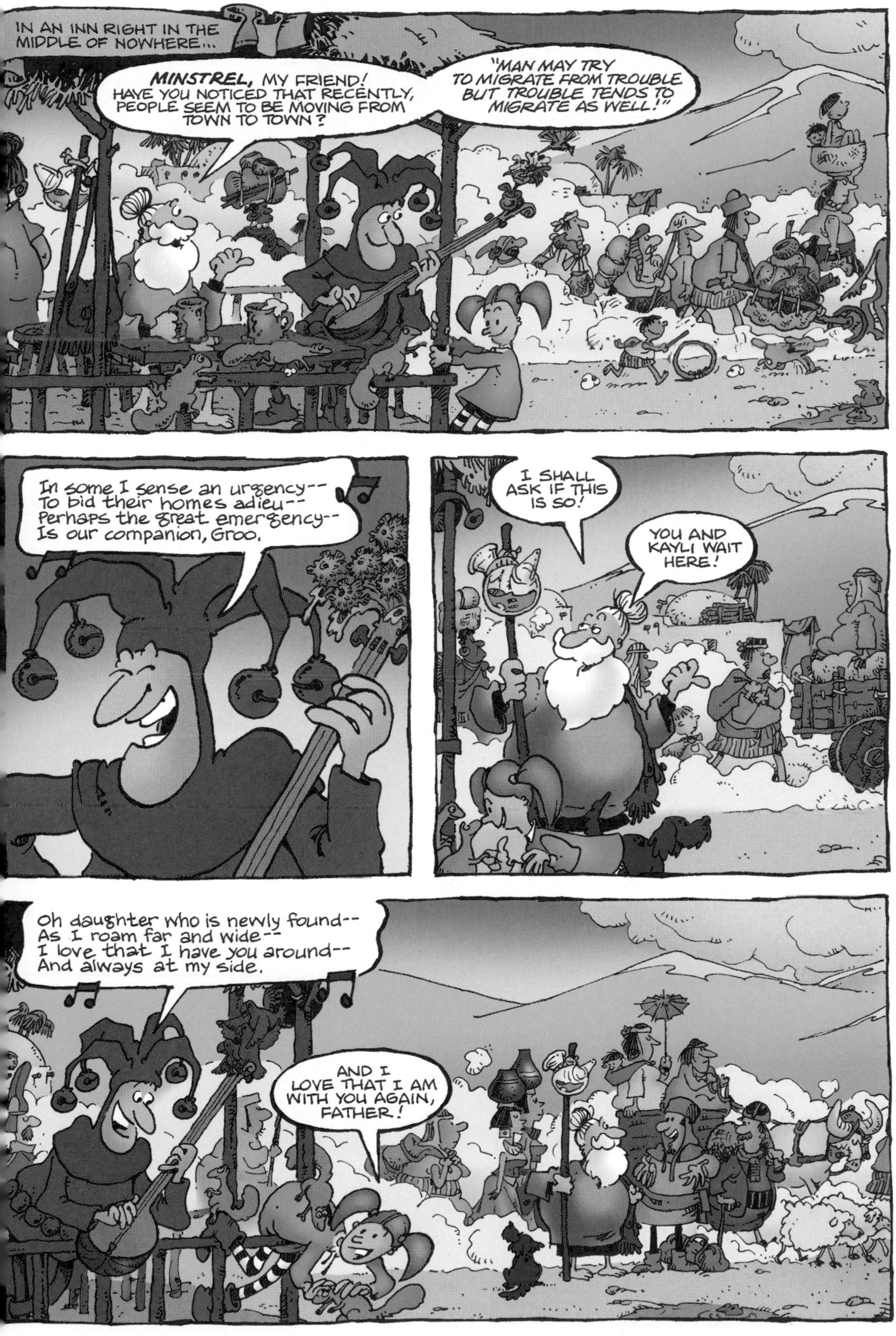

IN AN INN RIGHT IN THE MIDDLE OF NOWHERE...
MINSTREL, MY FRIEND! HAVE YOU NOTICED THAT RECENTLY, PEOPLE SEEM TO BE MOVING FROM TOWN TO TOWN?
"MAN MAY TRY TO MIGRATE FROM TROUBLE BUT TROUBLE TENDS TO MIGRATE AS WELL!"
In some I sense an urgency-- To bid their homes adieu-- Perhaps the great emergency-- Is our companion, Groo.
I SHALL ASK IF THIS IS SO!
YOU AND KAYLI WAIT HERE!
Oh daughter who is newly found-- As I roam far and wide-- I love that I have you around-- And always at my side.
AND I LOVE THAT I AM WITH YOU AGAIN, FATHER!

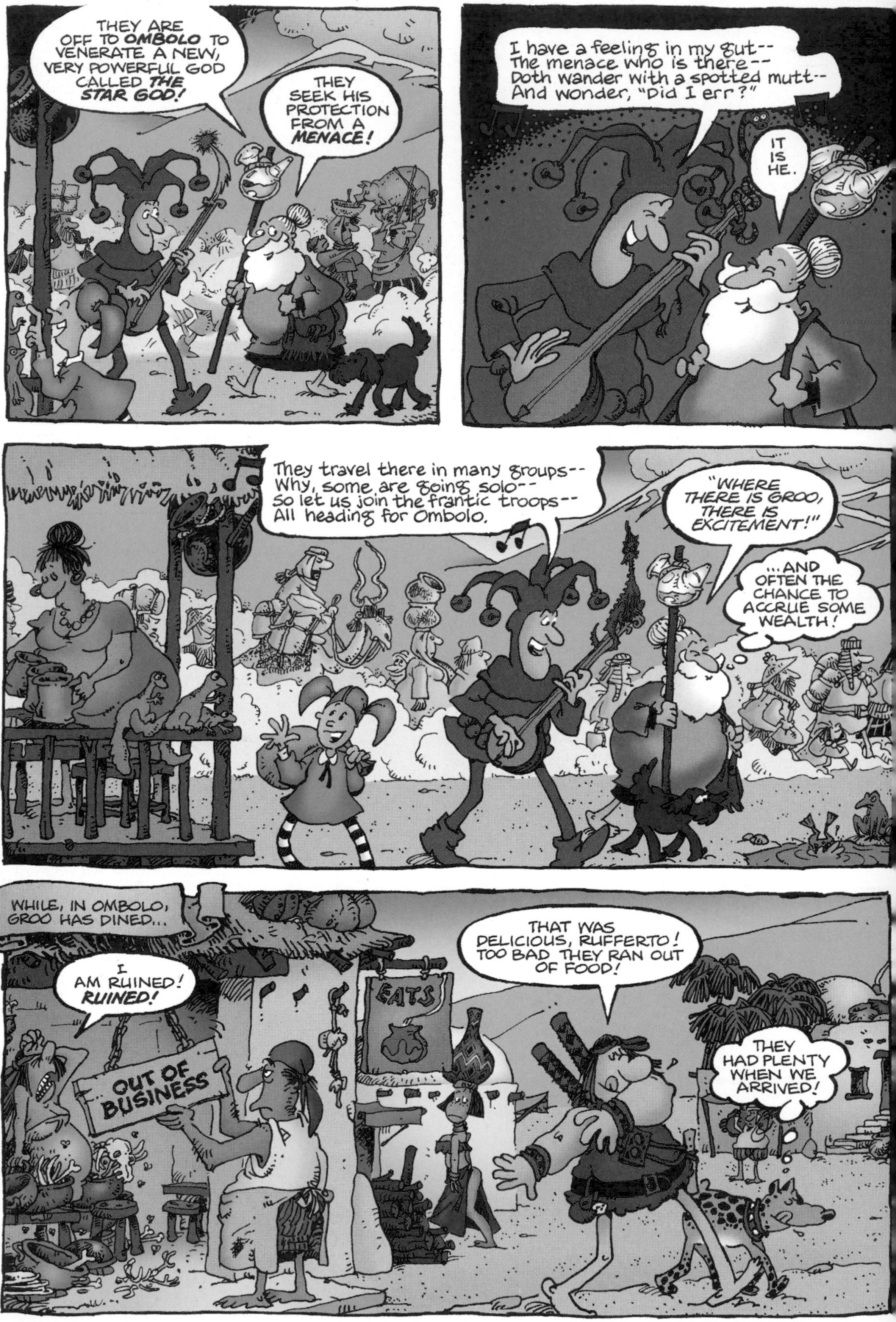
THEY ARE OFF TO OMBOLO TO VENERATE A NEW, VERY POWERFUL GOD CALLED THE STAR GOD!
THEY SEEK HIS PROTECTION FROM A MENACE!
I have a feeling in my gut-- The menace who is there-- Doth wander with a spotted mutt-- And wonder, "Did I err?"
IT IS HE.
They travel there in many groups-- Why, some are going solo-- So let us join the frantic troops-- All heading for Ombolo.
"WHERE THERE IS GROO, THERE IS EXCITEMENT!"
...AND OFTEN THE CHANCE TO ACCRUE SOME WEALTH!
WHILE, IN OMBOLO, GROO HAS DINED...
I AM RUINED! RUINED!
OUT OF BUSINESS
EATS
THAT WAS DELICIOUS, RUFFERTO! TOO BAD THEY RAN OUT OF FOOD!
THEY HAD PLENTY WHEN WE ARRIVED!

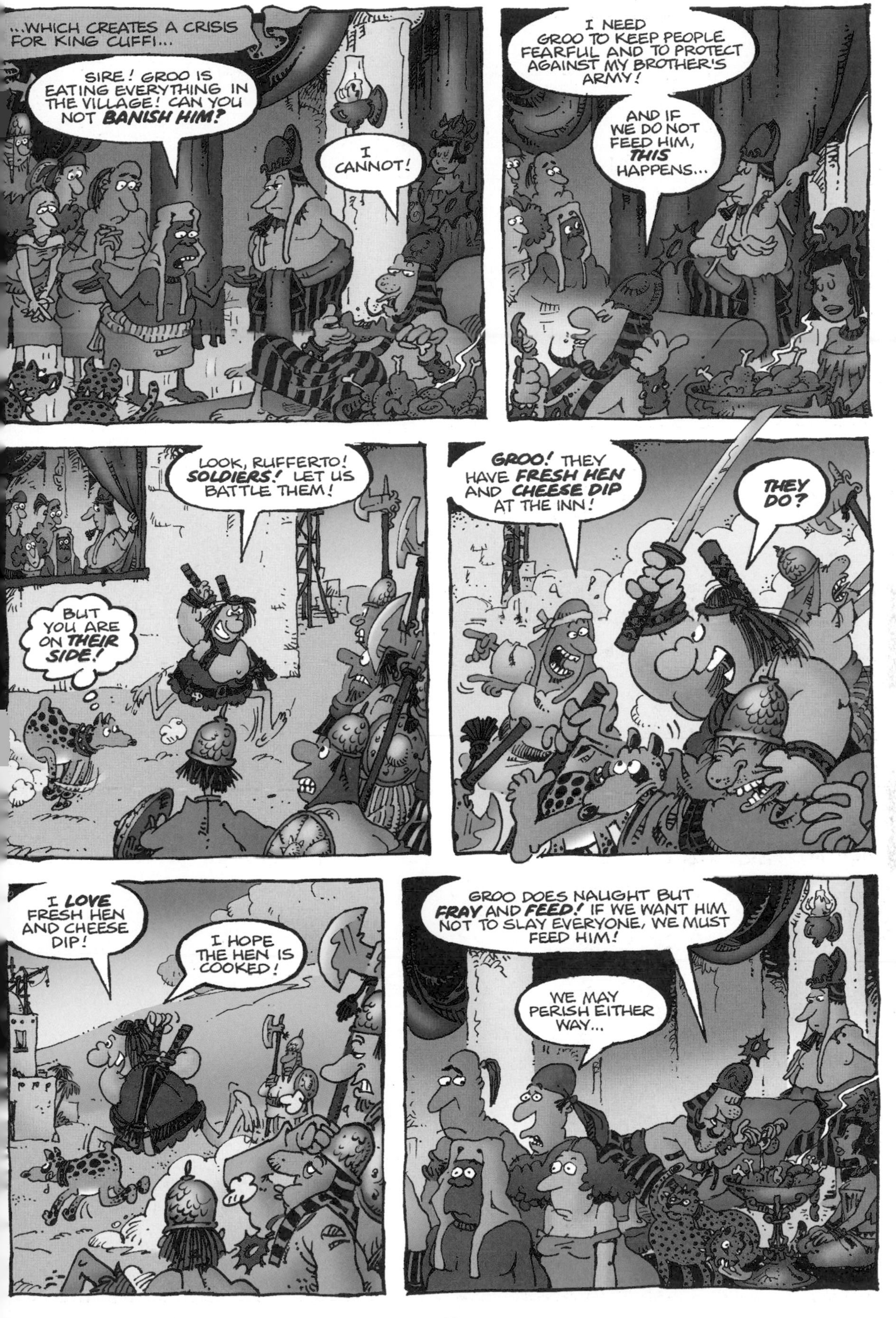
...WHICH CREATES A CRISIS FOR KING CUFFI...
SIRE! GROO IS EATING EVERYTHING IN THE VILLAGE! CAN YOU NOT BANISH HIM?
I CANNOT!
I NEED GROO TO KEEP PEOPLE FEARFUL AND TO PROTECT AGAINST MY BROTHER'S ARMY!
AND IF WE DO NOT FEED HIM, THIS HAPPENS...
LOOK, RUFFERTO! SOLDIERS! LET US BATTLE THEM!
BUT YOU ARE ON THEIR SIDE!
GROO! THEY HAVE FRESH HEN AND CHEESE DIP AT THE INN!
THEY DO?
I LOVE FRESH HEN AND CHEESE DIP!
I HOPE THE HEN IS COOKED!
GROO DOES NAUGHT BUT FRAY AND FEED! IF WE WANT HIM NOT TO SLAY EVERYONE, WE MUST FEED HIM!
WE MAY PERISH EITHER WAY...

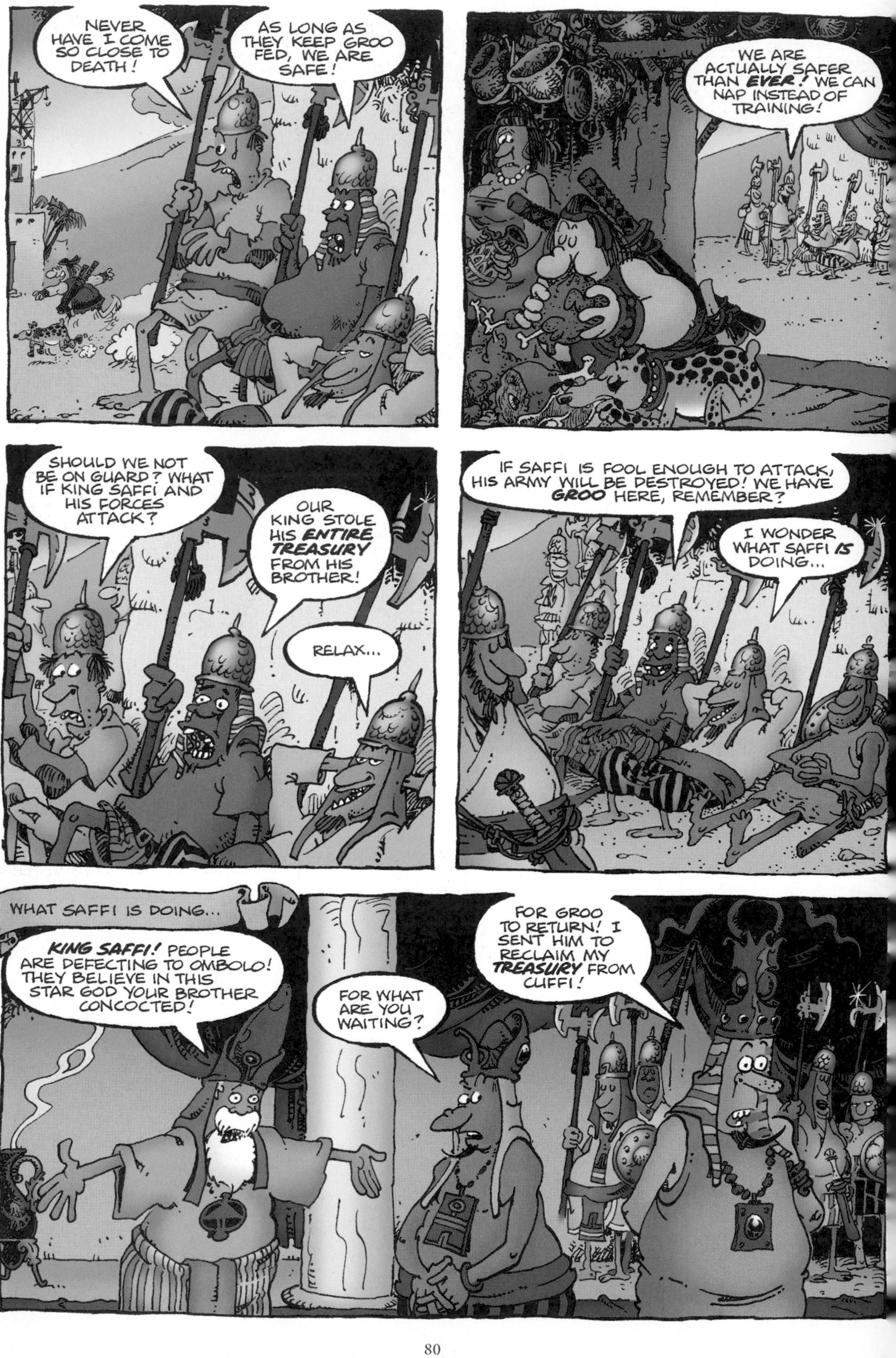

NEVER HAVE I COME SO CLOSE TO DEATH!
AS LONG AS THEY KEEP GROO FED, WE ARE SAFE!
WE ARE ACTUALLY SAFER THAN **EVER!** WE CAN NAP INSTEAD OF TRAINING!
SHOULD WE NOT BE ON GUARD? WHAT IF KING SAFFI AND HIS FORCES ATTACK?
OUR KING STOLE HIS **ENTIRE TREASURY** FROM HIS BROTHER!
RELAX...
IF SAFFI IS FOOL ENOUGH TO ATTACK, HIS ARMY WILL BE DESTROYED! WE HAVE **GROO** HERE, REMEMBER?
I WONDER WHAT SAFFI **IS** DOING...
WHAT SAFFI IS DOING...
KING SAFFI! PEOPLE ARE DEFECTING TO OMBOLO! THEY BELIEVE IN THIS STAR GOD YOUR BROTHER CONCOCTED!
FOR WHAT ARE YOU WAITING?
FOR GROO TO RETURN! I SENT HIM TO RECLAIM MY **TREASURY** FROM CUFFI!

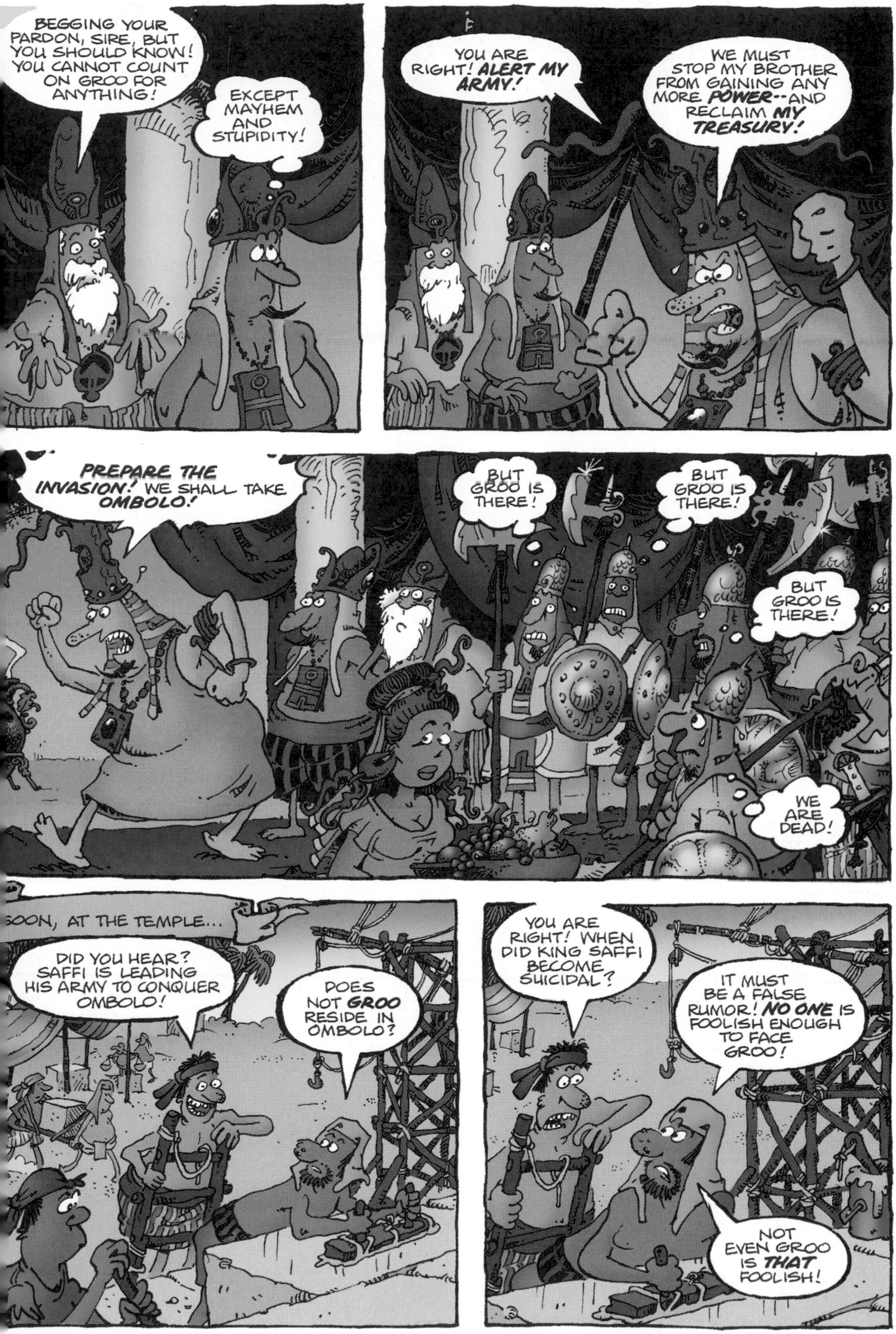
BEGGING YOUR PARDON, SIRE, BUT YOU SHOULD KNOW! YOU CANNOT COUNT ON GROO FOR ANYTHING!
EXCEPT MAYHEM AND STUPIDITY!
YOU ARE RIGHT! ALERT MY ARMY!
WE MUST STOP MY BROTHER FROM GAINING ANY MORE POWER--AND RECLAIM MY TREASURY!
PREPARE THE INVASION! WE SHALL TAKE OMBOLO!
BUT GROO IS THERE!
BUT GROO IS THERE!
BUT GROO IS THERE!
WE ARE DEAD!
SOON, AT THE TEMPLE...
DID YOU HEAR? SAFFI IS LEADING HIS ARMY TO CONQUER OMBOLO!
DOES NOT GROO RESIDE IN OMBOLO?
YOU ARE RIGHT! WHEN DID KING SAFFI BECOME SUICIDAL?
IT MUST BE A FALSE RUMOR! NO ONE IS FOOLISH ENOUGH TO FACE GROO!
NOT EVEN GROO IS THAT FOOLISH!

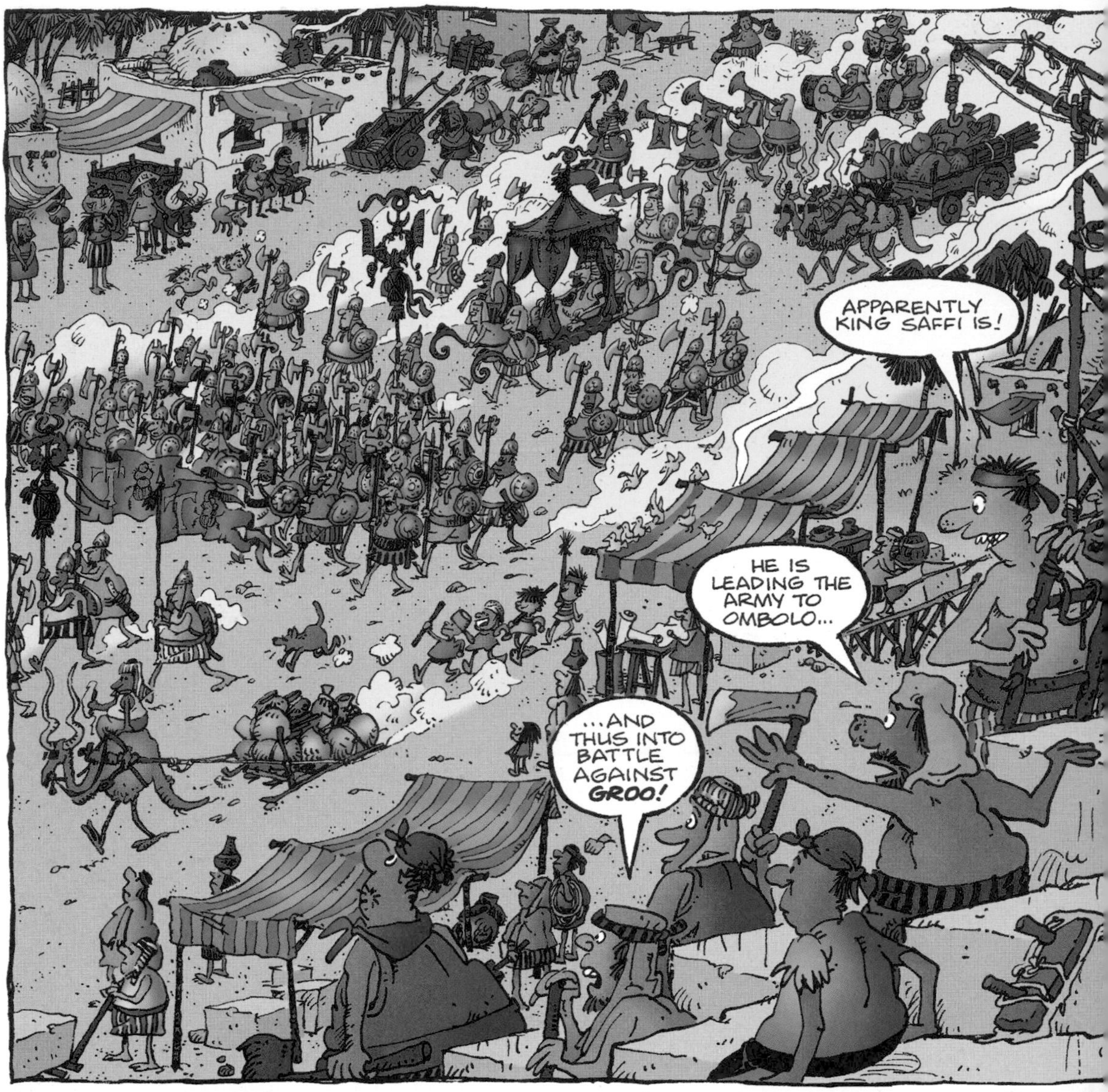
APPARENTLY KING SAFFI IS!
HE IS LEADING THE ARMY TO OMBOLO...
...AND THUS INTO BATTLE AGAINST **GROO!**

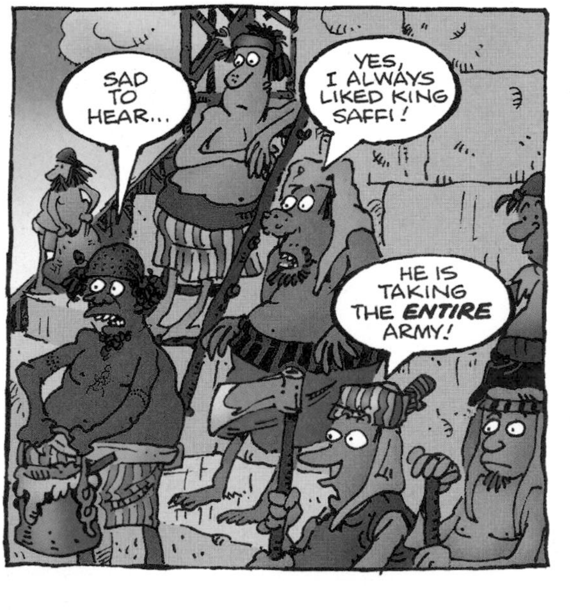
SAD TO HEAR...
YES, I ALWAYS LIKED KING SAFFI!
HE IS TAKING THE ***ENTIRE*** ARMY!

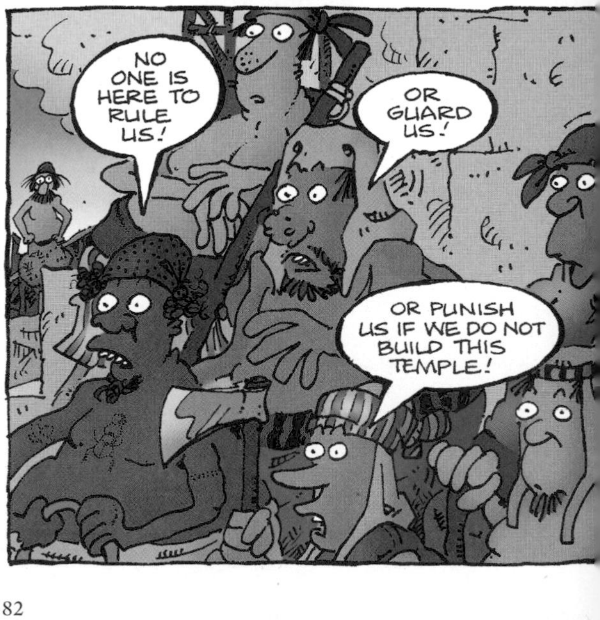
NO ONE IS HERE TO RULE US!
OR GUARD US!
OR PUNISH US IF WE DO NOT BUILD THIS TEMPLE!

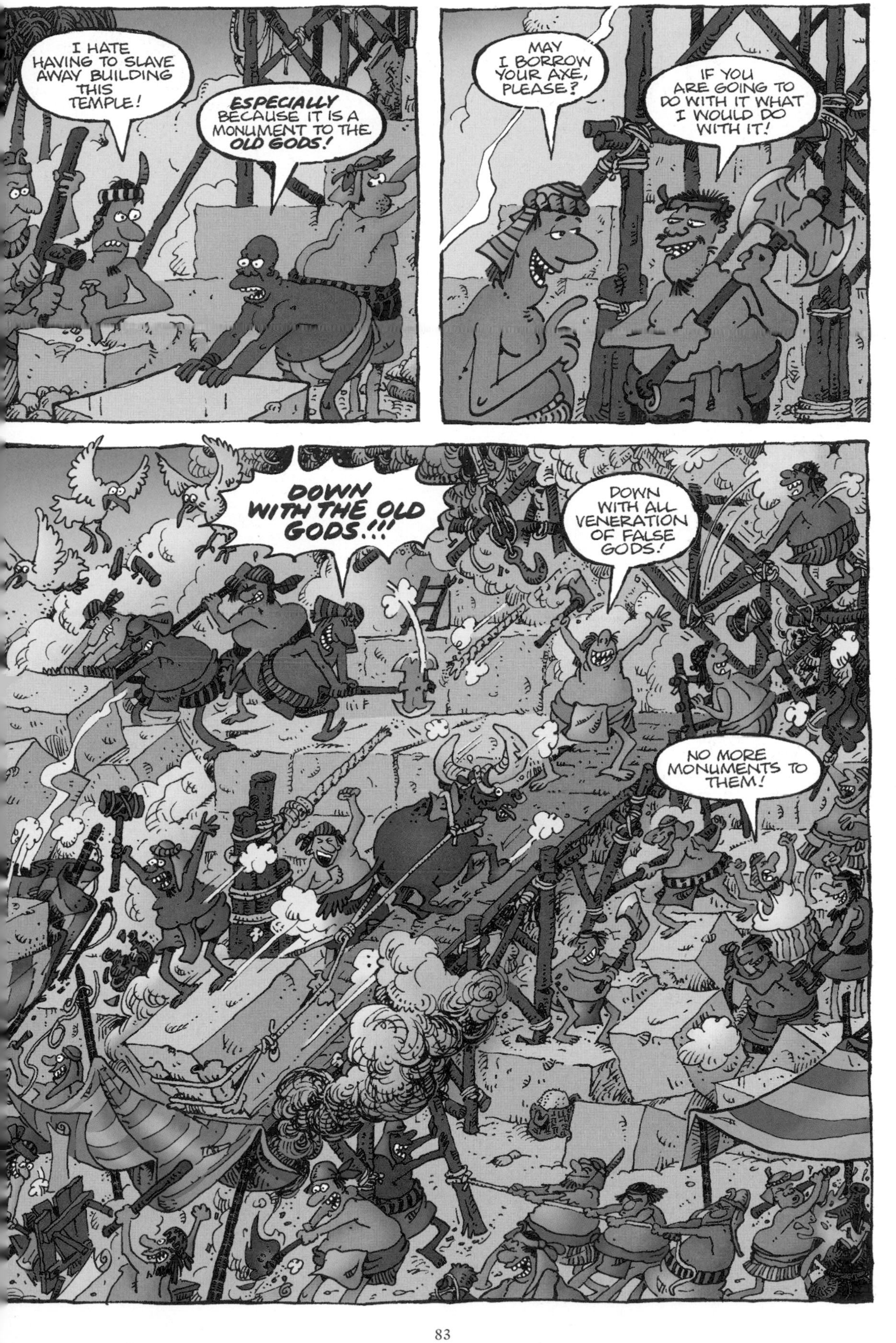
I HATE HAVING TO SLAVE AWAY BUILDING THIS TEMPLE!
ESPECIALLY BECAUSE IT IS A MONUMENT TO THE OLD GODS!
MAY I BORROW YOUR AXE, PLEASE?
IF YOU ARE GOING TO DO WITH IT WHAT I WOULD DO WITH IT!
DOWN WITH THE OLD GODS!!!
DOWN WITH ALL VENERATION OF FALSE GODS!
NO MORE MONUMENTS TO THEM!

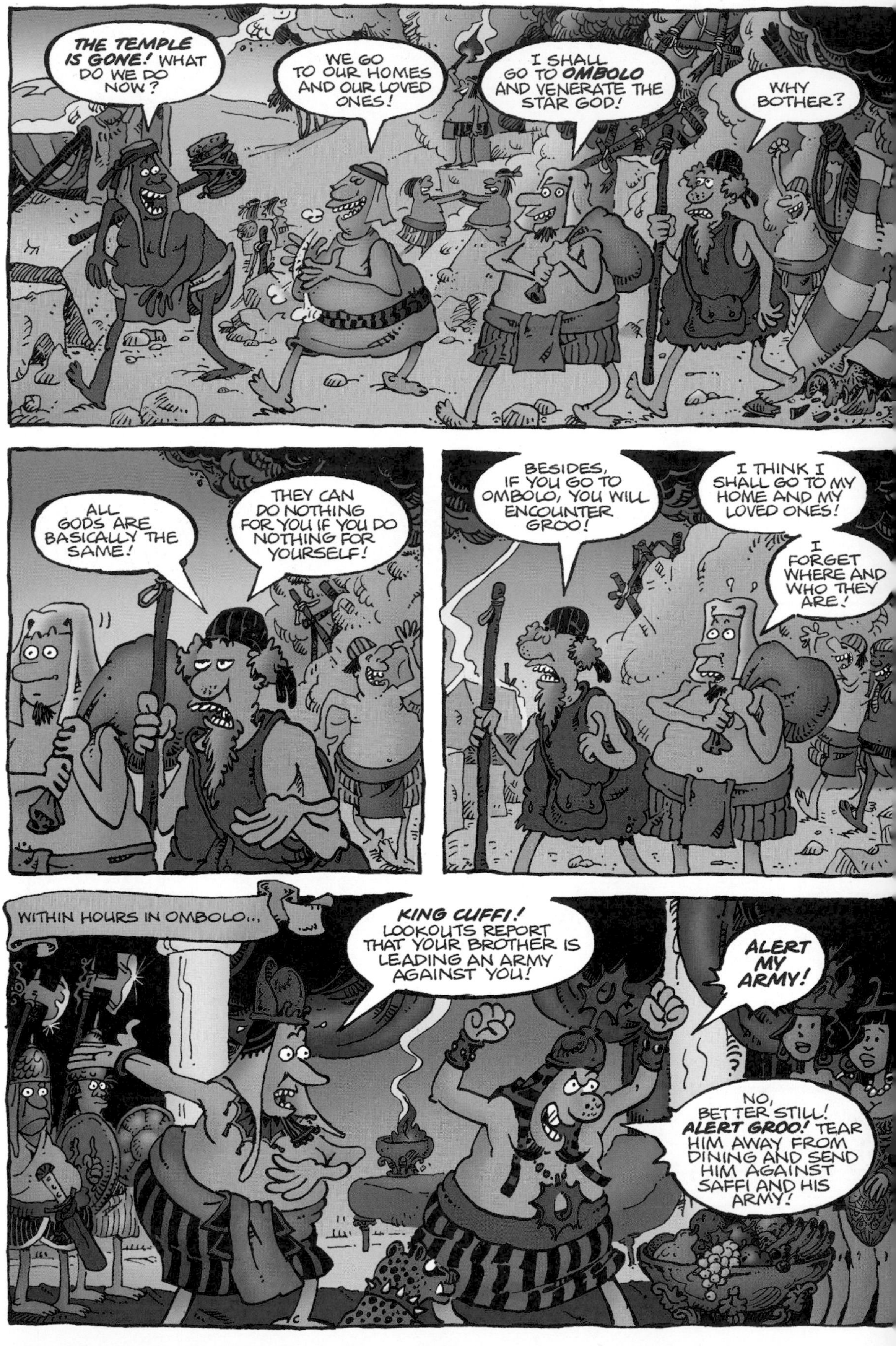

THE TEMPLE IS GONE! WHAT DO WE DO NOW?
WE GO TO OUR HOMES AND OUR LOVED ONES!
I SHALL GO TO OMBOLO AND VENERATE THE STAR GOD!
WHY BOTHER?
ALL GODS ARE BASICALLY THE SAME!
THEY CAN DO NOTHING FOR YOU IF YOU DO NOTHING FOR YOURSELF!
BESIDES, IF YOU GO TO OMBOLO, YOU WILL ENCOUNTER GROO!
I THINK I SHALL GO TO MY HOME AND MY LOVED ONES!
I FORGET WHERE AND WHO THEY ARE!
WITHIN HOURS IN OMBOLO...
KING CUFFI! LOOKOUTS REPORT THAT YOUR BROTHER IS LEADING AN ARMY AGAINST YOU!
ALERT MY ARMY!
NO, BETTER STILL! ALERT GROO! TEAR HIM AWAY FROM DINING AND SEND HIM AGAINST SAFFI AND HIS ARMY!

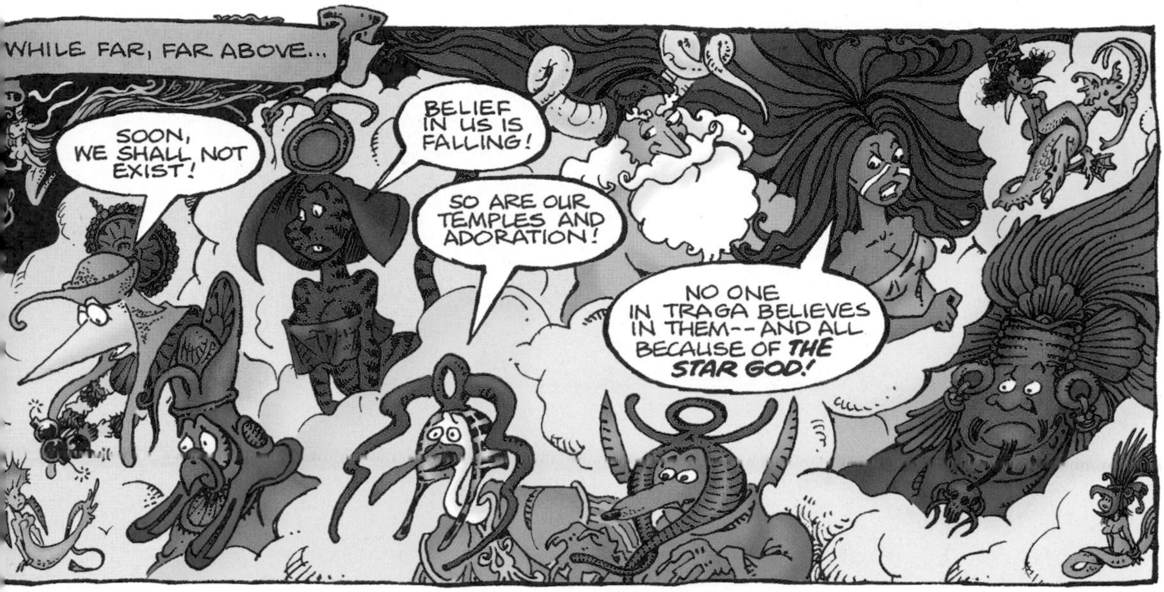

WHILE FAR, FAR ABOVE...
SOON, WE SHALL NOT EXIST!
BELIEF IN US IS FALLING!
SO ARE OUR TEMPLES AND ADORATION!
NO ONE IN TRAGA BELIEVES IN THEM--AND ALL BECAUSE OF THE STAR GOD!

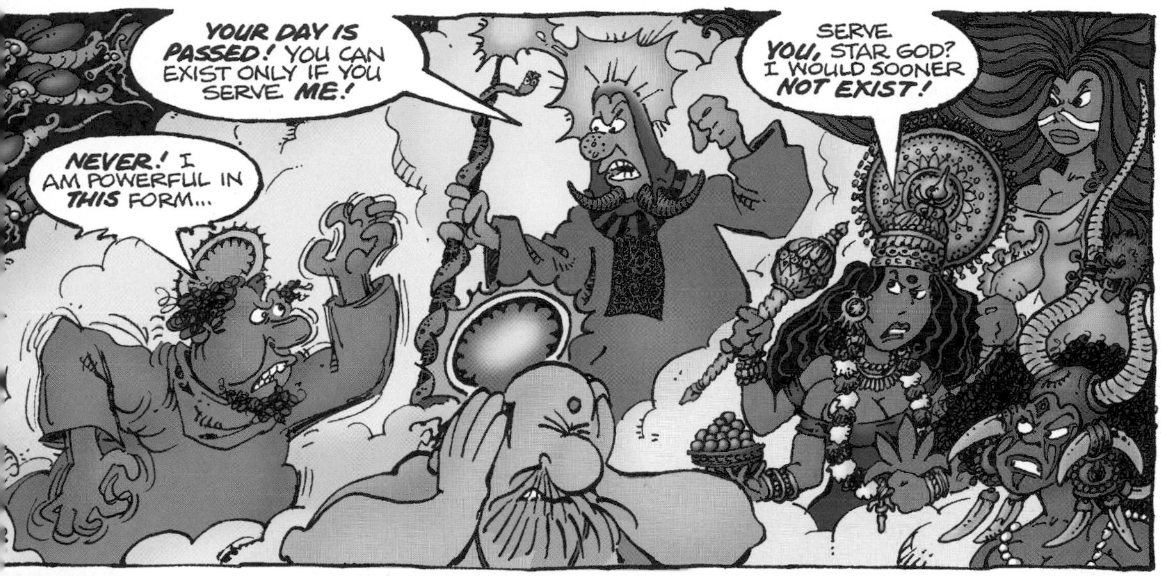

YOUR DAY IS PASSED! YOU CAN EXIST ONLY IF YOU SERVE ME!
SERVE YOU, STAR GOD? I WOULD SOONER NOT EXIST!
NEVER! I AM POWERFUL IN THIS FORM...

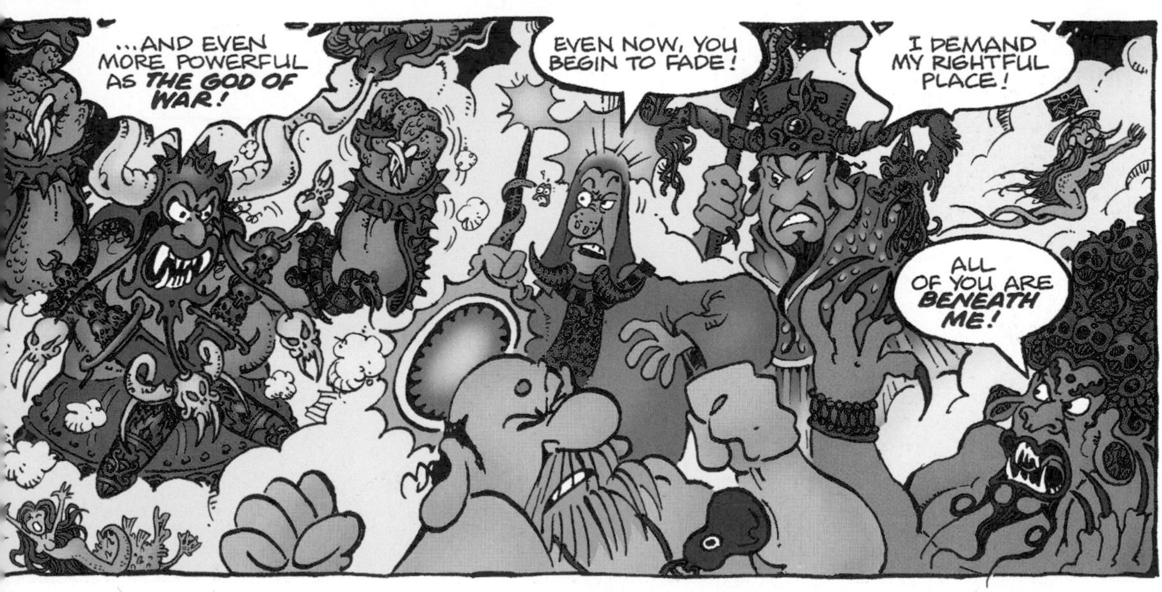

...AND EVEN MORE POWERFUL AS THE GOD OF WAR!
EVEN NOW, YOU BEGIN TO FADE!
I DEMAND MY RIGHTFUL PLACE!
ALL OF YOU ARE BENEATH ME!

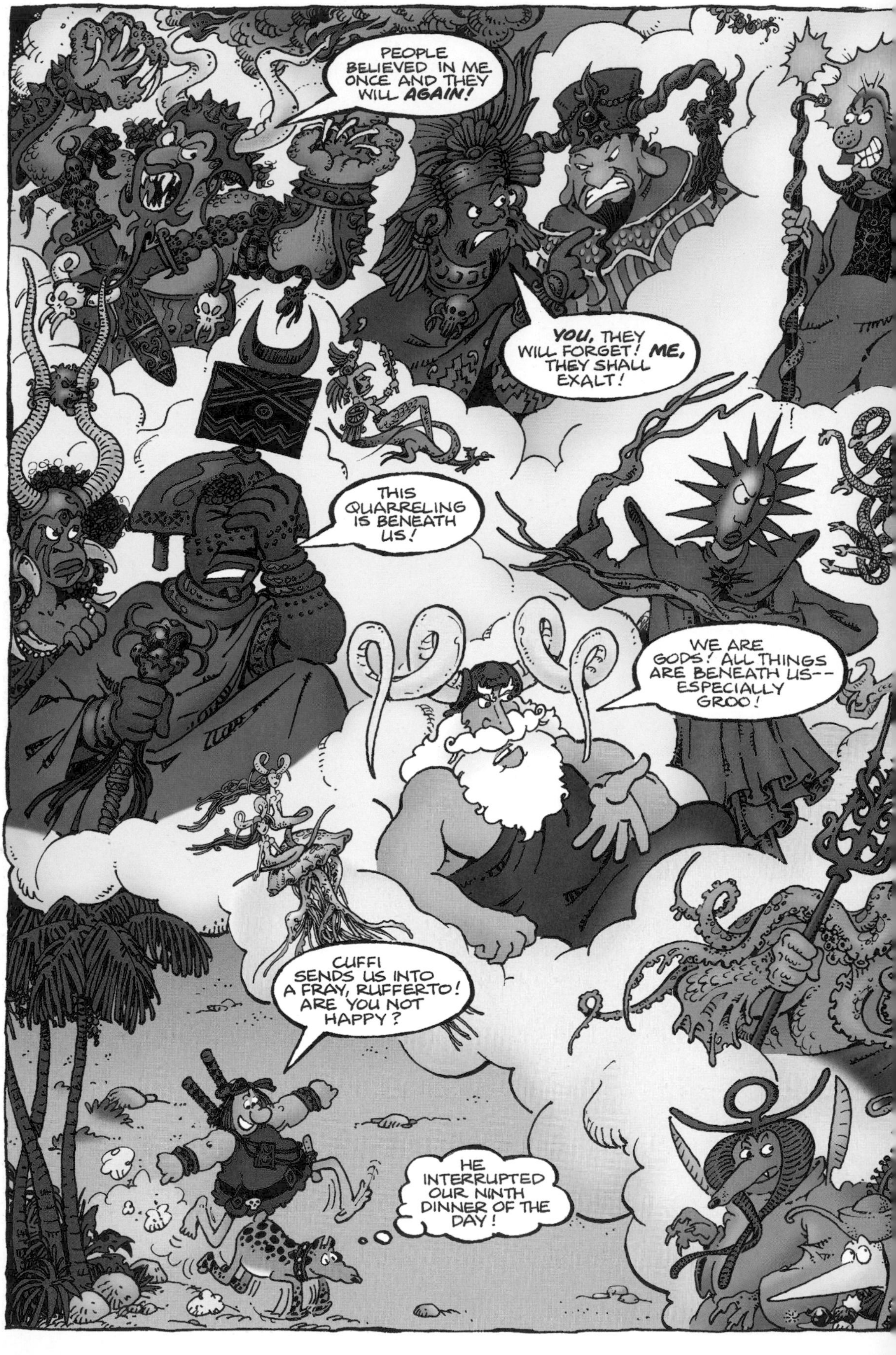
PEOPLE BELIEVED IN ME ONCE AND THEY WILL AGAIN!
YOU, THEY WILL FORGET! ME, THEY SHALL EXALT!
THIS QUARRELING IS BENEATH US!
WE ARE GODS! ALL THINGS ARE BENEATH US-- ESPECIALLY GROO!
CUFFI SENDS US INTO A FRAY, RUFFERTO! ARE YOU NOT HAPPY?
HE INTERRUPTED OUR NINTH DINNER OF THE DAY!

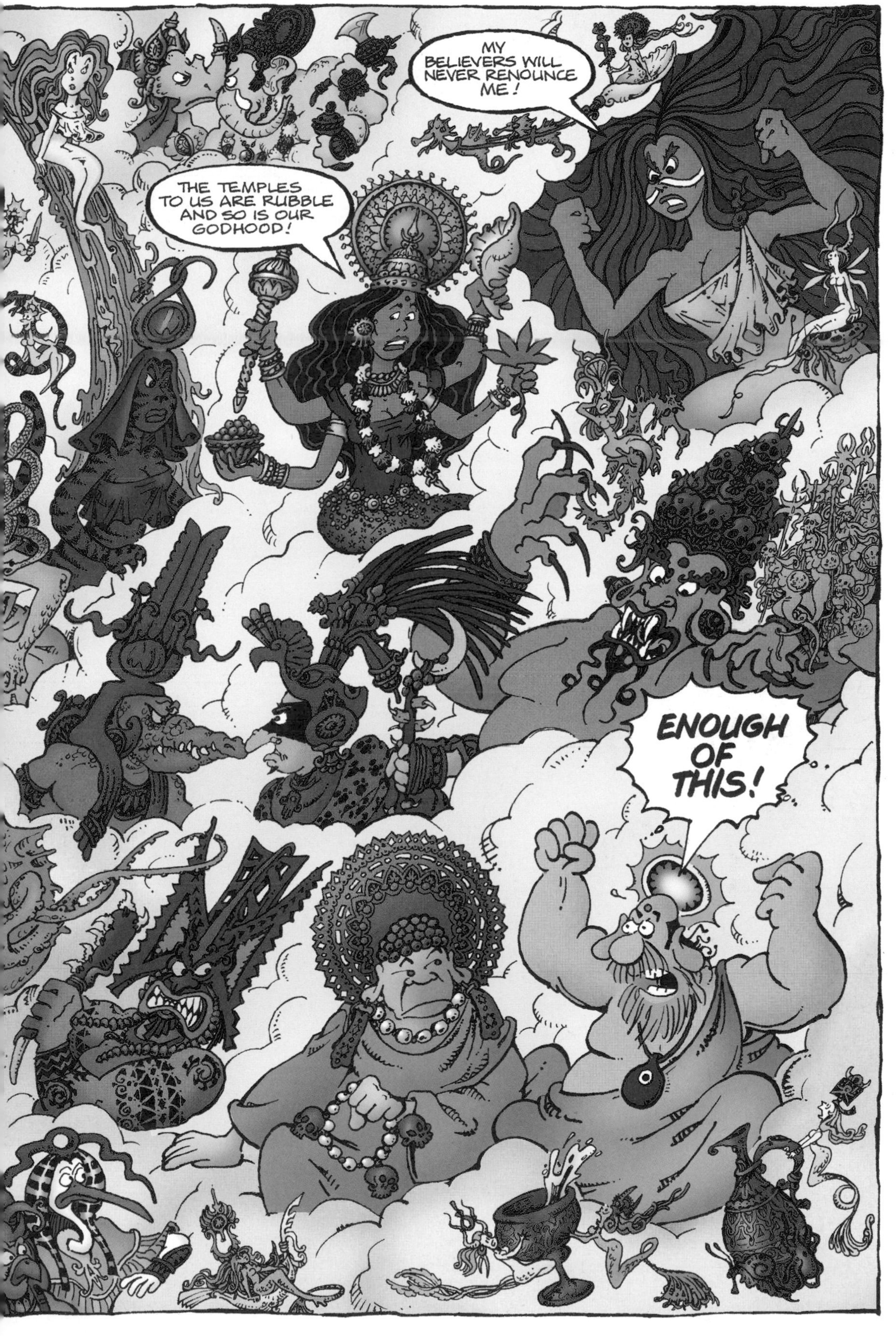
THE TEMPLES TO US ARE RUBBLE AND SO IS OUR GODHOOD!
MY BELIEVERS WILL NEVER RENOUNCE ME!
ENOUGH OF THIS!

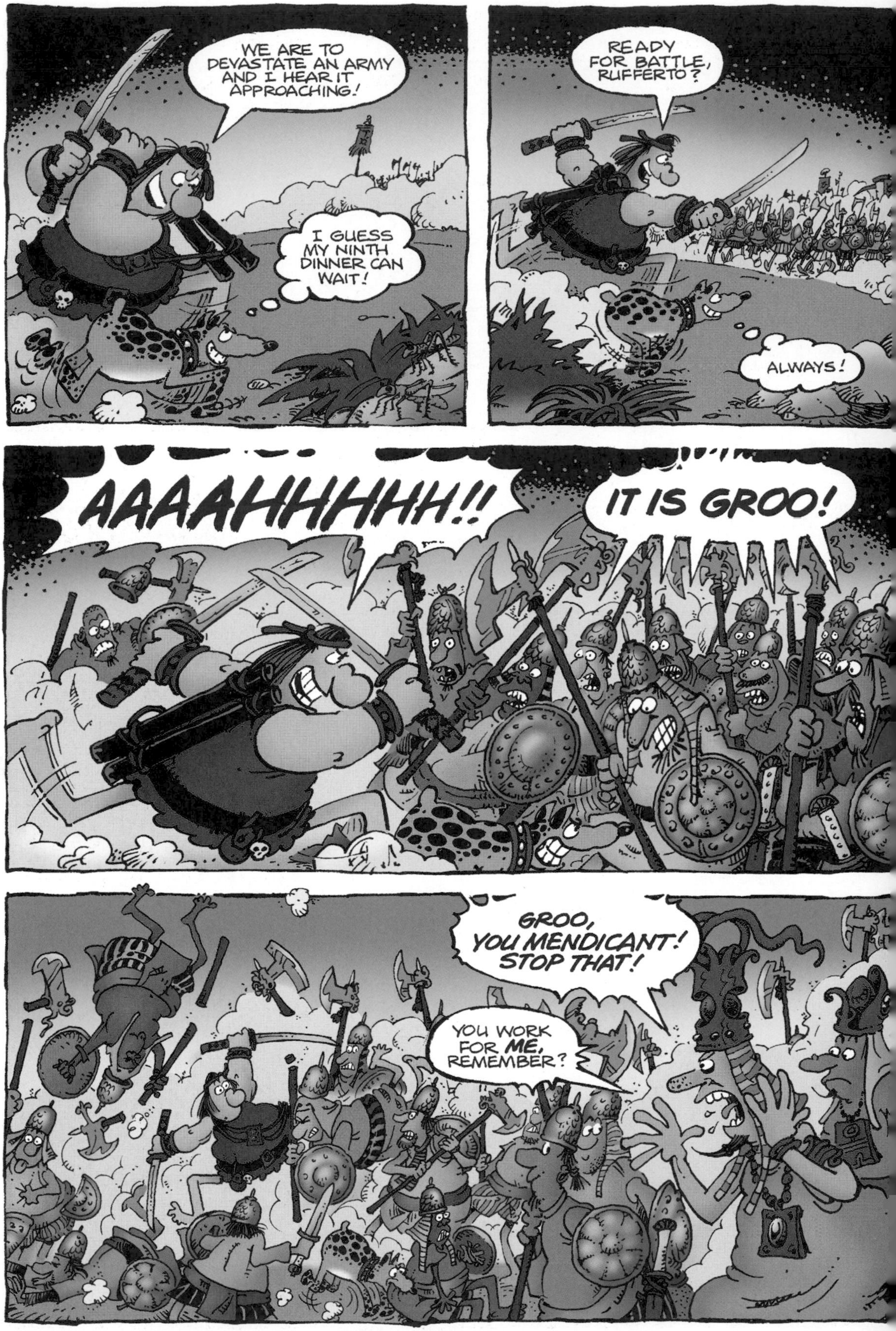
WE ARE TO DEVASTATE AN ARMY AND I HEAR IT APPROACHING!
I GUESS MY NINTH DINNER CAN WAIT!
READY FOR BATTLE, RUFFERTO?
ALWAYS!
AAAAHHHHH!!
IT IS GROO!
GROO, YOU MENDICANT! STOP THAT!
YOU WORK FOR ME, REMEMBER?

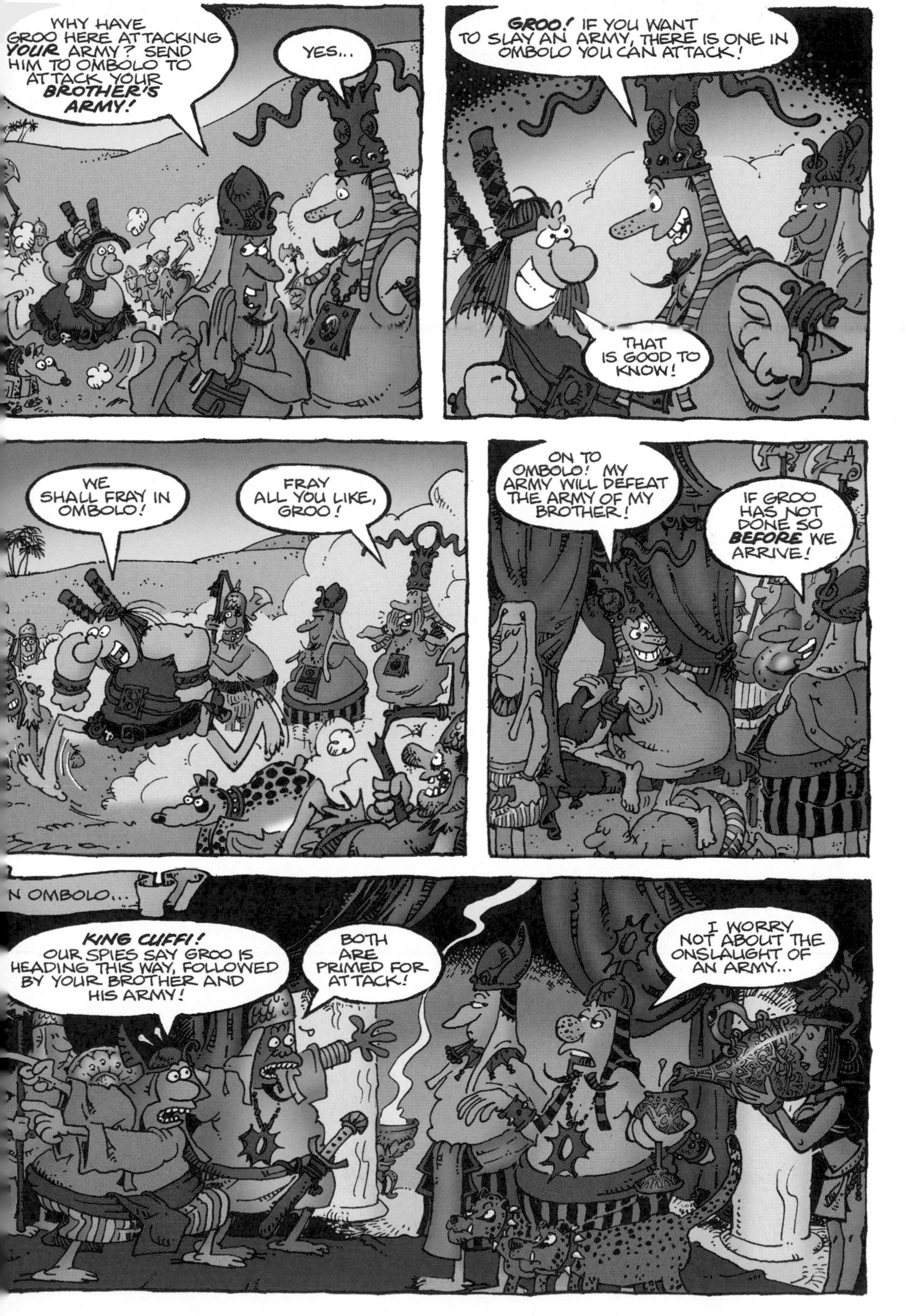
WHY HAVE GROO HERE ATTACKING YOUR ARMY? SEND HIM TO OMBOLO TO ATTACK YOUR BROTHER'S ARMY!
YES...
GROO! IF YOU WANT TO SLAY AN ARMY, THERE IS ONE IN OMBOLO YOU CAN ATTACK!
THAT IS GOOD TO KNOW!
WE SHALL FRAY IN OMBOLO!
FRAY ALL YOU LIKE, GROO!
ON TO OMBOLO! MY ARMY WILL DEFEAT THE ARMY OF MY BROTHER!
IF GROO HAS NOT DONE SO BEFORE WE ARRIVE!
N OMBOLO...
KING CUFFI! OUR SPIES SAY GROO IS HEADING THIS WAY, FOLLOWED BY YOUR BROTHER AND HIS ARMY!
BOTH ARE PRIMED FOR ATTACK!
I WORRY NOT ABOUT THE ONSLAUGHT OF AN ARMY...

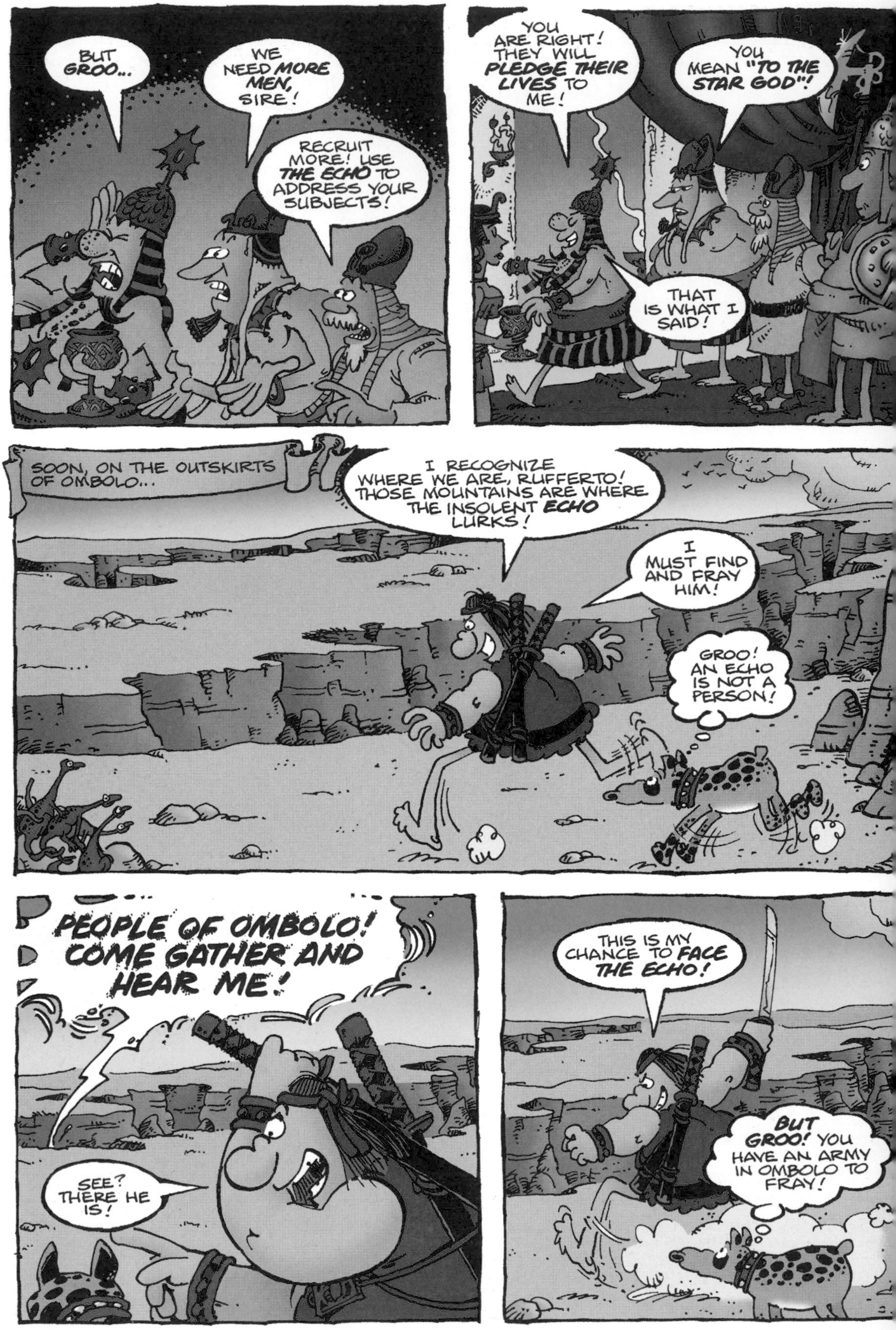
BUT GROO...
WE NEED MORE MEN, SIRE!
RECRUIT MORE! USE THE ECHO TO ADDRESS YOUR SUBJECTS!
YOU ARE RIGHT! THEY WILL PLEDGE THEIR LIVES TO ME!
YOU MEAN "TO THE STAR GOD"!
THAT IS WHAT I SAID!
SOON, ON THE OUTSKIRTS OF OMBOLO...
I RECOGNIZE WHERE WE ARE, RUFFERTO! THOSE MOUNTAINS ARE WHERE THE INSOLENT ECHO LURKS!
I MUST FIND AND FRAY HIM!
GROO! AN ECHO IS NOT A PERSON!
PEOPLE OF OMBOLO! COME GATHER AND HEAR ME!
SEE? THERE HE IS!
THIS IS MY CHANCE TO FACE THE ECHO!
BUT GROO! YOU HAVE AN ARMY IN OMBOLO TO FRAY!

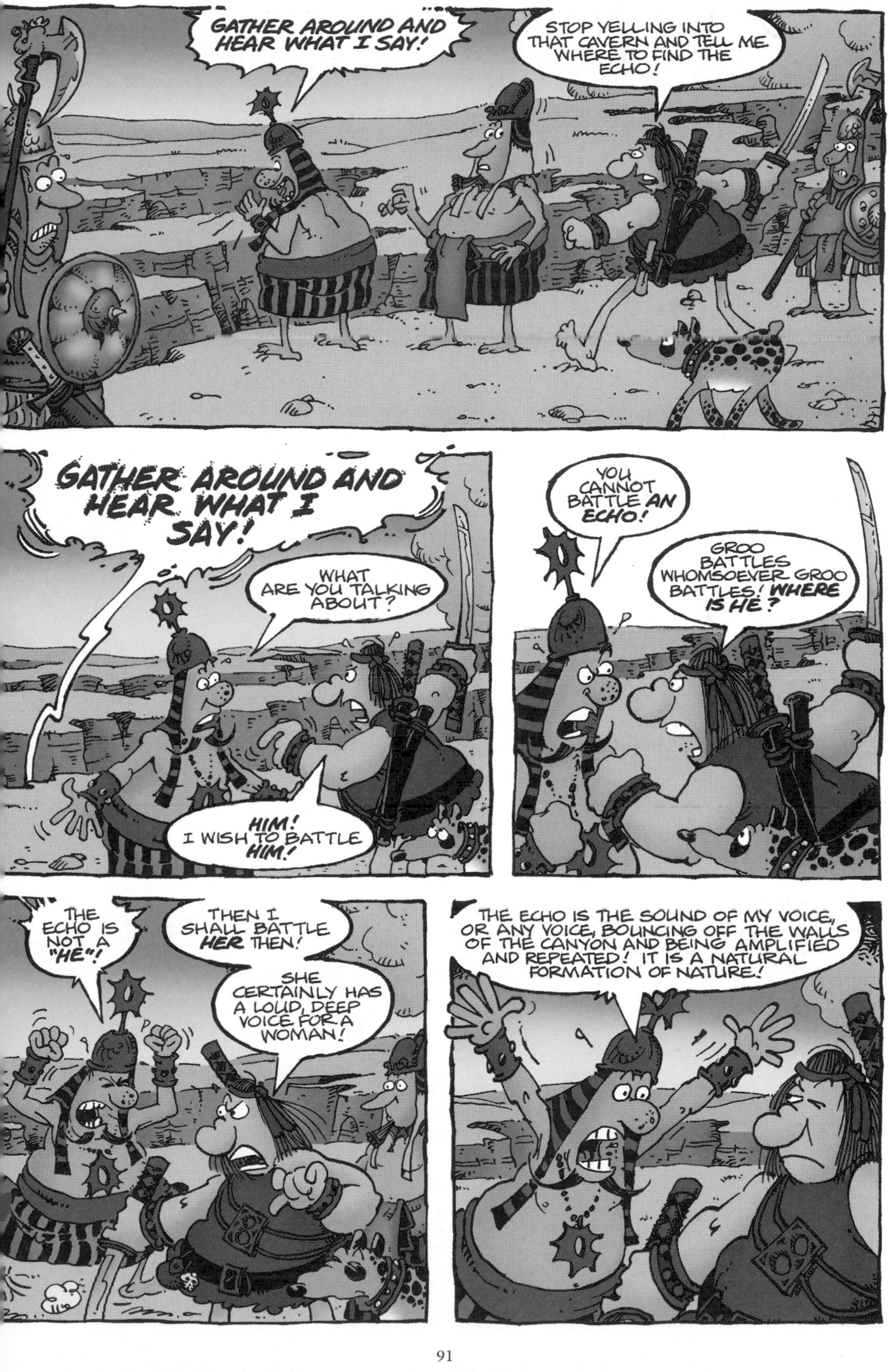
GATHER AROUND AND HEAR WHAT I SAY!
STOP YELLING INTO THAT CAVERN AND TELL ME WHERE TO FIND THE ECHO!
GATHER AROUND AND HEAR WHAT I SAY!
WHAT ARE YOU TALKING ABOUT?
HIM! I WISH TO BATTLE HIM!
YOU CANNOT BATTLE AN ECHO!
GROO BATTLES WHOMSOEVER GROO BATTLES! WHERE IS HE?
THE ECHO IS NOT A "HE"!
THEN I SHALL BATTLE HER THEN!
SHE CERTAINLY HAS A LOUD, DEEP VOICE FOR A WOMAN!
THE ECHO IS THE SOUND OF MY VOICE, OR ANY VOICE, BOUNCING OFF THE WALLS OF THE CANYON AND BEING AMPLIFIED AND REPEATED! IT IS A NATURAL FORMATION OF NATURE!

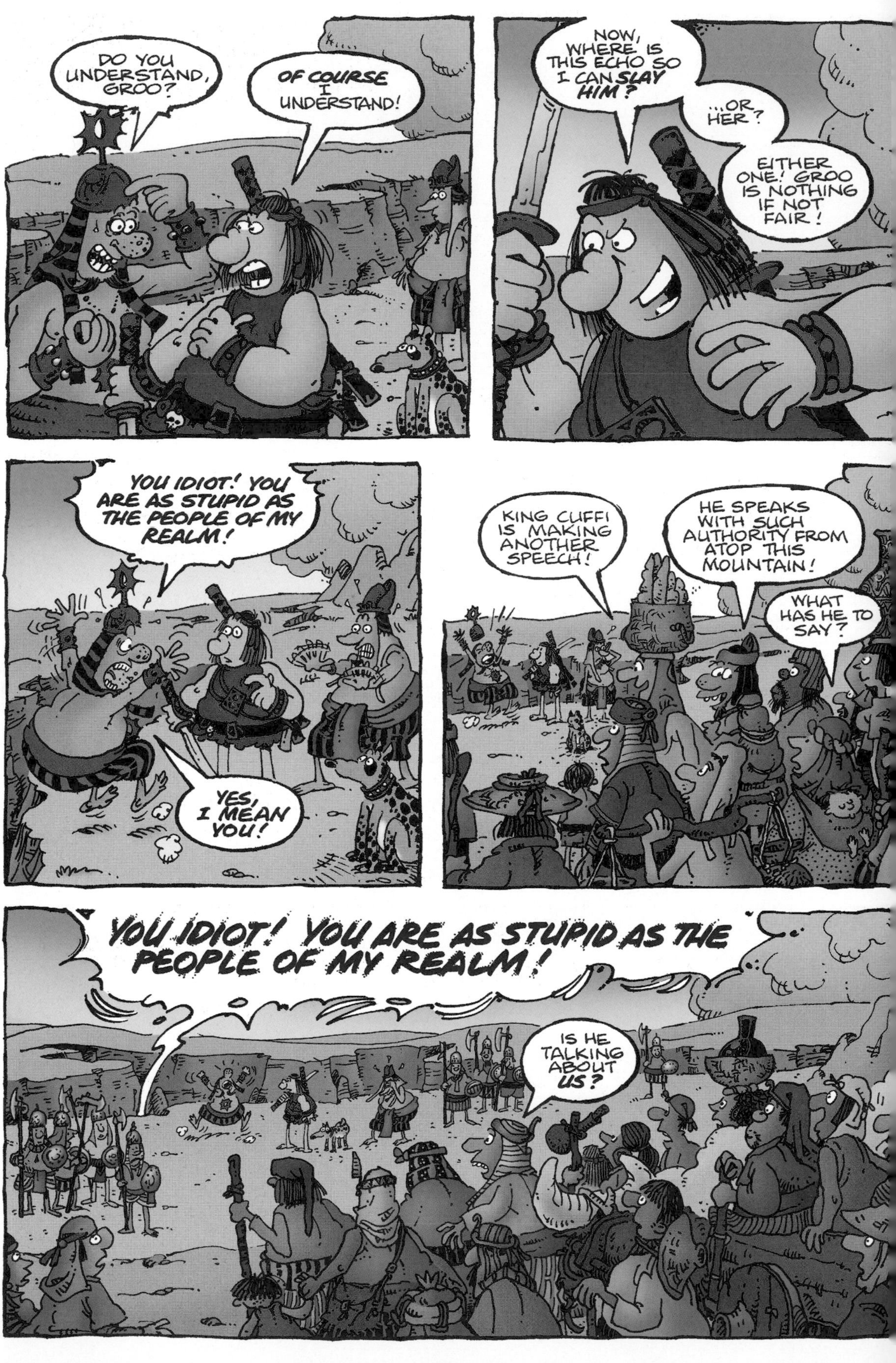
DO YOU UNDERSTAND, GROO?
OF COURSE I UNDERSTAND!
NOW, WHERE IS THIS ECHO SO I CAN SLAY HIM?
...OR HER?
EITHER ONE! GROO IS NOTHING IF NOT FAIR!
YOU IDIOT! YOU ARE AS STUPID AS THE PEOPLE OF MY REALM!
YES, I MEAN YOU!
KING CUFFI IS MAKING ANOTHER SPEECH!
HE SPEAKS WITH SUCH AUTHORITY FROM ATOP THIS MOUNTAIN!
WHAT HAS HE TO SAY?
YOU IDIOT! YOU ARE AS STUPID AS THE PEOPLE OF MY REALM!
IS HE TALKING ABOUT US?

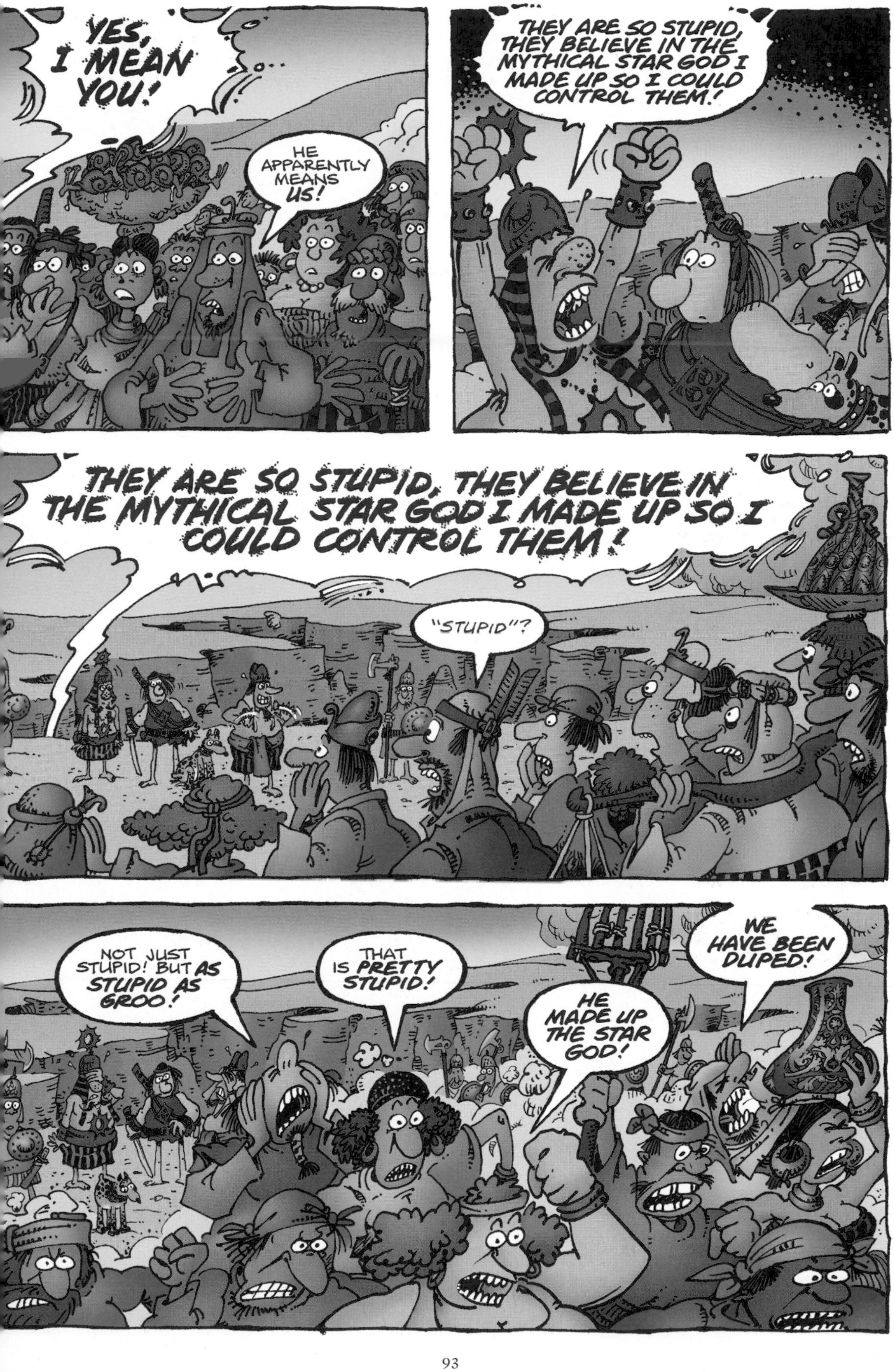
YES, I MEAN YOU!
HE APPARENTLY MEANS US!
THEY ARE SO STUPID, THEY BELIEVE IN THE MYTHICAL STAR GOD I MADE UP SO I COULD CONTROL THEM!
THEY ARE SO STUPID, THEY BELIEVE IN THE MYTHICAL STAR GOD I MADE UP SO I COULD CONTROL THEM!
"STUPID"?
NOT JUST STUPID! BUT AS STUPID AS GROO!
THAT IS PRETTY STUPID!
HE MADE UP THE STAR GOD!
WE HAVE BEEN DUPED!

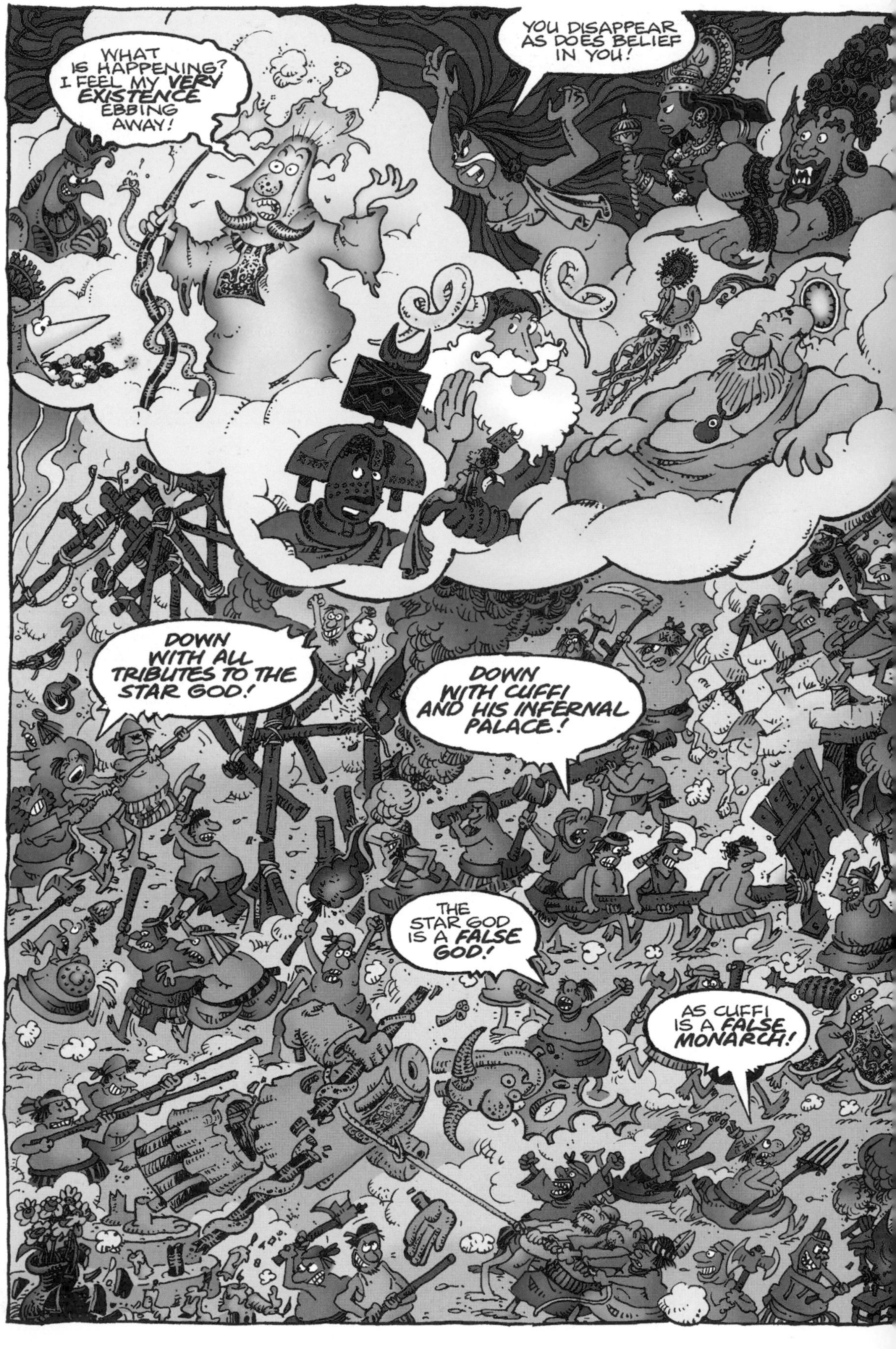
WHAT IS HAPPENING? I FEEL MY VERY EXISTENCE EBBING AWAY!
YOU DISAPPEAR AS DOES BELIEF IN YOU!
DOWN WITH ALL TRIBUTES TO THE STAR GOD!
DOWN WITH CUFFI AND HIS INFERNAL PALACE!
THE STAR GOD IS A FALSE GOD!
AS CUFFI IS A FALSE MONARCH!

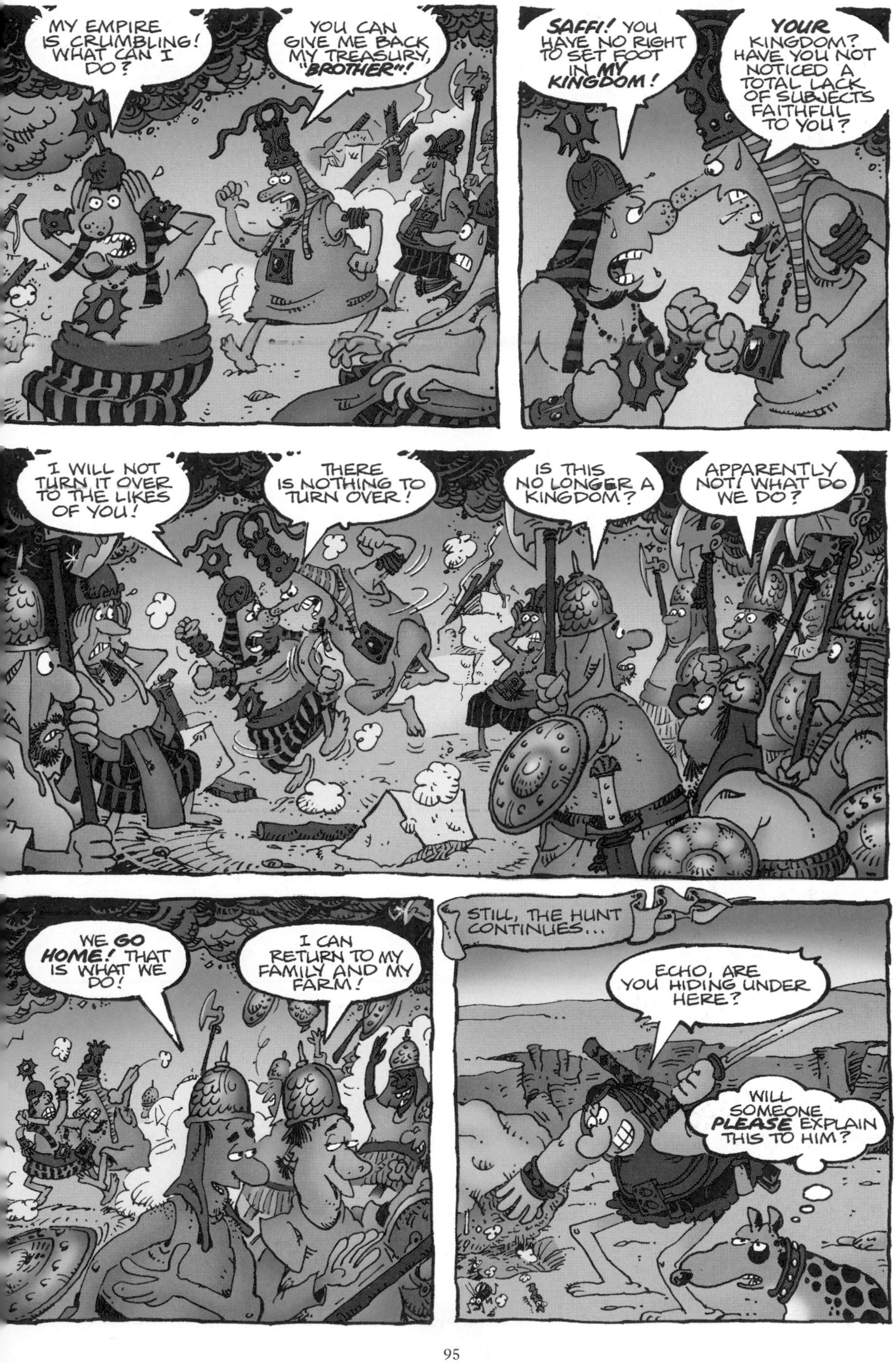
MY EMPIRE IS CRUMBLING! WHAT CAN I DO?
YOU CAN GIVE ME BACK MY TREASURY, "BROTHER"!
SAFFI! YOU HAVE NO RIGHT TO SET FOOT IN MY KINGDOM!
YOUR KINGDOM? HAVE YOU NOT NOTICED A TOTAL LACK OF SUBJECTS FAITHFUL TO YOU?
I WILL NOT TURN IT OVER TO THE LIKES OF YOU!
THERE IS NOTHING TO TURN OVER!
IS THIS NO LONGER A KINGDOM?
APPARENTLY NOT! WHAT DO WE DO?
WE GO HOME! THAT IS WHAT WE DO!
I CAN RETURN TO MY FAMILY AND MY FARM!
STILL, THE HUNT CONTINUES...
ECHO, ARE YOU HIDING UNDER HERE?
WILL SOMEONE PLEASE EXPLAIN THIS TO HIM?

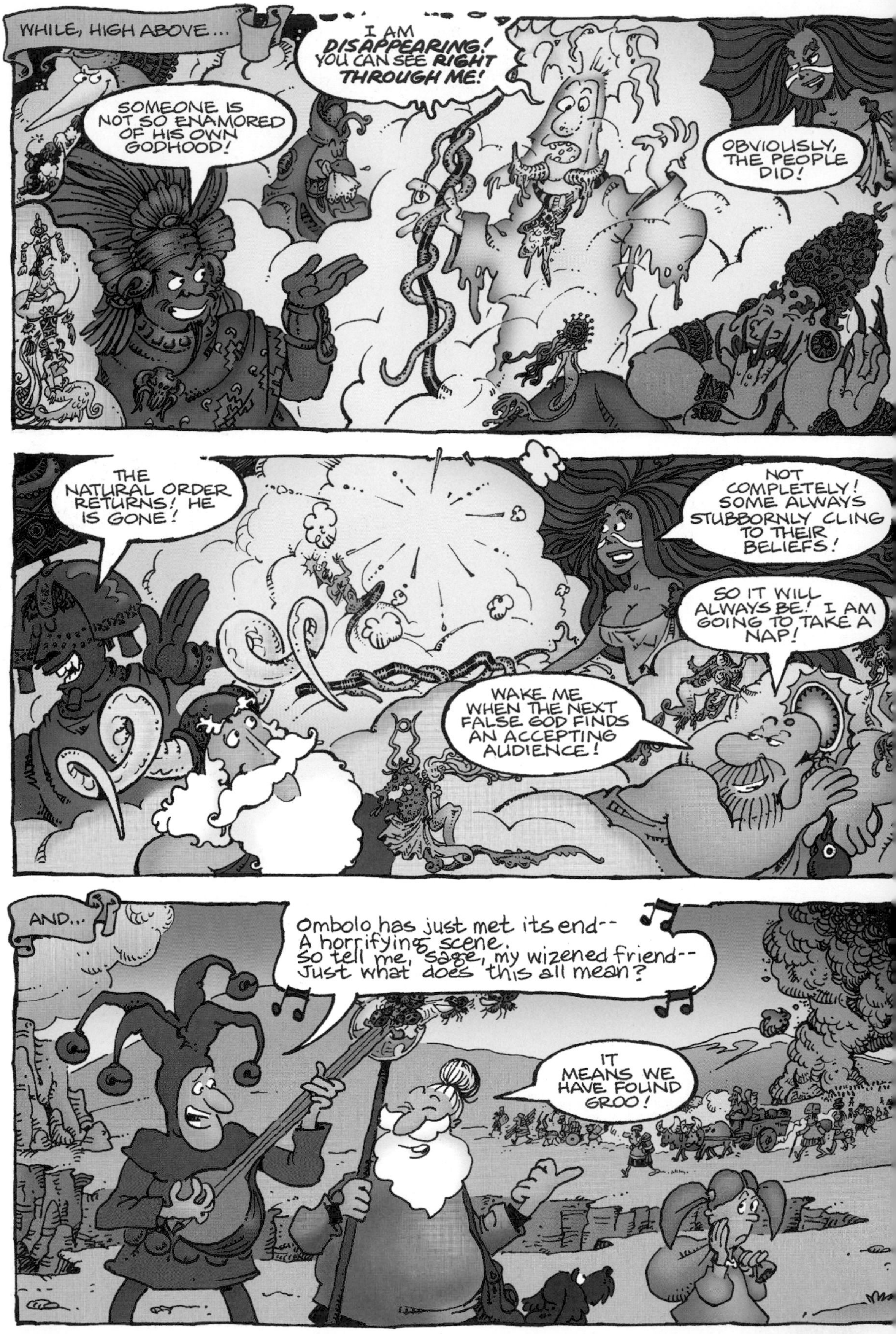
WHILE, HIGH ABOVE...
I AM DISAPPEARING! YOU CAN SEE RIGHT THROUGH ME!
SOMEONE IS NOT SO ENAMORED OF HIS OWN GODHOOD!
OBVIOUSLY, THE PEOPLE DID!
THE NATURAL ORDER RETURNS! HE IS GONE!
NOT COMPLETELY! SOME ALWAYS STUBBORNLY CLING TO THEIR BELIEFS!
SO IT WILL ALWAYS BE! I AM GOING TO TAKE A NAP!
WAKE ME WHEN THE NEXT FALSE GOD FINDS AN ACCEPTING AUDIENCE!
AND...
Ombolo has just met its end--
A horrifying scene.
So tell me, sage, my wizened friend--
Just what does this all mean?
IT MEANS WE HAVE FOUND GROO!

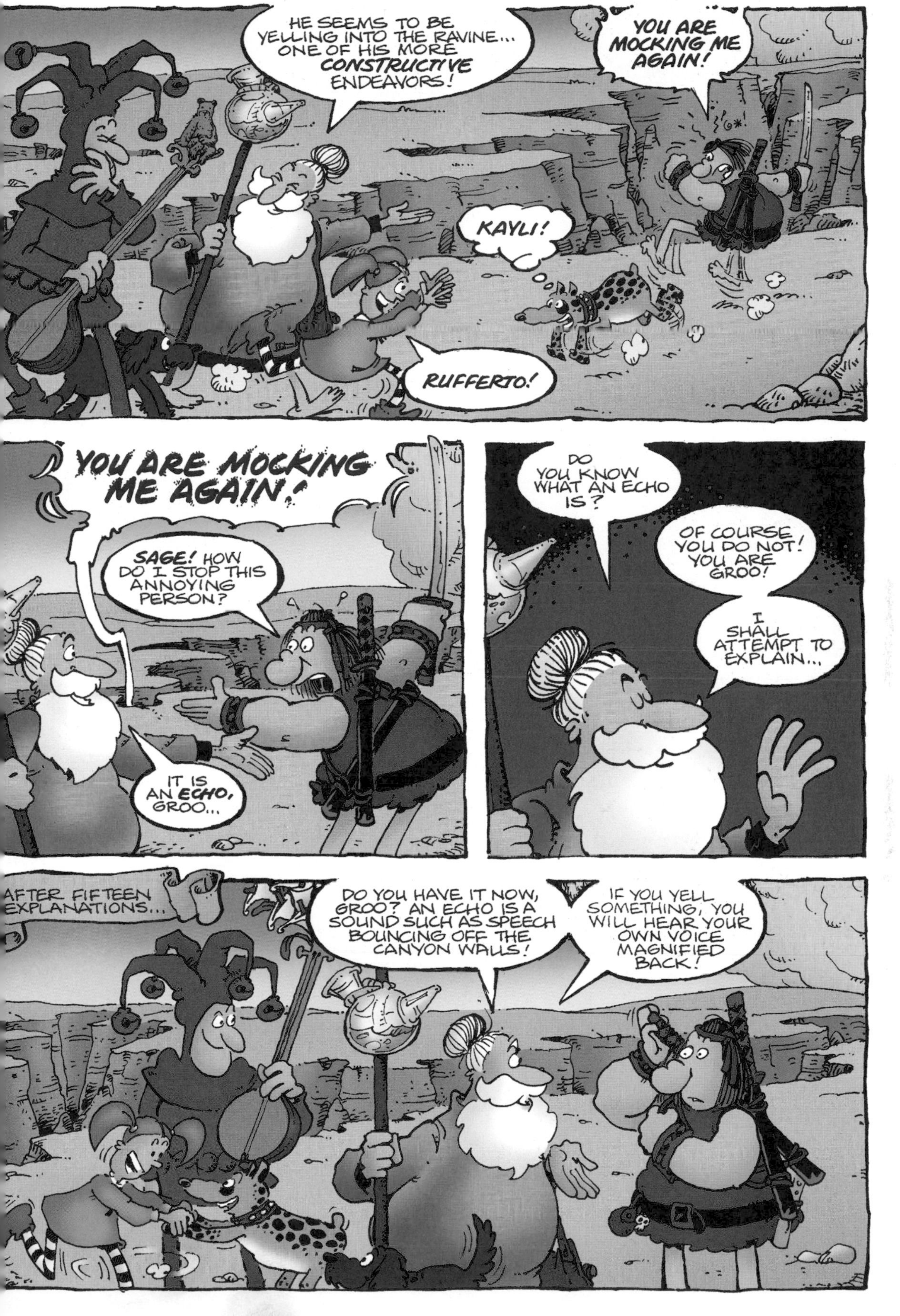
HE SEEMS TO BE YELLING INTO THE RAVINE... ONE OF HIS MORE CONSTRUCTIVE ENDEAVORS!
YOU ARE MOCKING ME AGAIN!
KAYLI!
RUFFERTO!
YOU ARE MOCKING ME AGAIN!
SAGE! HOW DO I STOP THIS ANNOYING PERSON?
IT IS AN ECHO, GROO...
DO YOU KNOW WHAT AN ECHO IS?
OF COURSE YOU DO NOT! YOU ARE GROO!
I SHALL ATTEMPT TO EXPLAIN...
AFTER FIFTEEN EXPLANATIONS...
DO YOU HAVE IT NOW, GROO? AN ECHO IS A SOUND SUCH AS SPEECH BOUNCING OFF THE CANYON WALLS!
IF YOU YELL SOMETHING, YOU WILL HEAR YOUR OWN VOICE MAGNIFIED BACK!

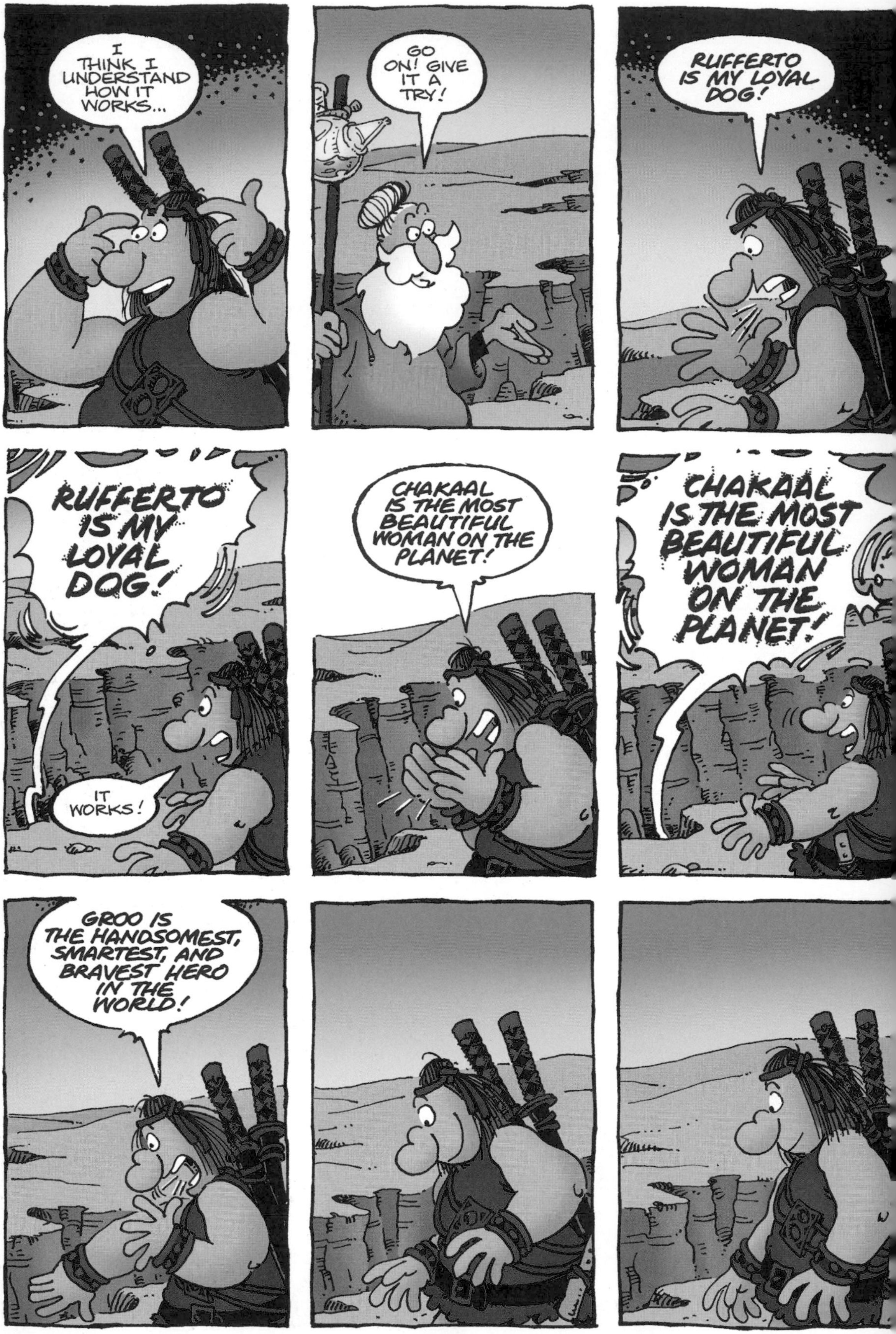
I THINK I UNDERSTAND HOW IT WORKS...
GO ON! GIVE IT A TRY!
RUFFERTO IS MY LOYAL DOG!
RUFFERTO IS MY LOYAL DOG!
IT WORKS!
CHAKAAL IS THE MOST BEAUTIFUL WOMAN ON THE PLANET!
CHAKAAL IS THE MOST BEAUTIFUL WOMAN ON THE PLANET!
GROO IS THE HANDSOMEST, SMARTEST, AND BRAVEST HERO IN THE WORLD!

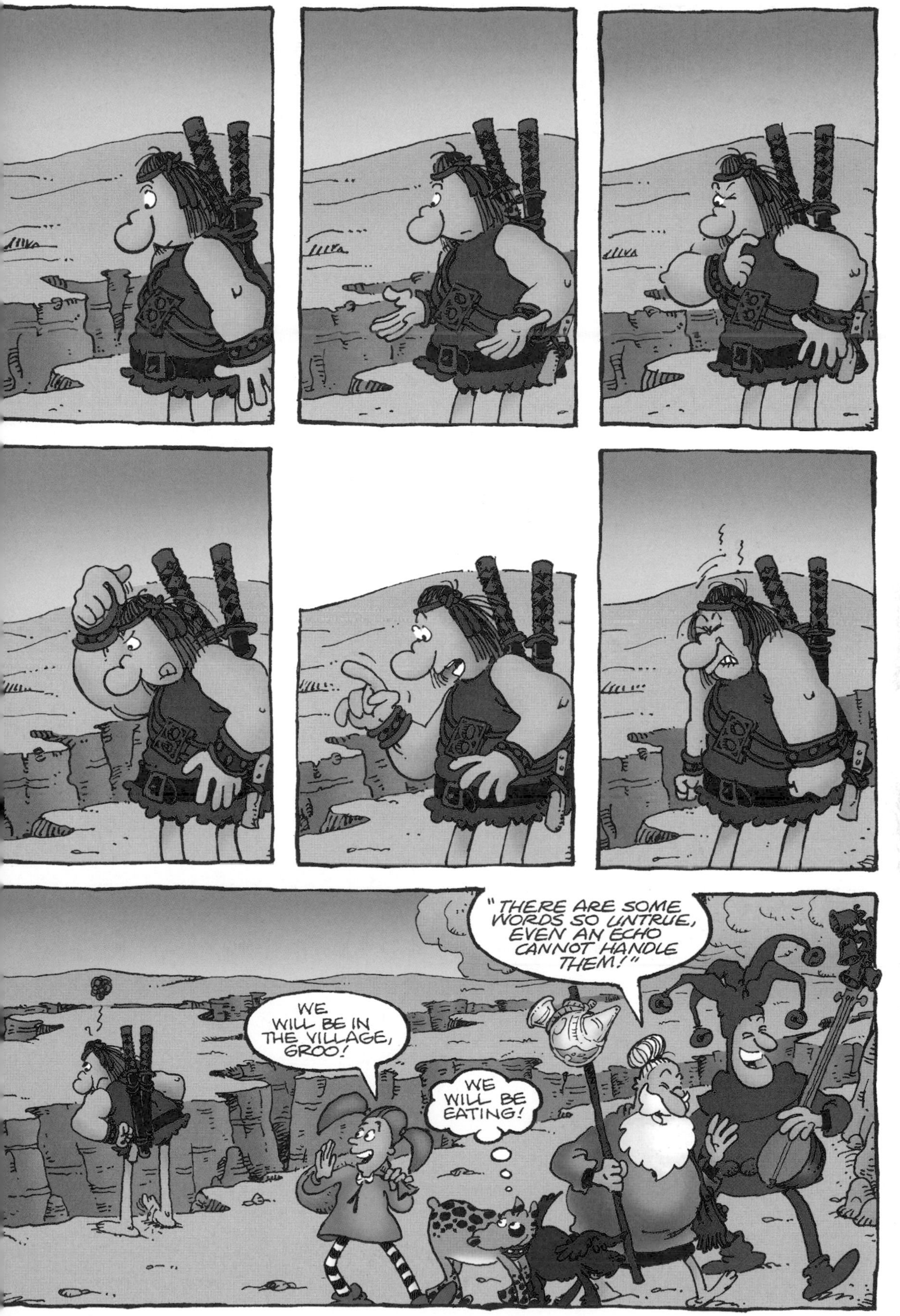
"THERE ARE SOME WORDS SO UNTRUE, EVEN AN ECHO CANNOT HANDLE THEM!"
WE WILL BE IN THE VILLAGE, GROO!
WE WILL BE EATING!

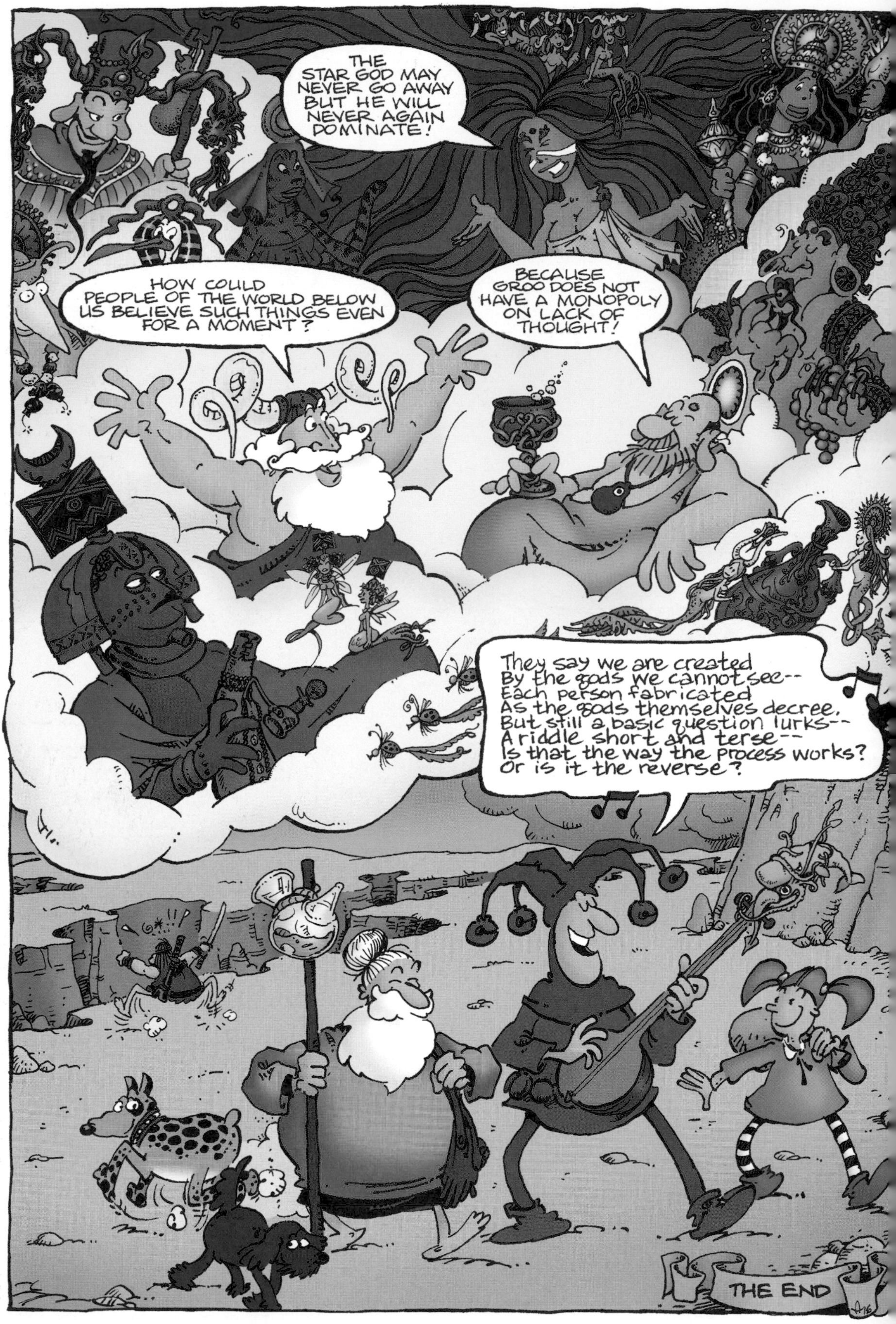
THE STAR GOD MAY NEVER GO AWAY BUT HE WILL NEVER AGAIN DOMINATE!
HOW COULD PEOPLE OF THE WORLD BELOW US BELIEVE SUCH THINGS EVEN FOR A MOMENT?
BECAUSE GROO DOES NOT HAVE A MONOPOLY ON LACK OF THOUGHT!
They say we are created
By the gods we cannot see--
Each person fabricated
As the gods themselves decree.
But still a basic question lurks--
A riddle short and terse--
Is that the way the process works?
Or is it the reverse?
THE END

Rufferto

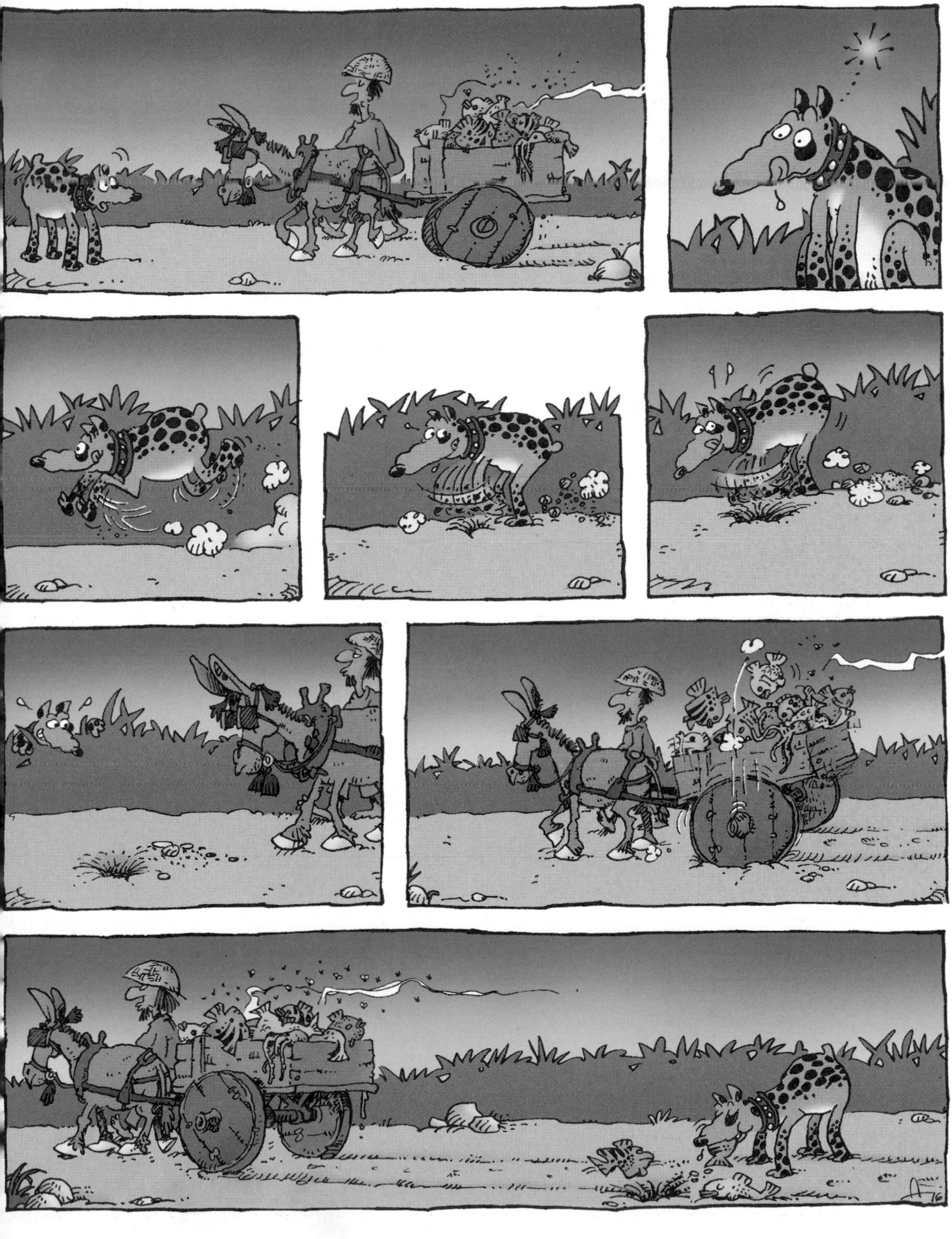

Rufferto

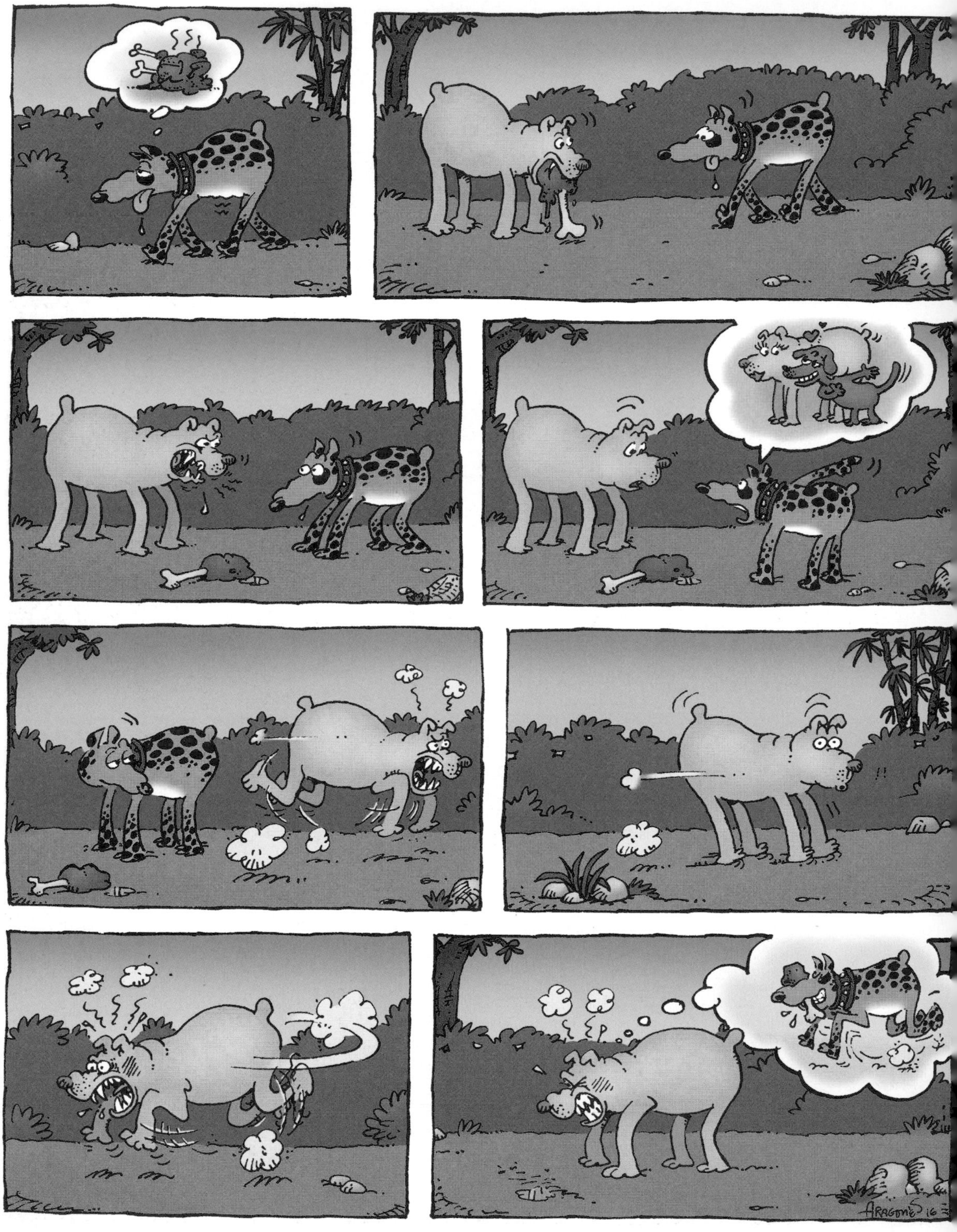
ARAGONÉS '16

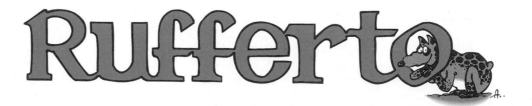

Rufferto

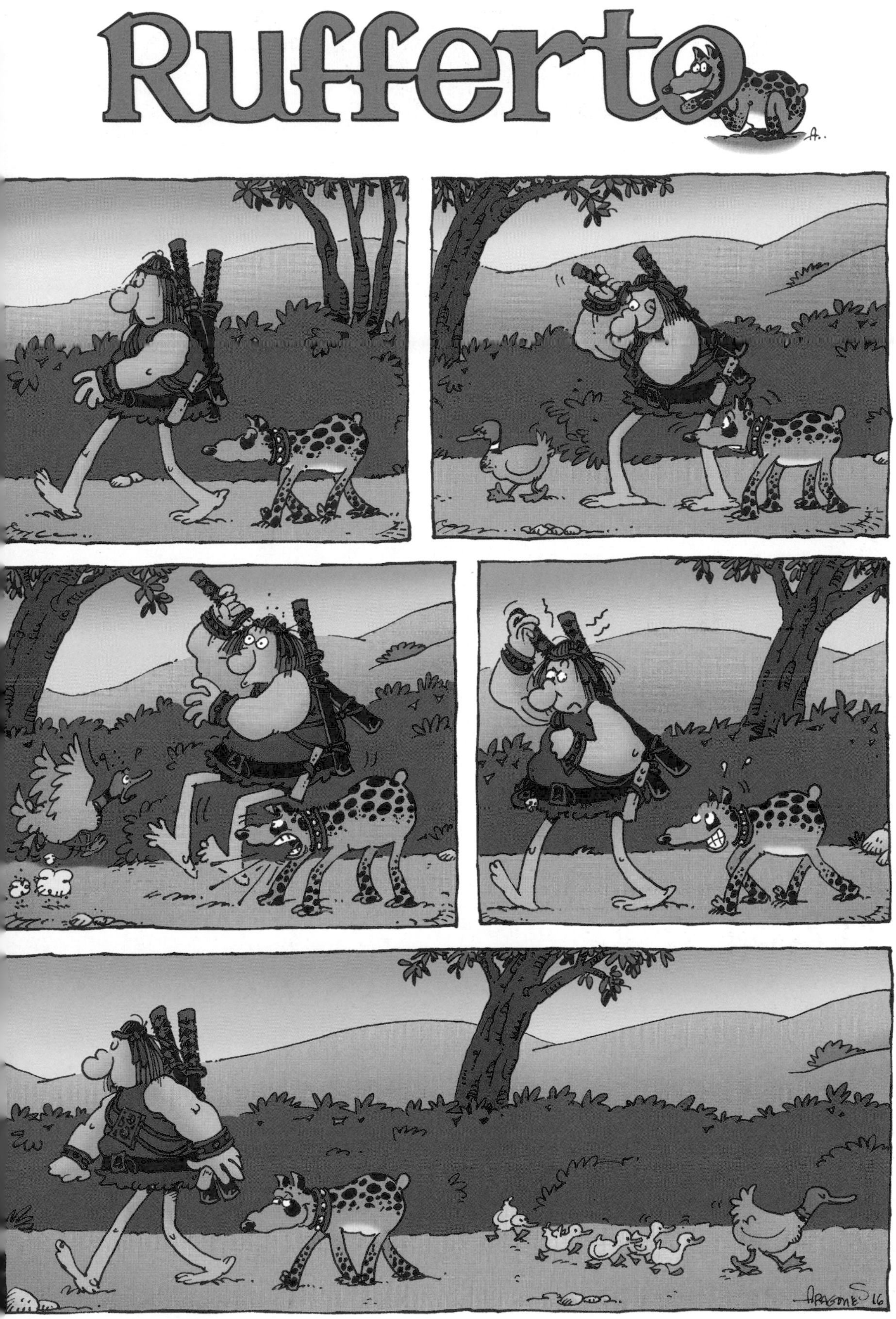

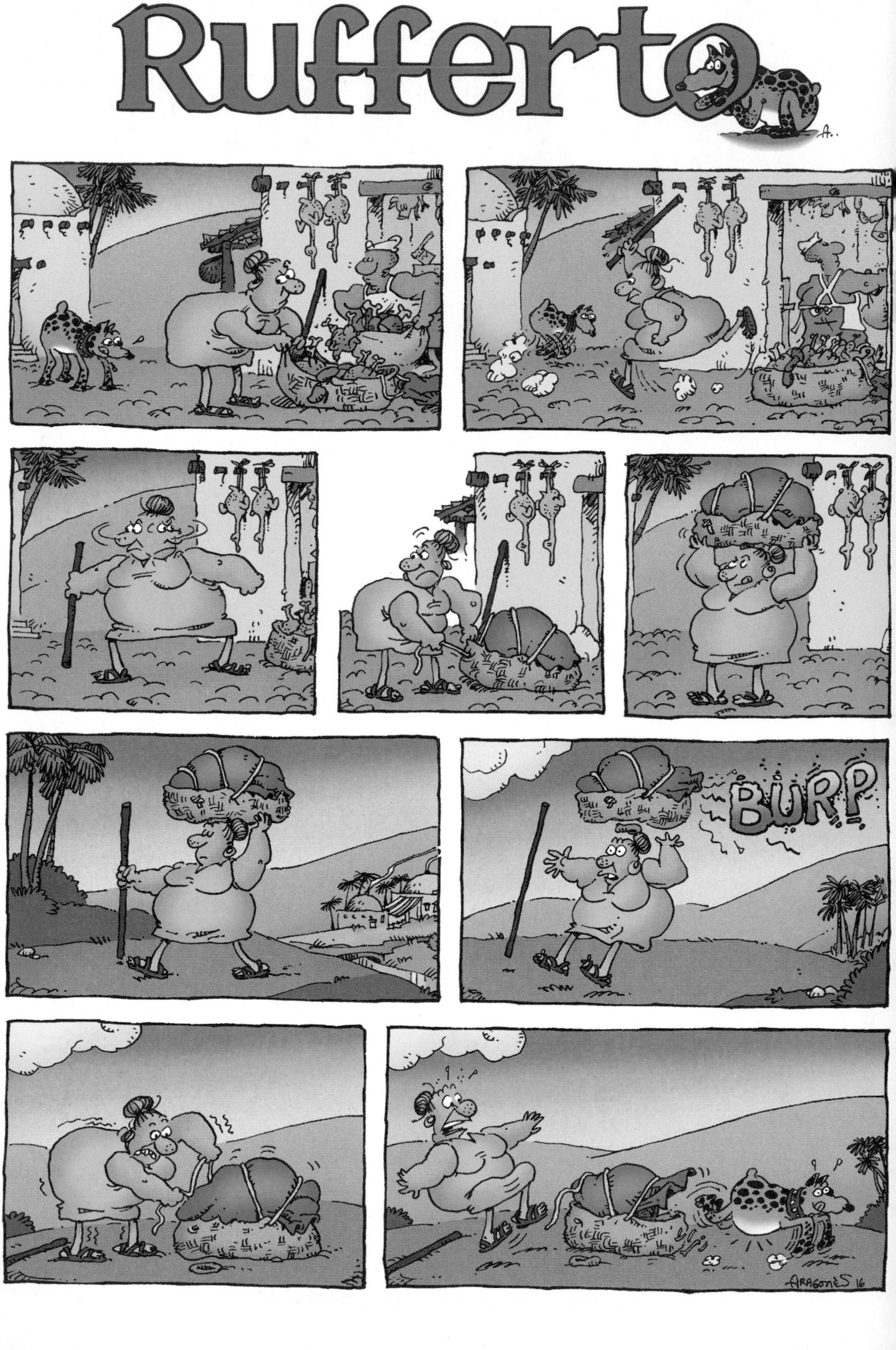
Rufferto
BURP
ARAGONÉS 16

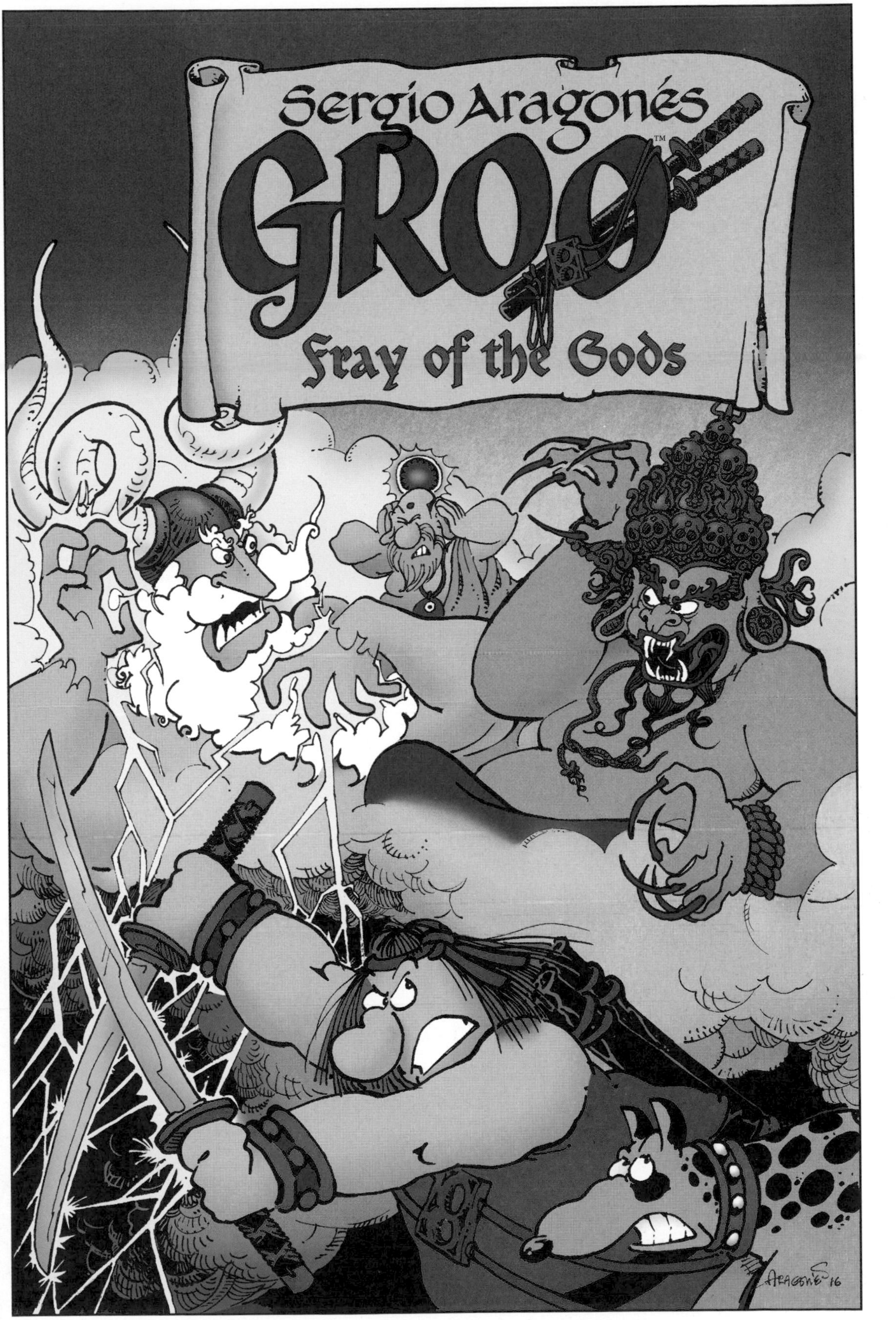
Sergio Aragonés
GROO™
Fray of the Gods
ARAGONÉS '16

Front cover art for *Groo: Fray of the Gods* #1

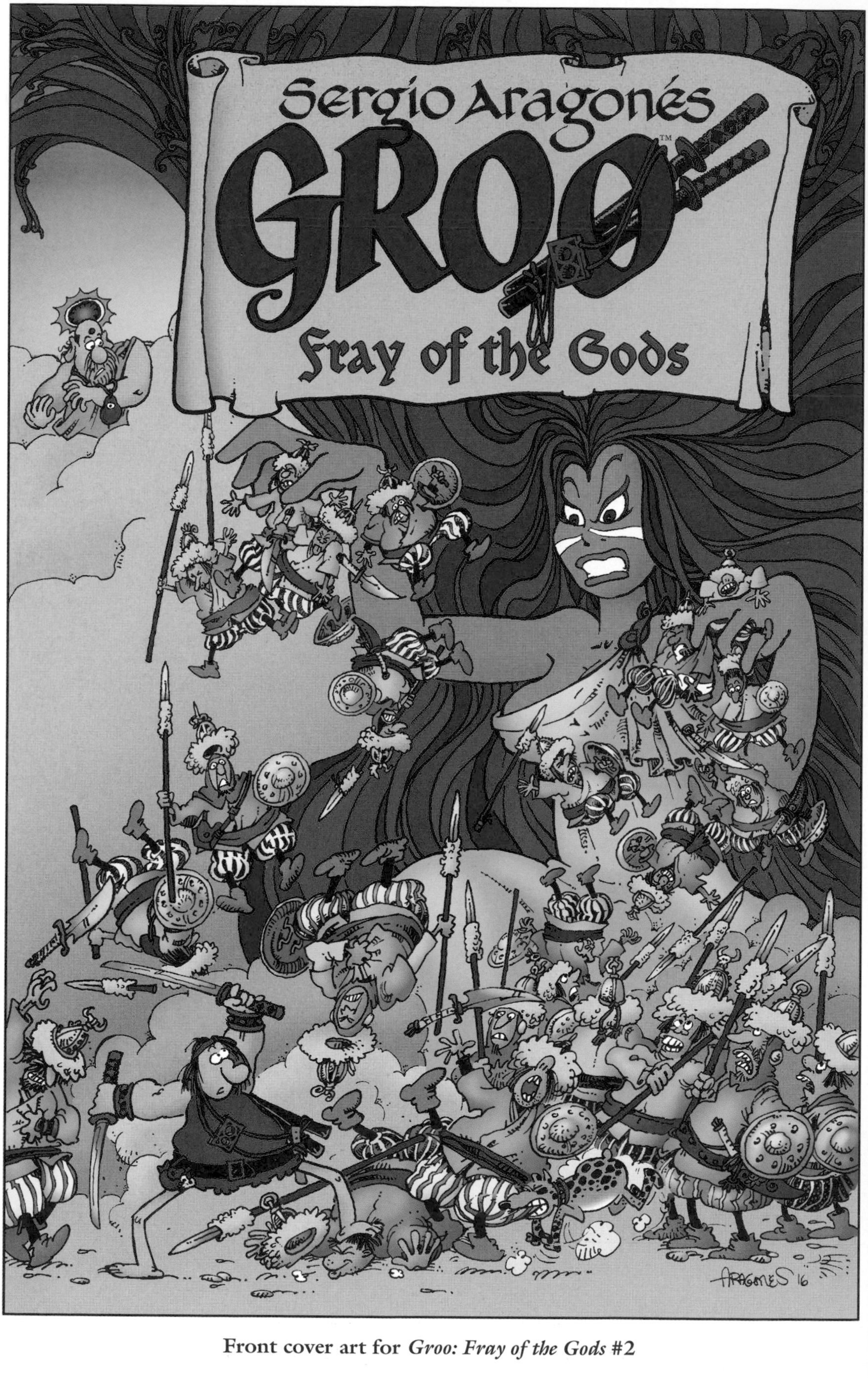
Sergio Aragonés
GROO
™
Fray of the Gods
ARAGONES '16

Front cover art for *Groo: Fray of the Gods* #2

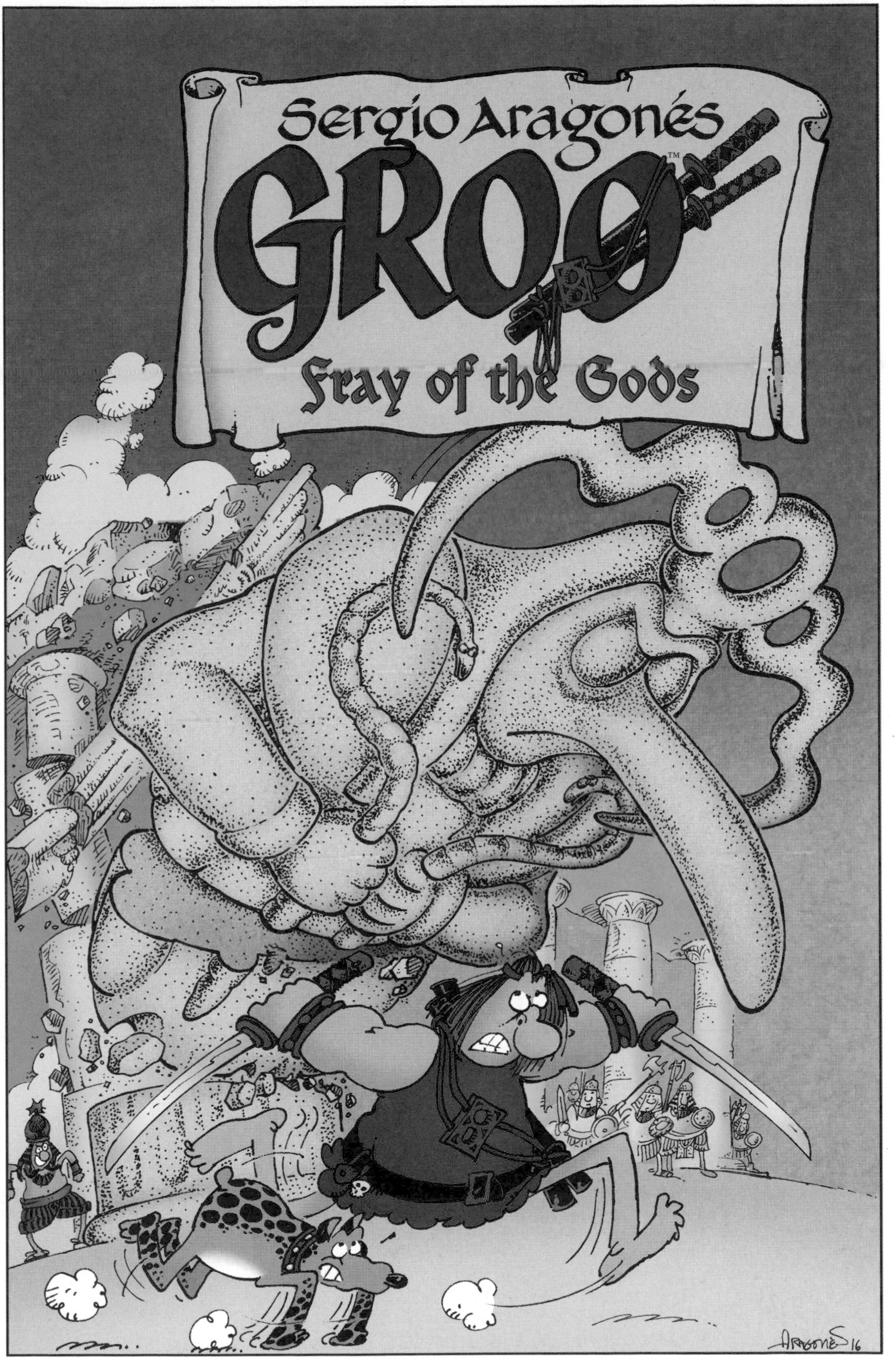
Sergio Aragonés
GROO
Fray of the Gods
ARAGONÉS 16

Front cover art for *Groo: Fray of the Gods* #3

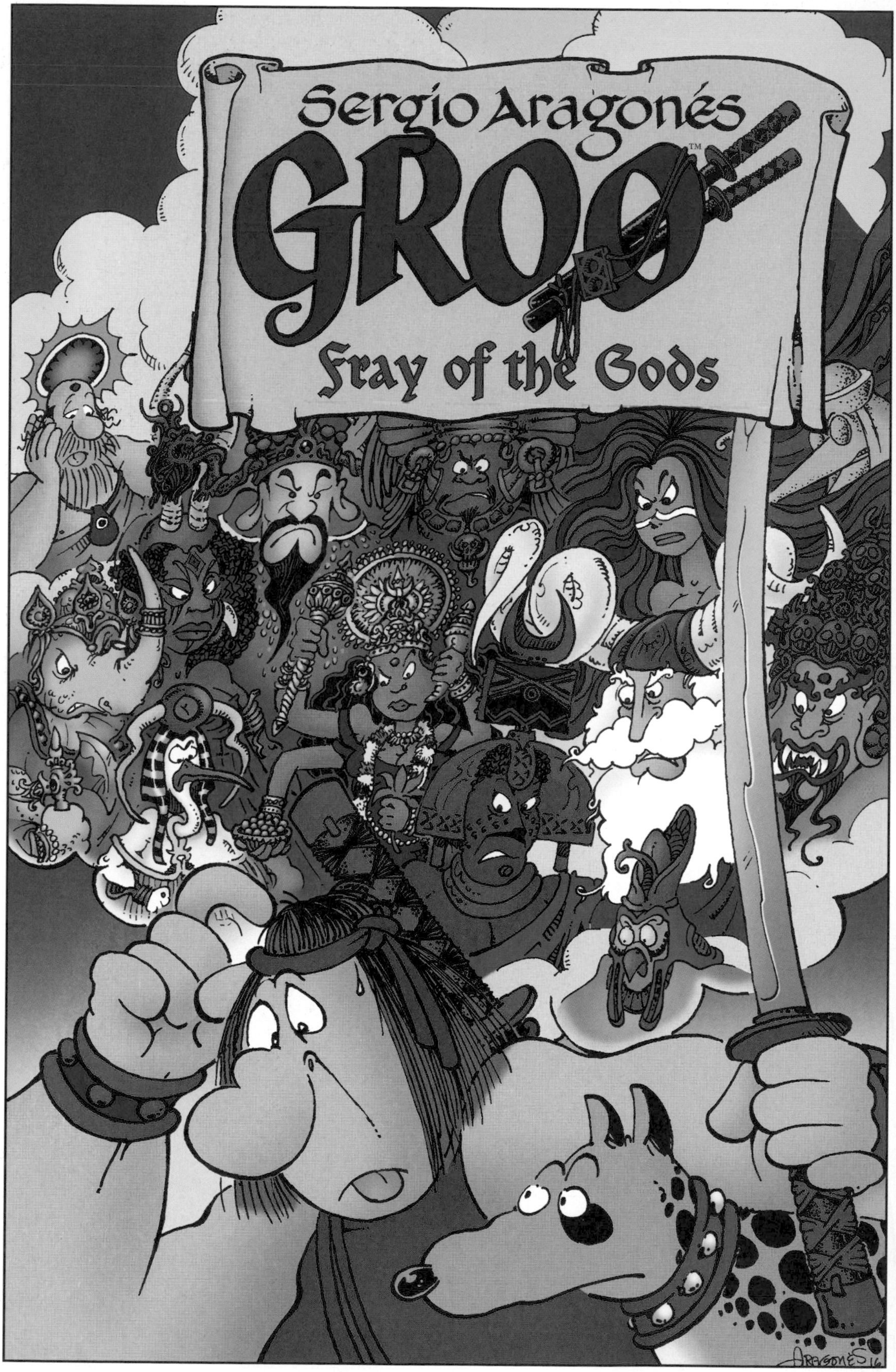
Sergio Aragonés
GROO™
Fray of the Gods
ARAGONÉS '16

Front cover art for *Groo: Fray of the Gods* #4

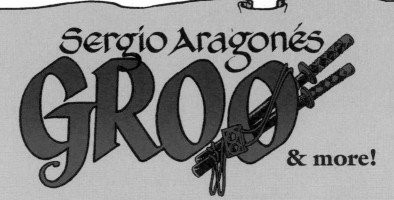

Sergio Aragonés GROO & more!

Dark Horse Comics presents the finest in humor with the master of pantomime on paper, one of the most beloved cartoonists in the world! Sergio Aragonés, veteran of *MAD* magazine and winner of the coveted Reuben Award and numerous Eisner and Harvey Awards, along with collaborator and partner-in-crime Mark Evanier, brings his unique magic and wit to these hilarious comics!

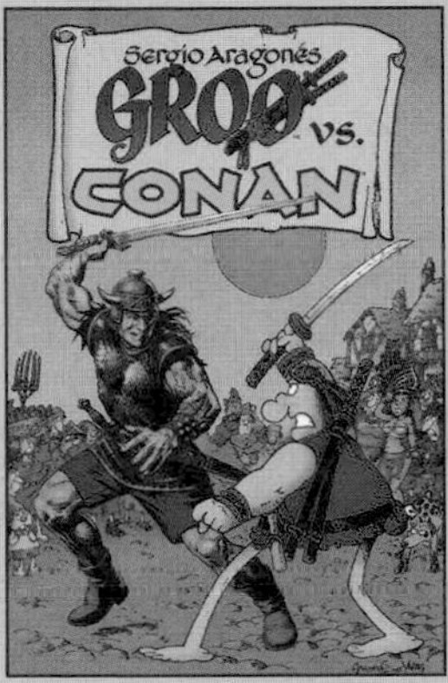
Sergio Aragonés
GROO vs. CONAN

GROO VS. CONAN
ISBN 978-1-61655-603-7
$16.99

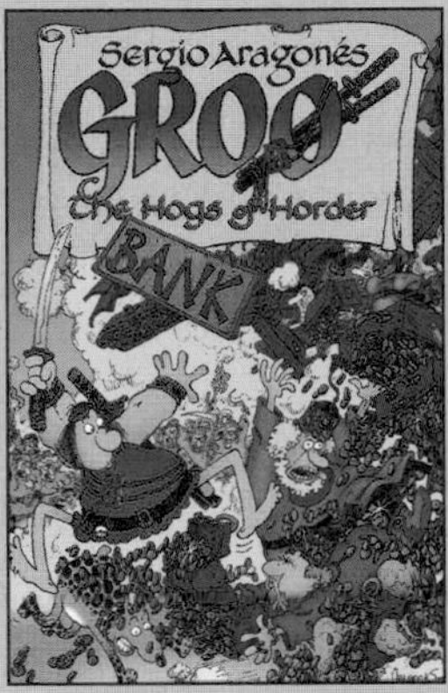
Sergio Aragonés
GROO
The Hogs of Horder
BANK

GROO: THE HOGS OF HORDER
ISBN 978-1-59582-423-3
$17.99

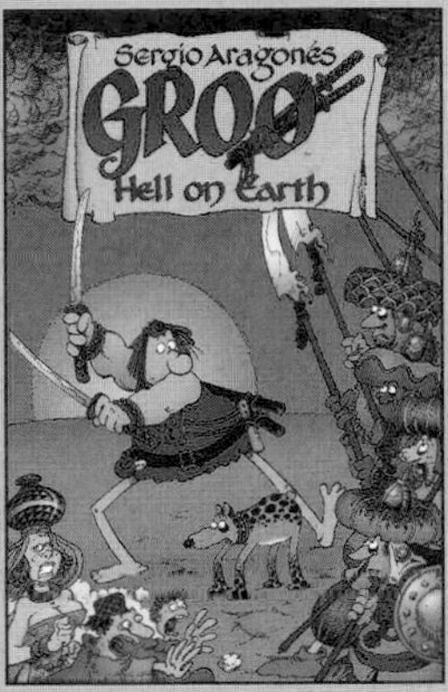
Sergio Aragonés
GROO
Hell on Earth

GROO: HELL ON EARTH
ISBN 978-1-59307-999-4
$17.99

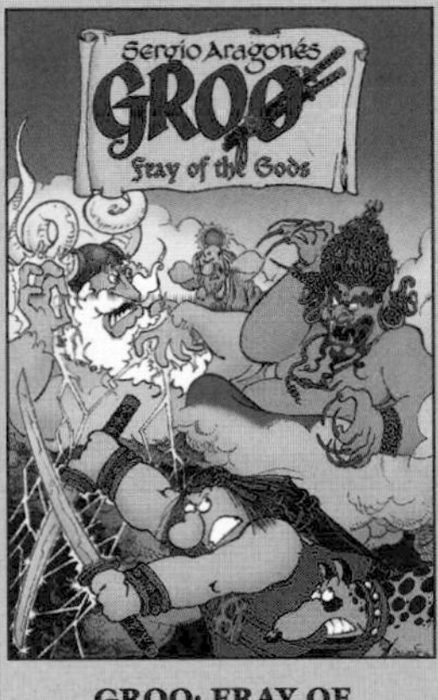
Sergio Aragonés
GROO
Fray of the Gods

GROO: FRAY OF THE GODS
ISBN 978-1-50670-241-4
$17.99

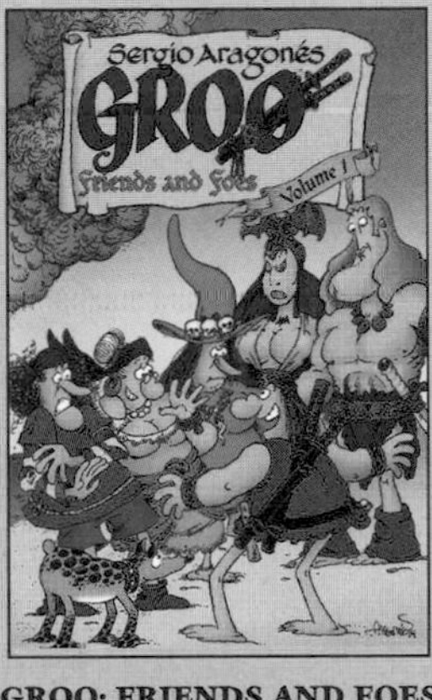
Sergio Aragonés
GROO
Friends and Foes
Volume 1

GROO: FRIENDS AND FOES
VOLUME 1
ISBN 978-1-61655-814-7
VOLUME 2
ISBN 978-1-61655-822-2
VOLUME 3
ISBN 978-1-61655-906-9
$14.99

AVAILABLE AT YOUR LOCAL COMICS SHOP OR BOOKSTORE!
TO FIND A COMICS SHOP IN YOUR AREA, CALL 1-888-266-4226.
For more information or to order direct: • On the web: DarkHorse.com • E-mail: mailorder@darkhorse.com • Phone: 1-800-862-0052 Mon.-Fri. 9 AM to 5 PM Pacific Time.

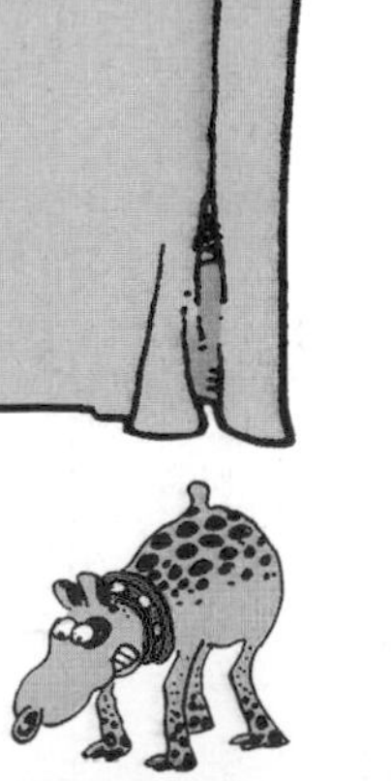

DARK HORSE BOOKS
DarkHorse.com

ALSO FROM

darkhorseoriginals | great creators original visions

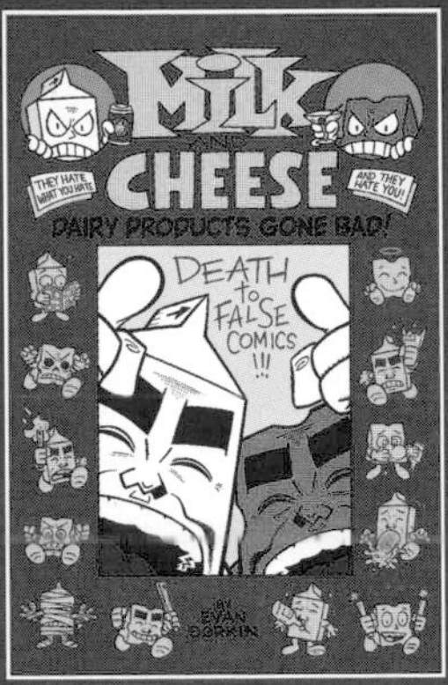
MILK
CHEESE
THEY HATE YOU
AND THEY HATE YOU!
DAIRY PRODUCTS GONE BAD!
DEATH to FALSE COMICS!!!
BY EVAN DORKIN

MILK AND CHEESE: DAIRY PRODUCTS GONE BAD

Evan Dorkin

The Eisner Award–winning dairy duo returns in this deluxe hardcover collecting every *Milk and Cheese* comic from 1989 to 2010 and a staggering array of extras, supplements, and bonuses.

ISBN 978-1-59582-805-7 | $19.99

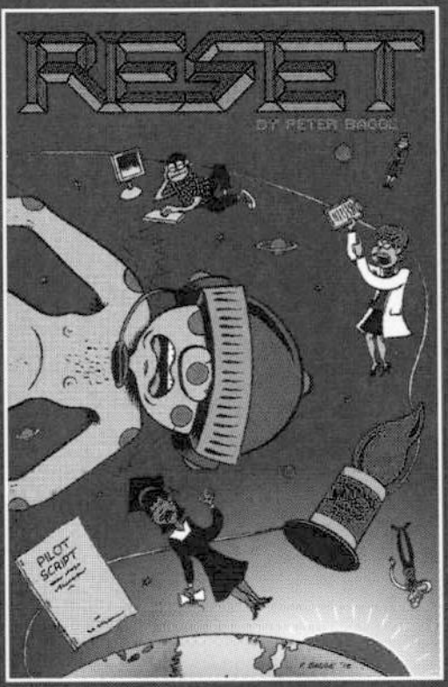
RESET
BY PETER BAGGE
PILOT SCRIPT

RESET

Peter Bagge

If you could relive major events in your life, would you try to make things better—even if your best attempts only make things worse? Or would you set your most twisted fantasies into motion? A hilarious new hardcover graphic novel from Harvey Award–winning writer/artist Peter Bagge!

ISBN 978-1-61655-003-5 | $15.99

CHIMICHANGA

Eric Powell

When Wrinkle's Traveling Circus's adorable little bearded girl trades a lock of her magic beard hair for a witch's strange egg, she stumbles upon what could be the saving grace for her ailing freak show—the savory-named beast Chimichanga!

ISBN 978-1-59582-755-5 | $14.99

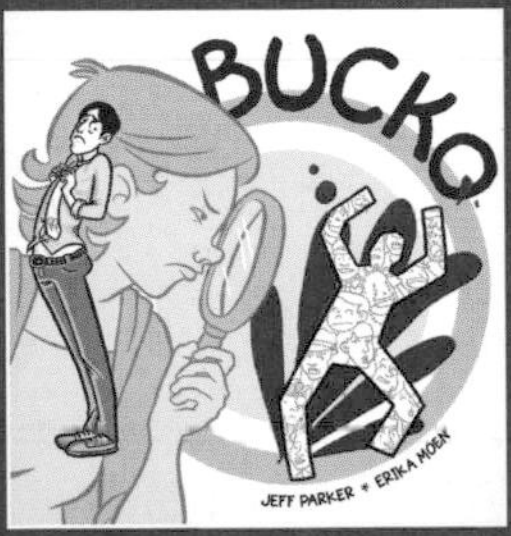
BUCKO
JEFF PARKER + ERIKA MOEN

BUCKO

Jeff Parker and Erika Moen

After discovering a body in an office bathroom, Rich "Bucko" Richardson becomes suspected of the murder. A quest to find the real killer becomes a romp through the wilds of Portland, Oregon. After taking the Internet by storm, Jeff Parker and Erika Moen's dirty, funny murder mystery is now a hilarious hardcover book!

ISBN 978-1-59582-973-3 | $19.99

THE MIGHTY SKULLBOY ARMY

Jacob Chabot

Skullboy stars in two volumes of manic fun, and the robotic, rascally Unit 1 and super-smart, simian Unit 2 await his orders. Are you ready for necktie-wearing bears in thinking caps, ninjas in tuxedos, police chases, giant squid battles, time-travel showdowns, not-so-evil duplicates, vengeful pigeons, flying dogs, wrestlers, jungle commando clashes, and more?

Volume 1 (2nd Edition) ISBN 978-1-61655-734-8 | $14.99
Volume 2 ISBN 978-1-59582-872-9 | $14.99

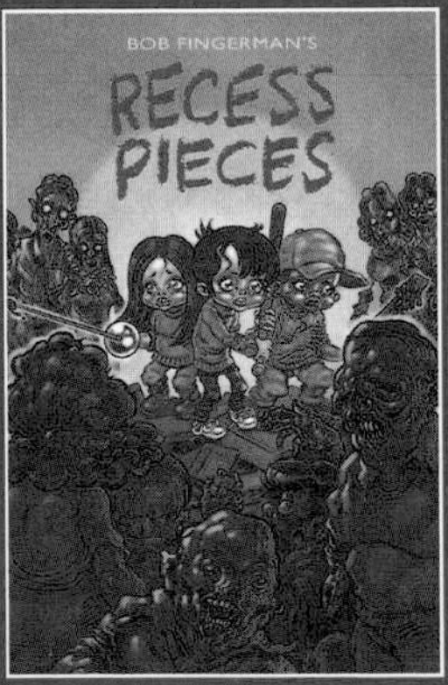
BOB FINGERMAN'S
RECESS PIECES

RECESS PIECES

Bob Fingerman

When a science project goes wrong, only the prepubescent children are spared the fate of zombification—which doesn't mean they're immune from being eaten alive! Bob Fingerman (*Beg the Question*, *You Deserved It*) dishes up a grisly combination of Hal Roach's *Our Gang* and zombies.

ISBN 978-1-59307-450-0 | $14.99

THE BOOK OF GRICKLE

Graham Annable

As befits his classically trained animation background, Graham Annable's fluid art pulses with life, in stories that practically jump off the page. Alternately poetic and hilarious, *Grickle* presents a strange twist on the everyday with heart and humor.

ISBN 978-1-59582-430-1 | $17.99

DARK HORSE BOOKS

AVAILABLE AT YOUR LOCAL COMICS SHOP OR BOOKSTORE • To find a comics shop in your area, call 1-888-266-4226.
For more information or to order direct: ON THE WEB: DarkHorse.com / E-MAIL: mailorder@darkhorse.com / PHONE: 1-800-862-0052 Mon.–Fri. 9 a.m. to 5 p.m. Pacific Time.